Social Change in Modern France describes and explains the radical transformations which have taken place within French society during the past thirty-five years. The authors contend that these changes constitute a revolution in French affairs as important as that of 1789. Since the late 1950s the traditional social structures of the Third Republic have been transformed: peasantry and bourgeoisie have disappeared or mutated; the great national institutions of church, army, trade unions and schools have declined or severely weakened, and a late and rapid industrialisation has wrought profound economic changes. Even the French Communist Party has become a virtual irrelevance. All these institutions, so characteristic of French society throughout the Third Republic, have now ceased to be the object of major conflicts and tensions. In their stead local institutions, voluntary associations and the family have acquired a renewed strength and serve as the basic network for social relations and social life. Traditional French 'joie de vivre' has become diversified, and expressed in a series of varied life-styles. In contrast to the conventional analysis of a conflictive, endemically unstable country, Mendras and Cole regard contemporary France as a sturdy and cohesive society, based on widespread consensus.

Social change in modern France

Towards a cultural anthropology of the Fifth Republic

HENRI MENDRAS

Directeur de recherche au CNRS;
Professeur à l'Institut d'études politiques de Paris
with

ALISTAIR COLE

Lecturer in Politics, Keele University

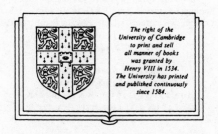

The right of the
University of Cambridge
to print and sell
all manner of books
was granted by
Henry VIII in 1534.
The University has printed
and published continuously
since 1584.

CAMBRIDGE UNIVERSITY PRESS
Cambridge
New York   Port Chester   Melbourne   Sydney

EDITIONS DE LA MAISON DES SCIENCES DE L'HOMME
Paris

Published by the Press Syndicate of the University of Cambridge
The Pitt Building, Trumpington Street, Cambridge CB2 1RP
40 West 20th Street, New York, NY 10011, USA
10 Stamford Road, Oakleigh, Melbourne 3166, Australia
and Editions de la Maison des Sciences de l'Homme
54 Boulevard Raspail, 75270 Paris Cedex 06

Originally published in French as *La Seconde Révolution française*
by Gallimard, Paris, 1988
and © Henri Mendras 1988

First published in English by Editions de la Maison des Sciences de l'Homme
and Cambridge University Press 1991 as
*Social Change in Modern France:
Towards a Cultural Anthropology of the Fifth Republic*
English adaptation © Maison des Sciences de l'Homme
and Cambridge University Press 1991

Printed in Great Britain by the Redwood Press Ltd, Melksham, Wiltshire

British Library cataloguing in publication data

Mendras, Henri
Social change in modern France: towards a cultural
anthropology of the Fifth Republic.
1. France. Society, 1958–
I. Title. II. Cole, Alistair III. Seconde Révolution
Française. *English*
944.083

Library of Congress cataloguing in publication data

Mendras, Henri.
Social change in modern France: towards a cultural
anthropology of the Fifth Republic / Henri Mendras with Alistair Cole.
p.   cm.
Includes bibliographical references (p.).
ISBN 0 521 39108 3. – ISBN 0 521 39998 X (pbk.)
1. Ethnology – France. 2. France – History – 1958– 3. France –
Social life and customs. 1. Cole, Alistair, 1959– . II. Title.
GN585.F8M46 1991   90–1493 CIP
306'.0944 – dc20

ISBN 0 521 39108 3 hardback
ISBN 0 521 39998 X paperback
ISBN 2 7351 0353 6 hardback (France only)
ISBN 2 7351 0354 4 paperback (France only)

Contents

Preface

Social Change in Modern France originated as *La Seconde Révolution française*, by Henri Mendras. It started from the precept that the social sciences had recently become too specialised, that social scientists were in danger of losing sight of the overall structure of society by concentrating too exclusively on their own specialisms. Taking as its object the post-war social revolution and the likely future evolution of French society, the book set itself the task of drawing together the main pieces of this complex mosaic, in order to give a comprehensive overview of the whole. This procedure is obviously open to the objection that it leads to a cavalier interpretation of each particular sphere of society, upon which specialists would prefer to deliberate alone. This risk is fully assumed by the authors. The dual ambition of *Social Change in Modern France* is to provide a considered analysis of the revolution which has changed French society during the past thirty-five years and to attempt to draw an outline of the new society of the third millennium, which is presently in the process of construction.

In its analysis of the Second French Revolution, the book concentrates initially upon the great institutions (such as the church, the army, the school and local government) and their working-class counterparts (the Communist Party and the trade unions), which have traditionally claimed so much attention. It charts the fundamental changes to which they have been subjected. It looks beyond these institutions, however, and seeks to discover the new social structures which organise the lives of groups and individuals. These institutions are frequently barely visible; indeed, they are often still in the process of being invented.

The great success of *La Seconde Révolution française* in France prompted Professor Mendras to have the book translated into English: Alistair Cole agreed to undertake the task. What began as a work of translation, however, was transformed into one of adaptation, interpretation and creation. The result is that *Social Change in Modern France* is more than a translation of *La Seconde Révolution française*: it is the fruit of a collaboration between Henri

vii

Mendras as author, and Alistair Cole as co-author. The authors hope that *Social Change in Modern France* will fill an important vacuum in the understanding of contemporary France in the English-speaking world. It attempts to provide a serious but accessible sociological study, we hope avoiding the pitfalls of journalese and impressionism which have characterised most other such works. The authors are grateful to Vincent Wright of Nuffield College, Oxford, who played no small part in the materialisation of this project, and to Shirley Letwin, who read the manuscript. Any mistakes are, of course, our own.

Introduction

The last thirty-five years have witnessed a new French Revolution. Although peaceful, this has been just as profound as that of 1789 because it has totally overhauled the moral foundations and social equilibrium of French society. This judgement must not be impaired by the fact that violence has had no part within this second French Revolution, except for the limited violence of May 1968. Despite the profound transformations that have occurred during the post-war period, the idea of the 'Revolution', in the form of the violent and brutal upheaval of society, has today become a myth. The hymn to the Revolution sung by the revolutionaries of May 1968 seems anachronistically utopian in an industrialised society at the end of the twentieth century.

A number of salient features have characterised the Second French Revolution, which has overhauled the equilibrium of French society as it had existed since 1789.

The demographic and economic expansion of the post-war period until the onset of the economic crisis in the 1970s (1945–1975) has been sufficiently analysed by economists to preclude further examination here. After a century of demographic stagnation (1840–1940) France's population rose dramatically after the war, from 42,000,000 to 56,000,000 within one generation. Simultaneously, economic production forged ahead and the structure of the French economy was radically altered. The nation's wealth increased in a totally unprecedented manner and economic production multiplied five-fold within several decades.

The two dominant social classes produced by the French Revolution, the peasantry and the bourgeoisie, have disappeared. The expansion of tertiary-sector employment and the birth of the *cadres* (see below) have produced a complete overhaul in the nation's social class structure.

Industry and the industrial working class are in decline, despite the post-war economic boom.

The opposition between the town and the countryside, which was born with the industrialisation of the nineteenth century, is becoming blurred because an urban lifestyle now prevails everywhere. However, the nature of life in the towns has itself dramatically changed.

The great national institutions such as the army, the church and the republic are no longer challenged in principle by particular sections of society, and they have lost their immense symbolic importance and ideological character. Alternative symbols, such as the red flag, and the hammer and sickle (which figure on the national flag of over twenty Communist nations), have lost their revolutionary meaning in contemporary France.

National unification has become complete because of the influence of the education system, the universal penetration of French (at the expense of minority languages) and the development of the mass media. The extent of centralisation has made the decentralisation of power both necessary and possible.

Individualism has made such progress that it is no longer considered as an ideology, but merely as a way of life shared by everybody.

It is clear that we are witnessing the collapse of the post-revolutionary France that came into existence during the nineteenth and early twentieth centuries. However, the contours and characteristics of the new France still appear uncertain. The objective of this book is to attempt to discern the architecture of this new French society.

THE 'THIRTY YEARS' WAR' 1914–1945

In order to understand the real extent of world upheaval between 1914 and 1945, we shall follow de Gaulle's advice and consider 'this thirty years' war as a whole', marked by two five-year conflicts, by the murderous Bolshevik Revolution and by an economic crisis which changed the equilibrium of Western capitalism. France emerged victorious but exhausted from the First World War. The glory of its armies and its field marshals could not hide the fact that the nation had suffered heavy losses in men and capital. The economic crisis of the 1930s became transformed in France into a political and social crisis, which was sanctioned by defeat at the hands of Hitler in 1940.

On the eve of the First World War, France remained a profoundly peasant society with almost half of its population making a living directly or indirectly from agriculture. Although it possessed its native bourgeoisie (see chapter 1), France had yet to become a profoundly industrialised society, in contrast with the UK, which since the end of the eighteenth century had sacrificed its agriculture to its industrial and commercial development. If its industry was less prosperous than that of the UK or Germany, the economic and financial power of France was nonetheless considerable. Large amounts of French capital were invested overseas: in China, in South America and in Eastern Europe (especially in Russia). Curiously, however, there was little investment in France's colonies.

In the political and ideological arena, France incarnated the liberal and humanitarian ideas of the Revolution and the Paris Commune for rebels throughout the world. In 1914, along with Switzerland, France was the only republic in Europe; all the other countries were still monarchies. Indeed, in many countries the republican anthem the *Marseillaise* was forbidden as a revolutionary song and still shocked traditionally inclined people in the French provinces. For Jews worldwide, France appeared a haven of tolerance and protection after the Dreyfus affair, which was viewed as a triumph for equal rights, invariably denied to Jews elsewhere. That representation was all the more paradoxical in so far as historians today see the Dreyfus affair as a manifestation of the anti-Semitism of a majority of the French people.

After the 1918 victory and the Treaty of Versailles, France presented itself as the head of the allied coalition against the vanquished German enemy. Alongside its initial politico-military domination of Europe after the First World War, France could also claim to be the prevailing cultural force in Europe. The League of Nations, whose existence had been willed by the USA, was dominated by the oratorical art of French politicians. Moreover, the 1937 Great Exhibition made Paris the centre of cultural attraction in the world. These great events left the French people in no doubt that their nation was still top. This position appeared to be disputed only by England: neither a defeated Germany, nor an impoverished and tyrannised Russia, nor even an isolationist America could pose a threat to France's leadership amongst nations. In the 1920s the French army became the strongest in Europe, and its colonial empire continued to develop in every region of the world. French culture remained dominant and the French language was the one used in diplomatic conversations and at the League of Nations. Paris was the unchallenged literary and artistic capital, and attracted artists and intellectuals from all over the world.

Although France continued to present a positive image to the world and to itself, the nation's sharp decline in the 1930s was felt by everybody. It was certainly recognised by Hitler, to whom it gave room for audacious military manoeuvres, as well as by Stalin, who eventually changed sides and preferred to ally with Nazi Germany. France's decline was also felt by the small peasant in his field, or by the artisan in his workshop. France's intellectual and artistic influence during the inter-war period masked a worrying economic and demographic stagnation. The Popular Front left-wing government of 1936/7 is celebrated by the left as a time of unprecedented social

Introduction

progress, but few can deny that it was an economic catastrophe, or that the Socialist-led government proved incapable of dealing with the economic constraints imposed by the existing social and economic machinery. In fact, whatever their political complexion, successive governments suffered from an inability to make decisions, which finally led to the allies ceding to Hitler at Munich in 1938. In less than ten years, the French nation had lost its nerve and its power. Such a rapid decline appeared to be the delayed effect of the exhausting effort and horrible slaughter of the First World War which had deprived France of its finest flower. The government's loss of willpower was only one manifestation of the rapid decay suffered by the country in between 1931 and 1939, which led it to the collapse of 1940.

Despite the image of national *grandeur* presented to the outside world, French society became completely introverted during the inter-war period and organised upon the basis of static, anachronistic social structures. The nineteenth-century bourgeoisie, described in chapter 1, was ruined after the war. Pre-war investments in eastern Europe and overseas collapsed in the political and economic crises of the late 1920s and the 1930s. More than one and a half million households, which held Russian bonds given in return for the large loans accorded by the French government to the Tsarist regime before the war, were completely dispossessed of their investments when the new Bolshevik rulers cancelled all overseas debts. Moreover, French stocks and shares yielded low dividends and their stock-market value fell constantly. During the inter-war period, around one-half of the working population was composed of non-salaried, independent workers, such as small businessmen, artisans, shopkeepers and professionals. These 'independents' survived in a subsistence economy, and refused to invest or start up businesses. Small family firms, which had made France prosperous before the war (especially in the South), survived only for as long as one gen-eration struggled to make them profitable, but they invariably closed once the first generation took retirement and its sons moved to the large towns to seek alternative employment. Both the small and medium-sized bour-geoisie and the peasantry lived increasingly modest lives during this period, and they had to cut back on all forms of expenditure. The overall impression was one of a period during which living standards were declining despite France's claim to greatness on the world stage.

In 1945, at the end of the last battles of this thirty years' war, the balance of power in the world had completely changed. The dismantlement of the colonial empires created a new political map in Africa and in parts of Asia which was conducive to all sorts of conflicts. Amongst the traditional monarchies, the only survivors were those which had conferred power to a parliamentary regime, and which conserved only a symbolic function. The remaining countries of the world were divided between pluralistic democracies and single-party states, which were to a greater or lesser extent totalitarian. The predictions of the great visionaries of the nineteenth century had at last come true: the world was dominated by two superpowers, the USA and the USSR. England, Germany and France became second-rate powers, and it was widely expected that Japan and then China (and later on perhaps Brazil and India) would take their place in the international hierarchy.

The French people rapidly understood the nature of this new world balance of power and France's position within it. Traumatised by the 1940 collapse and then by successive colonial defeats in the 1950s and early 1960s, they accepted that their country was a second-rate power. However, they did not renounce their aspirations for France to continue to play a world role, which de Gaulle presented to them as a 'burning obligation'. They readily understood that a strong economy and active diplomacy, supported by a powerful army, were the main instruments for playing this role. Although they had been overcome by foreign arms in 1940, the French people showed themselves to be capable during the post-war period of staging a dramatic demographic and economic recovery. Such a national recovery merits an explanation, which this book attempts to provide. Before undertaking the explanation, however, we must situate French society in its chronological context during the post-war period.

CHRONOLOGY OF THE SECOND FRENCH REVOLUTION

In 1944 France found itself in a state of destruction and disorganisation which had no parallel in any other country. During the war, it had been forced to fall back upon the basic networks of family and neighbourhood relations, which had ensured people's survival. In the immediate post-war period, the nation still used equipment and machinery which had not been replaced since 1930. By 1950 France had rebuilt its ruins, replaced outdated machinery and equipment, recovered its GNP of 1939, and launched itself into a giant industrial leap forward. By 1965, the country had caught up for the first time with the projected growth rate that had been made back in 1900–14.

Thus twenty years were needed to make up for the losses (and the failures to gain) that had been incurred during thirty years of wars and economic crises between 1914 and 1944. In other words, in 1965 France recovered the position that it ought to have occupied had its economic growth continued calmly along the upward curve established at the beginning of the century. In the years after 1965, economic growth in France continued at an astonishing 6 per cent annual average until the aftermath of the oil crisis of 1973.

The 'thirty glorious years' after the war enabled France to multiply its income five-fold and to triple its productive capital (see figure 1).

This fantastic enrichment was all the more spectacular in that it went hand in hand with a rapid upturn in population (see figure 2). In the half-century of demographic stagnation preceding the war, a low birth rate had been compensated by a strong influx of immigrants, which had just about managed to keep the population at its 1900 level. The post-war baby-boom and continuing high levels of immigration led to spectacular increases in population which helped to accelerate the move towards the towns in the 1960s. During the 1960s, economists, town-planners and developers confidently announced that France would soon be virtually entirely urbanised: 80 per cent of the population would live in towns. Despite these predictions, and despite a very real exodus of population, the rural infrastructure has maintained itself into the 1980s, and around one-half of the population continues to live in villages and small rural towns of under 20,000 inhabitants. After years of rural exodus, the population of the countryside and small towns has recently been growing more quickly than in the towns: between 1975 and 1982 the rate of demographic growth in rural communes was 7 per cent, compared with 3 per cent for the country as a whole and 1 per cent for the large towns. Notwithstanding thirty years of urbanisation, France remains the most rural of all the industrialised nations.

In 1945, the heads of almost half (45 per cent) of French households were independent workers, who lived by running a small farm, shop or business. Forty years later, the vast bulk of the active population (85 per cent) were wage-earners, working for employers other than themselves. The peasants, who represented one-third of the population in 1945, have been replaced by a far smaller group of farmers (6 per cent). Whereas the *cadres* did not exist

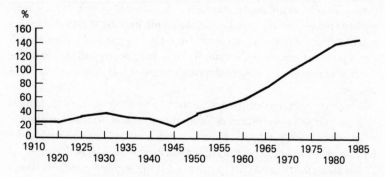

Figure 1 Growth of national income (1972 = 100).
Source: INSEE

in 1945 as a recognisable occupational category, forty years later they comprised around one-fifth of the workforce.

Several political landmarks more or less coincided with the beginnings of this fundamental social transformation: the signing of the Treaty of Rome in 1955, the birth of the Fifth Republic in 1958, and the end of the Algerian war and the process of decolonisation in 1962. Perhaps the last date was the most important of all, since for the first time since 1939, France no longer found itself at war. Moreover, for the first time in its history, the fear of war was about to disappear from the nation's life as the major anxiety of most French people. A new lasting era of peace had begun. For French people born since 1945, there is the virtually unanimous expectation that they will not have to fight in a war during their lifetimes, whereas every preceding generation had had to contemplate the possibility of armed combat and the honour and duty of dying for one's country.

In a number of spheres, the year 1965 represented the first major modification in the upward progress of post-war demographic and economic trends. The birth rate dropped for the first time since the war, and the productivity of fixed capital (which had been growing since 1946) began to diminish. These two reversals were symptomatic of a more general movement which was discernible in many other spheres. The length of the working week, which had risen slightly from 1946 to 1964, began a decline which has been continuing ever since and which has accelerated as a result of more paid holidays, the rise in unemployment and earlier retirement. Unemployment, which had been maintained at the level of around 3 per cent, began a slow increase which would reach 11 per cent of the working population in 1987 (see figure 3). Despite the increase in overall unemployment since 1965, female employment has expanded rapidly since then: whereas women comprised only 30 per cent of the working population in 1965, they

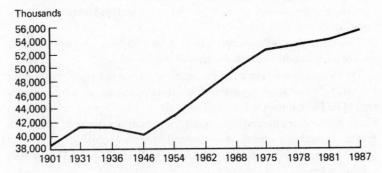

Figure 2 Growth of the French population. Source: INSEE

represented 44 per cent in 1985. Finally, immigration began to rise from 1965 onwards. As a result of all these partially contradictory movements, the number of those in work began to grow rapidly: an average of 19,000,000 from 1945 to 1965, 21,000,000 in 1975 and 25,000,000 in 1985. The result of this has been that the indices of the number of unemployed and of those in work have followed an almost parallel upward evolution. Amongst other demographic trends which can usefully be dated from 1965 are increases in life-expectancy for men and women, the rise in the divorce rate and a decline in the annual number of marriages.

If we shift our attention away from economic and demographic statistics towards significant events, the year 1965 clearly represents a turning point in the history of modern France.

For the first time the President of the Republic was elected by direct universal suffrage, which radically transformed the functioning of republican institutions.

The conclusion of the Second Vatican Council in Rome transformed the discipline and the rites of the Catholic Church.

Although the first hyper-market opened its doors in 1963, it was in 1965 that this new form of commerce began to expand with staggering rapidity. There would soon be no clearer sign that the lifestyle of French people was being transformed and that culture patterns were becoming more homogeneous.

Cheap paperback books (*livres de poche*), another instrument for the spread of mass culture, began to appear in bookshops from around this date.

The University of Nanterre opened its doors in 1965, the first new university created to cater for the massive, ten-fold increase in the number of students. Nanterre lay behind the initial spark which fired the May 1968 'revolution'.

The first nude pictures appeared in magazines and at the cinemas. A near two thousand-year-old practice of 'decency' was suddenly called into question.

The expression of hedonistic values, which had been repressed before the sixties, suddenly expanded within all strata of society.

These various indicators and events mark 1965 as the year which ended one stage of post-war development: that of economic and social reconstruction. The French people appeared suddenly to have become aware that a hard twenty-year effort to reconstruct the nation was about to bear fruit, that they could take a break, work less and have fewer children, in order to start enjoying the rewards of their labour. The Second French Revolution was beginning.

In relation to 1965, May 1968 appeared as the symbolic expression of a profound transformation that had been taking place for three years. During revolutions, symbols are more important than the events that they express, and are the moving forces of change. The causes of the May 1968 events have been analysed in numerous books. The reaching of adulthood by the first generation of the post-war baby-boom is one explanation that every-body agrees with. Such a phenomenon also occurred in other Western nations, and this helped to explain why similar events took place in the same year in a number of countries which were otherwise very different. How-ever, the events in France were different from those which took place in other countries, since it was only in France that a nationwide strike emerged from a mere student rebellion. Only a fundamental transformation of society could explain why such a movement emerged in France. The awareness and violent expression of this transformation gave the May 1968 movement its particular character. Both ideology and symbolism contain their own dynamism which can slow down or accelerate movements within society; they became the central moving forces of the May 1968 social uprising.

The fantastic leap-forward of the 1950s had occurred with scarcely any political change taking place by comparison to the inter-war period. The Fourth Republic was increasingly difficult to distinguish from the pre-war Third Republic, and its institutions soon became paralysed by the quarrels of factions and parties. After the war, the same politicians returned to power. Moreover, despite the profound transformations which were occurring within France's post-war system of social classes, the same bour-geois personalities dominated the real positions of power at every level of society. The economic miracle of the post-war period was largely achieved

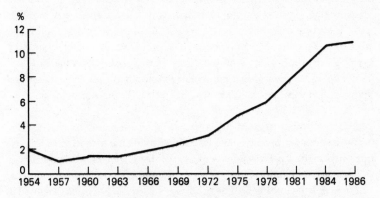

Figure 3 The unemployed as a percentage of the total
working population. Source: INSEE

thanks to economies of scale, which promoted the development of institutional giants (huge companies, dealing with large government departments) alongside of which the individual felt isolated and impotent.

The ideological reaction to the creation of vast institutions was commonly expressed in the slogan 'small is beautiful'. It is not so much what is small which is beautiful and seductive, however, as the diversity and complexity of contemporary western societies. Since 1968, all Western societies have abandoned ingrained ideas of the need for growth at any price, and recognised that the desire for economic growth must be set alongside the need to manage complex and diversified social structures in a cohesive manner. Within the French context, the compulsive drive for economic growth has been modified since 1968 to take into account the demand for more collective facilities, and for a greater cohesion amongst the different groups within society.

The young revolutionaries of May 1968 also demanded a more transparent society. Paradoxically, the May 1968 revolutionaries could be likened to the technocrats in the civil service, who dreamt up perfect descriptions of society in order to be able to manage that society more rationally. Both visions were equally naive, since at that very time French society was becoming increasingly complex, impenetrable and difficult to analyse in terms of categories or statistics. Neither the technocrats' nor the students' utopia, both of which promised a stifling world, has materialised.

The first oil crisis of 1973 was initially considered as the beginning of a new temporary hiccup in the economy which would be overcome as rapidly as others during the post-war period. This did not occur. Certain economic indices (for example inflation) began showing signs of a more durable crisis. The invention of 'stagflation' in the 1960s was the concrete sign that the post-war economic miracle was drawing to a close. Another indicator was that although the rise in GNP and average incomes continued after 1973, they did so at a slower rate and levelled off completely in 1983. Despite this, most social and demographic indicators continued in their earlier patterns: unemployment, female employment, life-expectancy and divorce all continued to rise; whereas the birth and marriage rates continued to fall.

The economic 'rules of the game' became unsettled throughout the world from 1965 onwards. The traditional industrial sectors in the developed nations became less and less of a motor for growth, and were replaced by service industries fuelled by growing consumption and by industries based on new technologies. The economists who had previously claimed to be able to manage growth suddenly found themselves at a loss to explain or control the profound transformations that were occurring in patterns of industrial production, international trade or finance. Whether governments of the left or right were in power, national economic policies could not provide easy solutions.

In 1981, the victory of the left in France provided the ultimate legitimisation of the Fifth Republic's institutions, and renewed the nation's political personnel by bringing a new generation of Socialist activists to power. Despite its attempted Keynesian-style relaunch of the economy upon taking office in 1981, the left was forced by the pressure of international constraints to return to a 'classical' deflationary economic policy in 1983. The left's economic U-turn demonstrated that the international economy has its own rules which cannot be lightly infringed. That it was the left which finally drove home this lesson to everybody is of crucial importance for the future. Across the mainstream political spectrum in contemporary France, a belief in the need for governments to conduct rational, sensible economic policies that take into account the surrounding international environment has been accepted. The businessman and the company are no longer the villains of the piece for the left, and profit is no longer regarded as an unmentionable word. The primacy of the economy over social, political and legal objectives has been accepted by everybody, except the extremes.

This ideological U-turn has been accompanied by the demystification of Marxism and the USSR, for which the PCF has paid the electoral penalty. Neither of the Soviet invasions of Hungary in 1956 or Czechoslovakia in 1968 had worried PCF activists and voters. In contrast, the 1979 Russian invasion of Afghanistan and the suppression of Solidarity by the Polish government in 1981 finally exposed the Soviet myth, which had already been badly shaken by Solzhenitsyn's revelations since 1973 on conditions in labour camps in the USSR. However, even the most seasoned observer must be somewhat surprised by the rapidity with which the ideological baggage of Marxism and the Soviet Union was abandoned by intellectuals and left-wing activists in the 1980s.

Finally, the conflict over the church schools, which the Socialist government attempted to bring under more rigorous state control in 1983/4, ended in a setback for the anti-clericals of the left: the proposed reform was abandoned once it became clear that it was opposed by a substantial majority of public opinion. The Catholic Church defeated the Republican School, and with that defeat a major part of the French left's traditional ideology disappeared. Suddenly primary school teachers and supporters of anti-clerical solutions appeared anachronistic, or even reactionary. The effect of this unexpected event was to bury a century of anti-clerical republican ideology (see chapter 5).

The Second French Revolution was over.

At the end of this second revolution, French society is entering into a new, unknown, world. The great social structures of the nineteenth century are crumbling, or else have disappeared. The four old antagonistic social classes (bourgeoisie, peasantry, industrial working class, middle class) are splitting up into a greater number of smaller social groups, most of which form part of a new central middle-class constellation (see chapter 2). Moreover, the old symbolic institutions of the nineteenth century – the Church, the Army, the Republic and the School – have all lost their symbolic value (see part II). They no longer divide the French people as they used to. The same can be said for the alternative institutions of the early twentieth century, since the Communist Party (PCF) and the trade unions no longer arouse such passions and their influence has been greatly reduced.

French society is becoming more diversified, more complex and more difficult to predict. Older symbolic institutions have declined in importance, but more discrete structures have increased their significance: local government, kinship relations and the role of age-groups all provide examples to confirm this shift in emphasis. Individual and group strategies are no longer perceived as endangering the cohesion of society as a whole. A new value system is in the process of emerging, emanating from social groups forming part of the central constellation. This value system places greater emphasis on the efforts of individuals and intermediary groups to achieve their objectives than ever before. Social change is no longer necessarily dictated from above, but is more likely to emerge from the central, intermediary groups within society. The contours of French society are more fluid than ever before. It appears probable that by the end of the century, French society will be scarcely recognisable even from the vantage point of the 1980s.

Part I

The breaking-up of traditional class structures

1

The bourgeois, the workers and the peasants

In 1914, French society was divided into four great social groups, each of which had its own particular characteristics: the peasants, the bourgeoisie, the proletariat and the 'middle classes'. The peasants represented the most important numerical group, but were themselves divided into countless independent local communities and for that reason remained relatively isolated from the rest of society. Each region spoke its own language and guarded itself against the intrusion of outside forces, especially the state. Because it was the dominant class, the bourgeoisie attempted to impose its values on the rest of society. Because it possessed its own independent wealth (see the definition of *patrimoine* below), the bourgeoisie did not need to work, and enjoyed a financial security which was denied to other social classes. By contrast, the industrial working class lived in a situation of total insecurity, because workers owned only the labour they could offer, and were often reduced to destitution by unemployment or sickness. In between these three major groups, the members of the 'middle classes' were few in number and were torn between their popular peasant origins and their bourgeois ambitions.

This schematic picture no longer corresponds in the least to today's France: the peasants have disappeared; the bourgeoisie has lost its wealth, and its culture has become more widely diffused amongst other social classes; popular culture is dead, and the middle class is no longer made up of a majority of shopkeepers, artisans and lesser clerical workers, but of *cadres* (see definition, chapter 2). In fact a complete social revolution has taken place since the war.

THE END OF THE PEASANTRY

At the beginning of the Second World War, France was the most peasant of all Western nations: 45 per cent of the population lived in 'rural' communes and one-quarter of the labour-force worked in agriculture. Forty years later

France has become a heavily urbanised nation, in which agriculture employs no more than 5 per cent of the working population and is responsible for only 3 per cent of national production. During the 1960s, at the height of the rural exodus, 100,000 workers left the land every year. The French economy has undergone its industrial transformation and lost its peasant base. France is today an industrialised nation comparable with other industrialised nations. Because it possesses more land than any of its neighbours, its agricultural sector is somewhat more important than in either the UK, West Germany or the Netherlands; however, this is a difference of degree rather than of structure.

In order to understand the swiftness of this transformation, we must first explain the historic significance of the peasantry in shaping French society. For two centuries, all political regimes and governments in France carried out policies aimed at maintaining a strong, numerous peasantry which seemed to be the best safeguard against the threat of revolution from Paris. It provided a solid backdrop of support for the political regime and seemed to successive governments to be the best foundation for national stability. Both the Second Empire (1852–70) and the Third Republic (1870–1940) supported themselves squarely on the peasantry as the central social class. Until 1950, French politicians were unanimous in seeking to maintain a balance between industry and agriculture, and to preserve a sizeable peasant population. For the right, the peasants incarnated all the traditional virtues of moderation and of respect for God and the authorities. For the left, the peasant was the model of the independent citizen who jealously guarded his autonomy against threats posed by external authorities. Both left and right thus lauded the countryside and the peasantry. This political agreement, based on an ideological disagreement, was justified in the last resort by the needs of national defence. The French army had always been mainly composed of peasant-soldiers, and a strong peasantry was thus considered to be indispensable in order to defend the nation against foreign aggressors. This fundamental belief underpinned government policy throughout the nineteenth century, and appeared to be vindicated by the stout performance of the peasant-dominated French armies during the First World War. However, the Second World War revealed how archaic this doctrine had become in military terms: because of technological advances, military victory depended upon creating a strong industrial sector, rather than preserving an outdated peasantry.

A changing perspective on the peasantry's future began to be adopted during the 1950s by military strategists, economists and peasants alike. Even farmers' leaders began to accept that the rural exodus was a necessary condition if agricultural modernisation was to take place. From a different perspective, economists declared that agriculture must cease leading its autarkic existence and must enter the market economy and become a client of industry. Increasingly large numbers of farmers were leaving the countryside and seeking employment in the expanding industrial sector of the economy. Indeed, the rural exodus became a precondition for general economic growth, as well as for prosperity for those remaining on the land.

The extraordinary technical revolution that French agriculture accomplished in the quarter-century after 1945 can be measured by several figures. In 1954, the total wheat harvest recovered to its 1907 maximum of 110 million quintals; in 1979 is exceeded 190 quintals. From 1950 to 1980 the production of beef more than doubled (from 650,000 tons to 1,400,000 tons per annum), while that of chicken increased ten-fold. By contrast, wine production has remained stable at around 60–70 million litres per annum. France has become self-sufficient in most of its agricultural products, although its population has increased from 42,000,000 to 56,000,000 and average consumption has rocketed. At the same time, France has become the largest food exporter after the USA.

These remarkable achievements occurred thanks to increases in productivity. There were as many as six million agricultural workers in 1946, and only just over one million in 1986, which meant that one-sixth of the workers were producing twice as much as forty years previously. To achieve this prodigious leap forward, French agriculture has become mechanised (230,000 tractors in 1945, 1,500,000 in 1980), and its farmers have learnt how to use fertilisers (1 million tons in 1945, 5.5 million tons in 1978), how to select their cattle and how to use animal-feed effectively. Indeed, agriculture is one of the branches of the French economy in which improvements in productivity have been most spectacular.

Such a development was completely unforeseeable in 1945. Certainly nobody had predicted it. Back in 1945 the average peasant was advanced in years, had only the barest minimum level of education, and had received no technical training, everything he knew having been taught to him by his father (who himself had learnt from *his* father). Peasant routine seemed to be inescapable. The idea of borrowing money to buy a tractor terrified the older generation, which was scared of falling into debt. By contrast, every young farmer today has an account at the agricultural cooperative bank, the Crédit agricole, and is perpetually in debt in order to finance investment on the farm.

The technical and economic knowledge of the young farmer in 1980 was incomparably greater than that of his grandfather, and yet their basic levels of education had hardly changed. The great difference between the opportunities open to the two generations lay in the creation in the 1950s of two pioneering organisations which continue to play a crucial role: the JAC (Young Christian Farmers) and the CNJA (National Centre of Young Farmers). These two bodies established an excellent system of general and technical training. Through the use of courses, study-days, and educational visits, they instilled an elementary technical and economic knowledge in young farmers and promoted a new pride in being a farmer. Within one generation, an entire population had learnt an updated occupation and adapted itself to the modern world. New forms of knowledge were accompanied by a new confidence in the future prospects of rural France. Above all, a new, more open conception of social relationships emerged, which buried ancient taboos and authorised greater cooperation between neighbours in farming communities, as well as more participation in professional associations and the use of technical experts. This opening up to others outside of the family triumphed over the older peasant morality and the rigidity of relationships in the traditional village, so much so that today's farmers are amongst the social categories which are the best informed, most alert and most open to progress.

The transformation of the modern farmer's mentality can best be understood by comparing it with that of the traditional peasant farmer who survived until the Second World War. Between the two wars, one French family in three lived on a farm and survived entirely off the goods produced on their land. There were four million such farms, all of which were broadly comparable despite regional contrasts and different products. If we except the large cereal farms in the Paris Basin and the big wine-producing farms of Languedoc, we can draw an ideal picture of the average French farm during this period. The whole household (including any servants or labourers who shared in every aspect of family life) would sit around the same table, and the typical farming family would eat only what was produced on the farm. There would be little, if any, new investment in equipment for the farm, and money played a minor role in this self-sufficient style of society. The men would buy virtually no new equipment for the farm, whereas the animals would eat fodder produced on the farm and provide manure for it. Tools, wagons and carts would all last for many years and were easily repaired. What money there was, acquired by the family selling farm produce at market two or three times a year, would go towards new tools, new land, or compensation to younger brothers and sisters who would not inherit the farm. This family-based peasant economy, which was largely self-sufficient and in which money played only a marginal role, seems totally archaic today. It must be remembered, however, that all peasants who are today over sixty years old were brought up in this lifestyle and that their experience was shaped by it.

Today everything has changed. Typically the oldest generation will continue to live in the old farm, besides which their children and families will have built new houses, which are comparable in every way with the townhouses of the suburbs. Both houses now enjoy the benefits of the most advanced domestic conveniences, such as a modern kitchen, television, electric cooker and freezer. The relationship between the two generations has been completely reversed: the son is his own boss, rather than remaining subordinate to his father as head of the family, as before; the daughter-in-law, rather than the mother, is in charge of her own children. In the modern farm, one or two tractors are sufficient to cultivate 25–30 hectares of land which can support a cowshed of twenty milking cows. Rather than aiming at self-sufficiency for the family, as before 1945, the modern farm is entirely geared towards the market and activity is concentrated upon intensively producing two or three products only. The high level of investment on the farm means that money plays a central role in the modern farming economy and today's farmers are frequently in debt. Moreover, modern farmers are far more mobile than in previous times, since they are usually forced to go into town every day in order to attend meetings of the union, the cooperative or one of the other farmers' organisations.

In one farm out of every two, a member of the family works full time outside of the farm and contributes his or her salary to the family budget. The son might be an industrial worker, for example, or the daughter a secretary, and it is increasingly frequent for the farmer's wife to work as a schoolteacher or a nurse. These outside earnings accounted for 72 per cent of the average farming family's income in 1982, compared with 45 per cent in 1970. In short, there is no longer a total identity between the family and the farm; indeed, the very notion of the farming household has been called into question by this diversification of economic activity. A modern farming household, which lives off at least two different incomes, is similar to most suburban households.

The village has undergone a transformation just as radical as the family or the farm. The village society of the nineteenth century, which is still alive in the memories of old people, used to be characterised by its relative isolation from the rest of French society. Of course, the old village was never totally cut off from the rest of French society, but the existence of the outside world did not prevent each village from preserving its originality and living on its own. The economic autarky of each farm meant that the village as a whole produced everything that was necessary for it to survive, and the local artisan would produce anything which the peasants could not produce but needed. During the eighteenth century, industry itself was based in the countryside before the development of modern towns: iron, paper, glass, textiles. Work in these industries was seasonally based and industrial workers lived on farms and became farm workers during harvest or planting time.

Amongst peasant families differences of wealth were considerable. The affluent peasant would own substantial property and would rule over a household with many children and servants. He might be compared in many respects to an English country squire. In contrast, the poor labourer cultivated his own garden and worked as a day labourer, when and if employment arose. An entire class of marginal people lived in the forests: beggars, woodcutters, victims of destitution. Finally, a class of *notables* oversaw and supervised the village's activities: landowners, priests, schoolteachers, lawyers and doctors. This remarkable social diversity went alongside a profound cultural homogeneity. From the lord of the manor to the beggar, everyone spoke the local dialect, and they all went to church, where the priest's sermon always reaffirmed the same universally applicable moral values. The manner in which the classes and sexes were segregated in church underlined the importance of social distinctions in the traditional peasant society: the children and adolescents would sit next to the choir, the women in the aisles and the men at the back, or in the gallery. The *notables* had their own separate pews or even their own chapel. Social distinctions were not only visible, but were imposed on everybody.

This intimate and coherent image seduces many town-dwellers today, especially amongst the young. But such a rosy image in no way corresponded to the total reality of village life. The violence of social relationships in the village is revealed by the accounts of the police and of trials that historians are only just beginning to study. Moreover, the intimate social relationships of the village meant constantly living in the view of others, and whereas individuals might amuse themselves with rumours or malicious gossip, they would also frequently be the victims of it. In addition, disputes about inheritance were frequently carried over from generation to generation and often became causes of hatred within the family. The village landlords exercised their power with violence and ruthless pride, whereas the priest was constantly brandishing the fires of hell. Finally, the outside authorities posed a continual threat to the survival of these communities. In short, the peasantry lived in constant fear of natural catastrophes (such as a storm which might destroy an entire year's work) or the misuse of power at their expense by the powerful.

Since the middle of the nineteenth century, the rural exodus has emptied the traditional village of between half and two-thirds of its population. Small workshops and their artisans were driven out by competition from urban industries, which attracted not only the rural poor to man the new industries and form an urban working class, but also the rich *notables* drawn by the wealth created in industry, so much so that after the First World War, the countryside was populated only by small and medium-sized farming families. The modernisation of agriculture in the post-war period then drove out the smallest farmers, with the result that by the mid 1970s only those farmers who had been able to modernise their production methods remained in the countryside.

From the mid 1970s onwards, everything seems to have changed. The French village has modernised itself and is recovering its population. Many of those who left the countryside have had difficulties in adapting to urban life; they return frequently to their native village, where they have transformed the old family home or the barn into a secondary residence. The population of today's village varies according to season: it increases during vacation periods, when city-dwellers spend their holidays there, and diminishes out of season. If the village is not too far from a town, those who work in the town are increasingly prone to buy houses in the countryside. In addition, a number of retired people continue to live in the village. In this way, there might be only two or three real farms in a village with twenty houses, whereas until the 1950s agriculture was the livelihood of virtually every village family. Above all, farmers live like any other middle-class category of the population.

The extraordinary post-war transformation of French agriculture was spread over a mere thirty years. In 1940 the peasant lived, worked and died in the same village as his ancestors had done since time immemorial, and was deemed to be an eternal human creation, imbued with an unchanging, timeless soul. This traditional peasant civilisation is passing away, however, with the dying-out of the last generation of genuine peasants born before 1914. Today's young farmer is totally different from his grandfather. The modern farmer is an urbanised producer living in the countryside. There is little to distinguish his lifestyle from that of other members of the middle class: he watches television, for example, or must ensure that his accounts are up to date just like a *cadre* or a businessman living in the town. Life in the modern village is fundamentally different from that which existed two generations ago. However, a curious sentimental reversal of this trend has appeared to be taking place since the late 1960s: peasants and the peasant civilisation are becoming ideologically attractive once again. Thirty years ago, the term peasant was synonymous with country bumpkin, while rustic meant coarse. Today the peasant has become a model for a new generation of neo-rural upwardly mobile people who see in the countryside the means of returning to nature and escaping the alienation of urban industrial society. This ideological volte-face has often left the experienced observer of the French countryside, who remembers the hardships of rural poverty, open-mouthed with surprise. However, the young people who have returned to the countryside have often been disappointed by how little the village corresponds to their idealised visions, and how its legendary sociability has become a myth.

After years of stagnation and decline, the countryside is becoming a living entity once again, although it has radically changed its character. A restored version of the old harmonious village continues to be a dream shared by ecologists and idealistic ex-town-dwellers alike. Many of these people have now moved back into the village in the belief that they can share in the values of the old rural society and escape from the alienation of the towns. However, these 'neo-rural' dwellers are helping to create a society in the village which no longer has anything in common with the old village society, although it has borrowed its surroundings and cultural traditions. Under pressure from the 'neo-rural' village inhabitants, local festivals are becoming increasingly numerous, and markets and fairs are rediscovering a new popularity. Regional cuisine is back in fashion and is codified in recipe books that these newcomers follow scrupulously. Restaurants which offer regional menus are growing rapidly in number. These and other examples confirm that the village is now enjoying a new vitality in contemporary France.

THE RISE AND FALL OF THE INDUSTRIAL WORKING CLASS

Unlike the French peasantry, whose ancestry was ancient, the origins of the French working class are recent, and span little more than two generations. Indeed, the survival of a large peasantry retarded the development of an industrial working class in France. Heavy industry developed late in France. Whereas industrialisation began in the United Kingdom at the end of the eighteenth century and in Germany during the nineteenth, it was only really at the beginning of the twentieth century that France began to industrialise. Throughout the nineteenth century French industry remained essentially small-scale and rural, concentrated in small companies employing fewer than 100 workers.

At the time of the Second Empire (1852–70) the textile industry employed half of the industrial workers in France, followed by the building and metallurgical industries. The first factories grew up around the textile industry, even though most spinning and weaving continued to take place at home. Historical enquiries into working conditions have drawn the distinction between the textile industry, in which women and children comprised a majority of the workforce, and other industrial sectors, where men predominated. By the end of the nineteenth century, only the metallurgical industries (such as iron and steel, or mining) were beginning to take the shape of modern heavy industries. Elsewhere, industrial workers remained in reality countryfolk, who divided their time between their industrial labour and working as farmers on the land. The great working-class strikes at the beginning of the twentieth century were as much the product of pre-industrial workers, such as winegrowers and woodcutters, as they were of genuine workers in industry.

France's industrial take-off began in earnest from 1900 and continued uninterrupted, despite the war, until 1930. The metallurgical industries developed particularly rapidly, and French industrial growth in this sector was more rapid than in any other country. The car-manufacturer Renault might be cited as an extreme example of this: in 1900 the company employed 100 workers, a figure which had risen to 4,400 in 1914 and to over 20,000 in 1930. The birth of heavy industry in urban conurbations brought about the creation of the modern working class and the beginnings of a new feeling of class-consciousness. The older artisanal 'pre-industrial' working class, which had prevailed until the turn of the century, had prided itself upon its trade-consciousness, based on the exercise of skilled occupations which gave it professional autonomy and self-confidence. The new industrial working class of the early twentieth century adopted a more genuine proletarian consciousness based upon poverty, deprivation and the performance of menial, unskilled tasks. Both these rival forms of class consciousness became an integral part of the modern working-class mentality in France. The French Communist Party (PCF) was traditionally the only party capable of expressing these two different forms of working-class consciousness and managed to bring them into harmony: under the party's direction, the skilled worker became the spokesman of the unskilled worker, who in turn derived pride from his work thanks to the example of the skilled worker.

The first generation of industrial workers came to age politically during the period of the left-wing Popular Front government (1936/7). As a direct result of the national strike movement which followed the left's victory in the 1936 election, industrial workers were able to impose the first really important social reforms on unwilling employers in the Matignon agreements, signed between government, unions and employers' organisations. Amongst the central tenets of this programme were the establishment of a forty-hour week and the creation of paid holidays. The success of the 1936 strikes led to massive increases in the number of workers joining trade unions, from which the CGT (whose Socialist and Communist wings were reunified into a single organisation in 1936) was the main beneficiary. The birth and stabilisation of a modern working class explained why the PCF made rapid political progress in the 1930s and 1940s, when it conquered unshakeable bastions in the working-class suburbs of most large towns, as well as in rural areas with a strong left-wing tradition.

This first working-class generation was still working after the Second World War, and it was largely thanks to its efforts that French industry took off in the post-war period. The high level of trade union membership and the frequency of strikes underlined the degree of class consciousness that existed during this period; French workers behaved as if the industrial working class had always existed and would always exist. They believed in the Marxist-inspired myth that the working class was the class of the future and that it was destined to play a central role in the creation of a Socialist society. The second generation of industrial workers, born during the inter-war period, came of age in the 1950s, remained faithful to its working-class roots and adopted as its own the ideas of a working-class counter-culture, as expressed by the PCF and the CGT. This laid great emphasis upon the workers' sense of apartness from the rest of society.

In France, as elsewhere, the strength of class-consciousness and the unity of the industrial working class have been challenged by the development of the post-war consumer society. Working-class living standards have rapidly improved since 1945, although these improvements took place later than in comparable industrialised nations. Back in 1934, working-class living standards in France were lower than those prevailing in most other industrial nations: according to one survey, 74 per cent of French working-class families lived in accommodation comprising fewer than three rooms, compared with 56 per cent in Italy, 52 per cent in West Germany, and 19 per cent in England. Even in 1976, almost one-quarter (22 per cent) of working-class families lived in conditions of 'critical overcrowding' (more than two people per room), but by 1985 that figure had declined to 8 per cent. The consumer society has not by-passed the working class, and nearly all working-class families possess televisions, washing machines, fridges and cars, although their quality is generally inferior to those used by other social strata. Thus, post-war economic growth transformed the French working class from a pauperised, politicised class-conscious entity into a more diversified, less unified class enjoying relative material and social security (for those in work) and the benefits of the consumer society.

Working-class consciousness reached its apogee during the 1950s, but it was precisely at that moment that structural and technical changes were beginning to transform its conditions of existence out of all recognition. As a result of these changes, working-class living standards rose, but industrial workers began to form a diminishing proportion of the overall labour-force. In 1954 industrial workers comprised 87 per cent of all those employed in industry, whereas employers represented 5 per cent and clerical workers 8 per cent. By 1985 clerical workers had come to represent 27 per cent of those working in industry. In absolute terms the number of industrial workers was highest in the 1975 census: 8,500,000, or 40 per cent of the working population. This figure began to decline from the mid 1970s onwards until by 1987 industrial workers comprised only 33 per cent of the workforce. Certain industrial sectors have been particularly hard hit by industrial unemployment. In the iron and steel industry, for example, the workforce was reduced by one-quarter between 1976 and 1983. Moreover, the nature and composition of the industrial working class have been profoundly transformed. Many of today's workers are more like clerical than manual workers: they perform a series of supervisory tasks which have little in common with the hard manual labour and sheer physical effort of their fathers' occupations. Half of today's industrial workers live in small towns or rural communities, rather than in vast industrialised ghettos, which have traditionally been more conducive to breeding class-consciousness. The industrial working class is no longer a male bastion, since 40 per cent of workers are women. Neither is it composed uniquely of native French: France's large immigrant community is concentrated within the working class, and performs most of those menial tasks that native French workers now refuse to do.

Having witnessed the demise of the peasantry during the post-war period, French society is now presiding over the decline of the industrial working class. Marx's proletariat, for which the great philosopher predicted a messianic role as the future harbinger of Socialist Revolution, will have lasted for only two generations in France.

THE BOURGEOIS LIFESTYLE

The bourgeois was an independent man who lived off his inheritance and other forms of unearned income, or *patrimoine* (see the definition below), an ideal which was aspired to and envied by everybody else in society. Except for a few notable exceptions, nobody in France today lives exclusively off his *patrimoine*. Even those people who can boast a sufficient fortune to be able to live without working usually feel obliged to have a paid job. This pattern is a complete reversal of that which existed during the nineteenth century. To be a landlord or a stockholder was itself a profession during the last century, and would be declared as such on census forms. Civil servants, especially magistrates and high-ranking officers, would receive a salary, but that would usually be insufficient to maintain a bourgeois household with dignity, so that earned income would usually be only a supplement to income derived from the *patrimoine*. A more active entrepreneurial bourgeoisie did exist, which created and developed many large companies in Paris and northern France. However, the bourgeoisie of the smaller towns corresponded to this image, especially in southern France, and was by far the more numerous.

The French word *patrimoine* has no exact English equivalent. It signifies the totality of the wealth possessed by a family which is transferred from one generation to another. The *patrimoine* of the bourgeois gentleman consisted mainly of rural and urban estate, state bonds and stocks (*la rente*) and shares in private companies. In general, the bourgeois gentleman preferred to invest in stocks guaranteed by a state – French or foreign – which gave him a feeling of eternal security, rather than to engage in hazardous investments in private companies. The French term *patrimoine* will be used throughout this book.

The traditional bourgeoisie placed considerable importance on the dowry and the 'arrangements' that preceded a bourgeois marriage. Every young married bourgeois couple had to have a sufficient *patrimoine* to be able to live in accordance with their rank in society; this wealth was provided by contributions from both families. A young married bourgeois couple, who had the prospect of inheriting or acquiring wealth, could always find willing money-lenders from whom to borrow sufficient money to be able to enjoy a bourgeois lifestyle. In this closed world, the *patrimoine* not only provided the means with which to enjoy a comfortable lifestyle, but also defined one's position in the social hierarchy. Its importance in the bourgeois world could be illustrated by the sophistication of the Civil Code on the passing down of wealth from generation to generation and in relation to marriage contracts.

The correct bourgeois lifestyle was codified in the minutest detail in various books and manuals which every *maîtresse de maison* (mistress of the household) consulted. These manuals would record every conceivable detail of the correct mode of behaviour for all different sorts of occasions: the visit of an engaged couple, how to wear a pocket handkerchief, how to lay the table when receiving a priest, polite expressions to be used when writing to a prince and so on. However, no mention was made in these manuals of money, which was the sphere of the husband, who was responsible for managing the *patrimoine*, and for providing the *maîtresse de maison* with adequate resources to maintain a bourgeois lifestyle. To refer explicitly to money was regarded as vulgar.

Servants were the most important part of the bourgeois lifestyle. Indeed, the number of servants was an important sign of hierarchy: three was the absolute minimum necessary for a small household. Their waiting upon the master, and the complete separation of their living and working accommodation from that of the master's, confirmed them in their double role as servants and spectators of bourgeois rituals. Because the master would do nothing with his own hands, all the daily duties were carried out by servants: doing the washing, preparing the fire, carrying water for the toilet, preparing meals and so on. These activities demanded a permanent presence and constant attention. But perhaps the most important role of the servant was that of spectator and judge: he obliged others to respect the ritual of which he was a servant and to which he was professionally dedicated. Without the ritual, the servant would have been out of employment, since the master would have had to do all those simple daily tasks himself, rather than acting out a detailed role play.

The dinner was the most important ceremony in this permanent liturgy. Members of the household and invited guests would gather in the large reception hall, before marching in line into the dining room. Unknown during the eighteenth century, the dining room was invented in the nineteenth century and will probably have disappeared by the end of the twentieth. It was a solemn temple entirely dedicated to the perpetuation of bourgeois rituals. In the middle there was a great table surrounded by chairs, while all along the walls there were smaller tables carrying side-dishes and desserts. Everything within the room was conceived for the dining ceremony. The ritual dinner would reproduce the fundamental social cleavages within the room. At the centre of the great table sat the parents, the masters of the house, who were surrounded by their guests; the children and others living in the house (governesses, poorer relatives) would sit at the end of the table. The servants would remain standing, serving the diners and watching the show offered to them. They would be coordinated by the bourgeois wife, the *maîtresse de maison*, who dominated the proceedings and who was determined that the dinner should be a personal triumph. In this way, the bourgeoisie, the middle class and the working class would each know its place within the dining room, as within the rest of society. This ritual could not have survived had the servants disappeared, or had the bourgeoisie itself not exploited every possible occasion to display its hierarchical superiority. The influence of the bourgeois filtered down to certain lower classes in society: the peasants and the middle classes were anxious to imitate their social superiors and maintained a separate dining room, although they did not use it.

The pleasure-garden was also invented by the bourgeoisie during the nineteenth century. The nineteenth-century garden was not merely a piece of scenery which adorned the house, as it had traditionally been in the

French and Florentine traditions, but was inspired by the English garden and was regarded as extremely important in its own right. The garden was an external extension of the house's complex internal organisation, with special places being set aside for particular activities, just like the different rooms of the house. The vegetable garden would be hidden away by the side of the kitchen and shielded by a hedge from the master's view lest he be offended by the sight of it. The bourgeois garden was organised so as to give the most pleasant views possible for family strolls, replete with steps, summerhouses and shady enclosures. These gardens were small compared with the English parks of the eighteenth century, but they were pleasant and comfortable and were tended by at least one full-time gardener.

The study of the humanities, especially Greek and Latin, used to form an important part of bourgeois culture. The structure of the Latin sentence was regarded as being of a great educational value because it promoted a meticulous intellectual vigour. These two languages introduced the bourgeois élite to ancient societies which were entirely different in their beliefs, morality and discipline from the Catholic society prevalent in France. Greek mythology and philosophy introduced young bourgeois men and women to a strange world composed of heroes with scandalous morals, and of young men fighting naked in hand-to-hand combat. The educated bourgeoisie shared a host of common cultural references based upon classical culture, such as the history of the Roman gods, the value of patrician morality, the discipline of the Roman legions, the poetry of Horace or the pomposity of Cicero. These common cultural references, shared by all bourgeois people and repeated by classical French authors, formed a tacit unspoken language which only the bourgeoisie understood. This language was impenetrable to those who had not studied the classics and it gave the bourgeoisie a consciousness of its difference, its class status and as a consequence its indisputable and undisputed social superiority.

From the works of Max Weber or Schumpeter we have become accustomed to the idea that the bourgeois was an ascetic entrepreneur who deprived himself of everything in order to accumulate wealth and who was so imbued with the work ethic that he never allowed himself any relaxation. This image might have been valid for several large entrepreneurs and captains of industry. But it was false for the French bourgeoisie as a whole, which transformed the comfort of daily living into an art. Indeed, never before had any society so entirely consecrated its efforts to satisfying its material needs and tastes with such great anxiety for perfection and sophistication. To live well, in an ostentatious manner, was in reality the common ambition and daily preoccupation of nearly all of the French bourgeoisie during the nineteenth century.

FROM CLASS CONFLICT TO SOCIAL MOBILITY

Mobility in between the three central groups in French society during the nineteenth century was rare. A worker's son had virtually no statistical chance of rising up the social hierarchy, and it was just as unlikely that the son of a bourgeois gentleman, irrespective of his wealth, would descend the social scale and lose his bourgeois status. If it was virtually impossible for a bourgeois or worker to leave his social class, mobility within this class was frequent. A bourgeois family might become financially ruined, whereas another might make a fortune. Similarly, a worker might excel in his job and become a highly valued technician or a respected foreman, whereas a lazy or unlucky worker would probably reduce his family to misery. Finally, within the village a family might increase its wealth generation after generation and multiply the number of its oxen and horses; however, bad management might lead to the disintegration of this wealth within a generation.

The possibilities for upward social mobility were thus extremely limited and were reserved for certain categories whose children were prepared to attempt the transition from one social class to another. The army, the church and above all the school were the only organisations through which upward social mobility could take place. The son of a well-off peasant, for example, could leave the village to work in his cousin's shop in town and eventually open his own shop. More frequently, however, he would do well at school, be noticed by his teacher and then be sent to the élite *école normale* (the best college in the region at which to train to become a schoolteacher). Once he was established in such a position, the possibility of a prestigious social ascent would open up for his son, who might just become President of the Republic (like Georges Pompidou, President of France from 1969 to 1974). Similarly both grandfathers of former Prime Minister Jacques Chirac were schoolteachers. These trajectories were narrow and difficult but they did exist, even though they usually required two generations for success.

During the period preceding the Second World War, the middle classes did offer a number of intermediary positions, such as shopkeepers, clerical workers, civil servants and especially teachers, which sometimes served as stepping stones on the way to greater upward social mobility. The diversity of the middle classes during this period thus corresponded to their mid-way position, as well as to their function of acting as intermediaries between the three great social classes. Their members were few in number and, like the peasantry, frequently concentrated on running small family firms.

Prior to 1945, relations between the main social classes were characterised by violence and fear. Workers lived in constant fear of the foreman and even more so of the boss, who had the power to sack them, thus condemning them to unemployment and misery. Likewise, the farm labourer or tenant-farmer feared the landowner, who could deprive him of his livelihood. The bourgeoisie lived in perpetual fear of social revolution which threatened its property and social superiority; many interpreted the left-wing Popular Front government (1936/7) as a dangerously subversive, potentially revolutionary movement. The wartime resistance movement and the liberation of 1944 represented the last occasions in recent French history when one category of French people feared for its physical safety at the hands of another. In May 1968 the threat of violence was brandished by both sides, but applied by neither. In fact, mutual fear and violence have virtually disappeared between different social classes in contemporary France.

The bourgeoisie and the proletariat are two complementary but mutually antagonistic classes which cannot exist without one another. By disappearing, the bourgeoisie, the proletariat and the peasantry have ensured that the class system, in the strong sense of the term, has been weakened. By class system, I mean on the one hand different class universes or civilisations which controlled every aspect of the lives of their members, and on the other a series of competing macro-groups which struggled for power and for the global domination of society. The bourgeoisie exercised this domination by its economic strength, its political power and its cultural hegemony. It exercised its power in an ostentatious manner, which reflected its own lifestyle. It could count upon the support of the peasantry in its exercise of political power. None the less, the peasantry was always anxious to defend itself as well as possible against the intrusion of the national authorities and to guard its autonomy. This could account for the incredible regional and local diversity of political and cultural structures that the peasantry displayed. For its part, although it ensured that industrial production took place, the industrial working class, or proletariat, opposed itself in every aspect to the bourgeoisie, against which it had built itself up, as well as to the peasantry, from which it had originated. Once the bourgeois, the peasant and the worker began to disappear together in the post-war period, it became clear that a new society was coming into existence out of the ashes of the three great classes of the nineteenth century.

2

The transformation of the social classes: the triumph of the central constellation

The class system has traditionally been regarded as a pyramid: a small number of people at the top form an élite which accumulates wealth and prestige. This élite holds the levers of power in all areas; other social groups attempt either to imitate the élite's behaviour-patterns (middle classes), or else to seek consolation in a counter-culture (proletariat). Beneath the élite, ordinary citizens form an amorphous mass, which is capable only of adapting to ideas and models transmitted from the élite. The mass might reject the élite, but it is incapable of proposing any alternative. According to the pyramidical model of the class system, there exist a number of intermediary strata between the élite and the mass. These 'middle classes' initially imitate the élite in terms of lifestyle, in an attempt to establish boundaries separating them from the mass. This pyramidical model of the class system is unsatisfactory in a number of ways. The division of society into three ill-defined social categories – élite, intermediary strata, mass – cannot adequately explain the range of social divisions within French society. It is possible, of course, to subdivide these categories almost infinitely, but the notion of social class then becomes of little value as an indicator of and explanatory factor for social divisions.

Marx rejected the simplicity of the pyramidical model, and replaced it with that of a class struggle in a society divided into two mutually hostile classes – the bourgeoisie and the proletariat. A steady bipolarisation between these two mutually antagonistic social classes would lead to revolution. Other social groups on the margins of the bourgeoisie and the proletariat would progressively be forced to choose their camp, siding either with the historically doomed bourgeoisie or the proletariat, the class which embodied the future hopes of humanity. Amongst the peasantry, for example, there would be a division between the rich landowning peasants, who would side with the bourgeoisie in defence of property, and the poor landless labourers, who were natural allies of the proletariat. In this century, however, the tendency has been for there to be a diversification of social groups within capitalist society, rather than a polarisation around bourgeois and proletarian poles. Despite the overwhelming evidence to support the idea of diversification, some Marxists still engage in exercises of mental contortion to try and reconcile the emergence of new social classes (apart from the traditional bourgeoisie and proletariat) with Marx's vision of steady polarisation, and the disappearance of intermediary strata.

At the turn of the century, the German sociologist G. Simmel postulated an alternative model of the evolution of social classes within capitalist societies. Simmel stood Marx's schematisation upon its head, by arguing that the middle class was becoming a genuine social class with its own identity, originality and class logic. According to Simmel, the development of capitalist societies was such that their class structure evolved into the shape of a triad: ruling class, middle class, popular class. Within any triad, it has been observed that the latest arrival is able to manipulate the conflict which divides the other two, sometimes allying with one, sometimes with the other. The third member of a group of three is thus able to act as a referee, mediator or simply ironic observer. The central location of the middle class, and its status as the last arrival, greatly increased its strategic leverage vis-à-vis the other two main classes, since both attempted to call upon the middle class as an ally against its traditional adversary. Moreover, the existence of the middle class as a referee has also limited the consequences of the class struggle, since it is inconceivable that one of the traditional antagonists could completely triumph over the other when both sides can be called to order by a third, more disinterested party.

Because of its central location, the middle class is in constant conflict with both the bourgeoisie and the proletariat; it gradually influences both these traditional classes by imposing its own characteristics upon them. In fact, the traditional classes come increasingly to resemble the central middle class, so much so that they lose many of the specific traits associated with their origins. The result of this development is that the boundaries between different social classes become confused, as each class adopts characteristics associated with the central middle class. Within the middle class, there is considerable diversity in occupation, lifestyle, income and education. The concomitant of this diversity is that a high degree of social mobility occurs within the middle class, and that this model of social mobility has become the central characteristic of society as a whole.

This new middle class first appeared within the USA during the 1920s and 1930s. In France, by contrast, the stagnation of the inter-war period delayed its development until the 1960s. The development of the middle class has reached new levels in the France of the 1980s. Paradoxically, although Simmel's analyses have been supported by the evolution of capitalist societies during the past century, their success has called into question the very notion of a middle class. When all groups within society begin to resemble the central middle class to a greater or lesser extent, then analysis in terms of social class loses much of its pertinence. This is certainly true for the traditional adversarial classes – bourgeoisie and proletariat – whose sense of class identity has been weakened by the intrusion of middle-class values in their midst. It is also true of the middle class itself, since its values are accepted with varying degrees of enthusiasm by nearly all groups within society.

A COSMOGRAPHIC VIEW OF SOCIETY

If both the Marxist and the pyramidical views of social class must be rejected, it is possible to propose a 'cosmographic' vision in their place. French society could be compared to the night sky, in which clusters of stars form a number of different constellations, which are variable in size and more or less clear to behold. Of course, such a schematisation is difficult to measure by relying merely on statistics, as the French national statistical office, INSEE, does when attempting to measure social class. In France, as in other developed nations, analyses of social class are classically based upon two sets of variables: income and degree of educational attainment. These two measures usually reinforce each other, so that the higher an individual is on the income scale, the more likely he is to have received a given level of education. Indeed, INSEE operates on the assumption that there is a broad measure of correlation between the two. But this is not always the case. Numerous examples exist of instances where a high degree of educational achievement does not correlate with an elevated income and vice versa. The two classic examples are those of the university lecturer, highly qualified but in receipt of a modest salary, and the self-made businessman, with considerable wealth but few if any formal educational qualifications. These examples are, however, exceptions which prove the general rule that there is usually a correlation between formal education and income (see table 1).

Most social groups can be stratified according to education and income. Within the popular constellation, a low income coincides with an absence of educational qualifications, whereas within the central constellation there is a higher level both of income and of educational achievement. The independent constellation is the most composite: it is separated both from the popular constellation on account of its members' greater income and independent status, and from the central constellation because of a general lack of formal qualifications, except amongst the liberal professions. The dynamism of the different class constellations can be measured by whether

Table 1. *Class constellations and socio-professional position*

Popular constellation	Industrial workers
	Employés
Central constellation	*Cadres moyens*
	Most *cadres supérieurs*
	Teachers
	Civil servants
	Engineers
	Most other salaried non-manual workers
	Most technicians
Independent constellation	Businessmen
	Independent professions
	Shopkeepers
	Artisans

Note: Central and independent constellations share many of the same characteristics: both form part of the middle classes. Excluded from this schema are: farmers, too varied to constitute a distinct group; the unemployed and paupers, at the bottom of the social hierarchy; and the ruling élite, recruited from the cream of the *cadres supérieurs*, the professions, and business.

The French expression *cadre* has no direct English equivalent. The *cadres* are divided by INSEE into two units: *cadres supérieurs*, and *cadres moyens*. *Cadres supérieurs* generally occupy top management positions in public-sector organisations and private companies; *cadres moyens* occupy middle-management positions. Both groups are composite: the *cadres supérieurs* category includes (besides top management) professors, secondary school teachers, the scientific and literary professions, and engineers and is linked by INSEE with the liberal professions. The *cadres moyens* category includes (besides intermediary management) primary school teachers, various intellectual professions, social and medical workers, and technicians. To minimise ambiguity, the French expression *cadre* will be retained throughout.

There is no exact translation either for the French *employé*, which refers to both low-status clerical workers (secretaries, clerks, office boys) and shop assistants and other poorly qualified staff working in commercial firms. To avoid ambiguity, the French expression *employé* will be retained.

they have grown or declined during our period of analysis. Census figures illustrate clearly the growth of those social groups forming part of the central constellation.

As we can see from table 2, social groups forming part of the independent constellation declined for most of the period, but this trend has recently started to reverse, probably reflecting government efforts to stimulate employment in this area. Within the popular constellation, manual workers are in slow long-term decline, but clerical workers and technicians have expanded, thereby shifting the centre of gravity away from manual work within the popular constellation. Within the overall expansion of the central middle-class constellation certain groups have developed more rapidly than others: the spectacular growth of the *cadres* is the most significant post-war development, although this has recently slowed down. There has also

Table 2. *The development of the French working population since 1954 (%)*

	1954	1962	1975	1982	1988
Farmers	21.0	15.5	7.5	6.5	6.0
Business people, shopowners, artisans	13.0	10.5	8.0	8.0	8.0
Cadres supérieurs, liberal professions	3.0	4.5	7.0	8.0	11.0
Cadres moyens	9.0	11.5	17.0	18.0	20.0
Employés	17.0	18.5	24.0	26.5	27.0
Industrial workers	37.0	39.5	36.5	33.0	28.0
	100.0	100.0	100.0	100.0	100.0

Source: INSEE

been a strong development within the teaching profession, and within medical and social work.

The cohesion of the main constellations is increased by the widespread practice of homogamy: the tendency for marriage to occur only amongst people of similar social backgrounds. Within the popular constellation, manual workers and *employés*, who are close in terms of the financial and cultural capital they possess, tend to marry each other. Likewise, *cadres supérieurs*, engineers, and the professional classes all share a similar degree of culture and lifestyle which makes it almost certain that they will marry within the central constellation, frequently within the same profession. Upward social mobility is thus rarely achieved by an individual from a popular background marrying into the central constellation; and it is more common for girls than for boys.

At the top of the social scale, the ruling class is composed of the members of the élite from the spheres of politics, business and the main professions. Members of the ruling élite often possess a substantial *patrimoine* and have nearly always obtained the highest level of education the system can provide, usually having studied at one of the Parisian *grandes écoles* (see chapter 5). It would appear that access to the ruling élite was more socially bound at the end of the 1980s than it had been ten years earlier, its members being recruited overwhelmingly from more privileged strata within society. This undoubtedly reflected the fact that the ruling élite has stopped growing in size and closed ranks against newcomers as a consequence.

The popular constellation is composed of all categories of manual workers, and *employés*. Within this group, women are more likely to be *employés* (secretaries and shop assistants), and men are more likely to be manual workers. The typical popular household is thus composed of a male manual worker and a female office worker or shopworker, although women are more likely to be housewives in the popular constellation than in groups higher up the social scale. Approximately half of popular households live in rural areas or in small towns. In general, they dispose of a strictly limited income and are unlikely to possess formal educational qualifications. Until the mid 1970s manual workers tended to vote in considerable numbers for the French Communist Party, identifying with the Communists' 'workeriste' discourse and ideology. *Employés*, by contrast, were more likely to vote for the Socialist Party. The popular constellation thus forms a relatively homogeneous social grouping, although *employés* can be ranked higher than manual workers with regard to their level of cultural awareness and cultural practices. The symbol of the solidarity of the popular constellation is the figure of the foreman, who despite his control over shopfloor workers preserves a lifestyle which has more in common with members of the popular constellation than it does with the prevalent middle-class model.

The situation of the poor and the structure of poverty has been transformed during the post-war period. Classical studies of the poor in France have illustrated that they constituted a relatively stable urban population. They had not so much been excluded from society as never formed a part of it. They came from families which had always occupied a marginal position and depended upon the different social services for their survival. Their children had little chance of joining society because they had never learnt its moral codes, habits or mysteries, and had a totally false image of it. For example, they believed that they stood virtually no chance of finding work, which became a justification for not looking. They were confined to a ghetto, which was an accurate description both of their objective position, and of the way they perceived their relationship with the rest of society. This traditional pauper represents a declining proportion of the population.

During the last fifteen years a new category of pauper has joined the traditionally marginal figure. The 'new poor' have experienced society, but have fallen into poverty accidentally, as the result of unemployment, illness, divorce or a similar catastrophe. These 'new poor' are often able to reinsert themselves into the mainstream of French society at a later date, although evidence suggests that they are frequently prone to fall back into the trap of poverty. In the USA, the 'new poor' represent two-thirds of the total; they are largely composed of blacks and Hispanics with problems of cultural integration into American society. In France, the statistical evidence is too meagre to allow similar conclusions, but local studies strongly suggest that in large cities unemployment is the main cause of the growth of the 'new poor'. Extreme poverty would appear to be confined mainly to the large cities, and is rarely visible in small towns and rural areas. Finally, many old people who survive only on state pensions live in extreme poverty,

Table 3. *Immigrants according to nationality (%)*

Nationality	1931	1954	1975	1982
Europeans (including USSR), of whom:	90.5	81.1	61.1	47.8
Germans	2.6	3.0	1.2	1.2
Belgians	9.3	6.0	1.6	1.4
Spanish	13.0	16.4	14.4	8.7
Italians	29.0	28.8	.13.4	9.1
Poles	18.7	15.3	2.7	1.8
Portuguese	1.8	1.1	22.0	20.8
Yugoslavs	1.2	1.0	2.0	1.8
Africans, of whom:	3.9	13.0	34.6	42.8
Algerians		12.0	20.6	21.6
Moroccans	3.2	0.6	7.6	11.7
Tunisians		0.3	4.1	5.1
Americans	1.2	2.8	1.2	1.4
Asians, of whom:	3.2	2.3	3.0	8.0
Turks	1.3	0.3	1.5	3.4
TOTAL	100.0	100.0	100.0	100.0

Source: INSEE

although their number is declining. The same is true for the mentally and physically handicapped, who often suffer from extreme disadvantage and poverty.

Immigrants form a category of the French population whose problems are somewhat different. The first forms of 'immigration' in modern France were internal, when Norman and Breton peasants migrated to Paris during the nineteenth century. However, it is more accurate to label as immigration the process whereby Italians and Spanish settled in Mediterranean France at the turn of the century, as well as Poles in the North, and Armenians throughout the country. After the Second World War, Spanish and Italian were succeeded by Portuguese immigrants and then, increasingly, by North African Arabs. By 1931, France had approximately the same percentage of immigrants as in the mid 1980s, around 7 per cent of the population.

French society has shown a remarkable capacity for assimilating all these various groups of immigrants. Within the space of one generation, each of the immigrant groups has become integrated into the mainstream French culture (even when it has retained elements of its unique racial or national identity). There are numerous examples of the sons of Polish miners or Italian masons becoming engineers, university lecturers, top civil servants and so on. Alongside these success stories, of course, many members of ethnic minorities have not managed to achieve such upward social mobility, but the vast majority of immigrants have become completely integrated into the mainstream of French culture. It must not be assumed, however, that the cultural integration of immigrants has always been an uncomplicated, unproblematic affair. All the immigrant communities have had to face a greater or lesser degree of ostracism and have often had to make considerable efforts before succeeding in being recognised as fellow citizens by native French people. None the less, immigrant communities have been well absorbed into French society, with the result that France is a nation with heterogeneous ethnic origins, but a remarkably homogeneous and uniform culture. The same can be said neither of the United States (which is becoming more and more of a pluri-cultural society), nor of the United Kingdom or Germany (both of which have placed their immigrants in a marginal situation).

In the 1970s, it was feared by certain observers that the onset of economic crisis and the growth of unemployment would create economic, social and psychological conditions conducive to the development of a pervasive, even violent racism. Such pessimistic predictions have not generally been validated, despite the openly racist outlook adopted by a minority. It is true, of course, that Jean Marie Le Pen, leader of the extreme right-wing National Front, has exploited the diffused anti-immigrant sentiment of a minority to build up a new, ultra-conservative political movement in the 1980s. However, the importance of Le Pen must not be exaggerated, and his ideas are completely alien to the large majority of French citizens. Indeed, Le Pen has probably served a useful social function, since it is eminently preferable that racist sentiments should be expressed by means of verbal rather than physical violence. Most French people have developed a powerful sense of racial tolerance, as well as accepting modes of behaviour and existence which differ from the norm (be they social, psychological or cultural). Few can deny that the young *beurs* (the children of North African Arab immigrants) have expressed an overwhelming desire to be considered no different from other young French people.

It is important to recall the context in which North African immigration occurred in the 1950s and 1960s. As France divested itself of its remaining colonies in those decades, members of colonial communities (mainly North African immigrants, from Morocco, Tunisia and Algeria) were attracted to France in order to provide a cheap, unskilled labour-force, to perform the menial, unskilled tasks that French workers were only too willing to relinquish to them. Because these workers were unskilled, they were the first to be affected by the economic crisis of the 1970s; indeed, unemployment rates are far higher amongst immigrant communities (except the Portuguese) than they are within the rest of French society. This is especially the case for young people, who suffer more than anybody from the inadequacies of the education system. Such inadequacies prevent a sufficient number of them from acquiring technical training, their only guarantee of a job. Most immigrants find themselves in a worse (although not a fundamentally different) situation than those French people on the bottom rung of the social ladder. Demonstrations of racism in contemporary France have been provoked primarily by the country's difficult economic position since the 1970s, and have been concentrated mainly in those social categories which perceive themselves to be most at threat from the apparent competition of immigrant workers. It is surprising that the anti-immigrant backlash has not expressed itself in a more brutal manner.

One area in which the assimilation of racial minorities is likely to prove difficult is that of religion. The new religious fundamentalism aired by sections of France's ethnic minority groups might be interpreted as an attempt to rediscover a group identity in the context of rapid social change. Such a development is entirely consistent with the sociological model according to which rapid social transformation is invariably accompanied by a proliferation of fundamentalist religious sects. The importance of Muslim fundamentalism in France must not, however, be exaggerated, since the number of Muslim fundamentalists is still smaller than that of practising Jews. The dominant impression left from a brief survey of France's immigrant community is that the new North African immigrants are gradually becoming integrated into the mainstream of French society, especially those of the second generation. Moreover, the problems immigrants have to face (education, unemployment, poverty) are those which afflict other sections of French society as well, although they are usually experienced in a more acute form by immigrants. Finally, new religious beliefs introduced into France by immigrant communities illustrate the increasing diversity of French society. In spite of this diversity, the strength of French culture will probably tend in the long run to promote the integration of immigrants into the social mainstream, making it less likely that they will seek refuge in ethnic subcultures.

THE CENTRAL CONSTELLATION

The key to an understanding of the changing structure of social classes in the past decades lies in an analysis of the central constellation, defined above. In the traditional French society described in chapter 1, when social cleavages were well defined and barriers between social classes rigid, the rare individual who experienced upward social mobility was under intense pressure to conform with the behaviour-patterns of his new social group, and to abandon those of his group of origin. This traditional pattern has lost its pertinence in a period of extreme social mobility. In the new, extremely fluid French class structure, in which new social groups are constantly emerging, the differences between groups are naturally blurred. This means that the individual who rises in the social scale is under less pressure to accept the norms and values of his new group, and reject those of his group of origin. He has a considerable degree of freedom to decide what lifestyle to adopt, or, if necessary, to invent his own.

To continue with the cosmographic analogy evoked above, within the central constellation there exist a number of different galaxies, each with a greater or lesser degree of homogeneity and dynamism. The *cadres* form the core of the central constellation (see definition above). Their number has grown dramatically during the post-war period. This growth has been accompanied by an increased sense of consciousness as a social class: 63 per cent of *cadres* declared themselves to belong to a social class in 1987, as against 57 per cent in 1976, a development which is in strong contrast with the declining sense of class identity amongst manual workers. The *cadres* represent not only the core of the central constellation, but also the obligatory model to which other social groups refer, either in order to imitate or to reject.

As a new social class, the *cadres* have experienced a number of problems within contemporary French society. Firstly, they suffer from a problem of identity: the *cadres* are of sufficiently recent invention not to be able to draw upon a precise identity forged through centuries of existence. Secondly, they suffer from a problem related to status: how are they to be situated in relation to existing social and professional hierarchies? They are salaried staff working for employers; as are the manual or clerical workers of the popular constellation. But they have a higher level of educational attainment and (usually) income than manual or clerical workers, and are involved in work of a more intellectually demanding character. Unlike manual workers, the *cadres* enjoy an organised career structure, with regular prospects of promotion as they get older, and increasing opportunities for responsibility within their organisation. The manual worker does not have such prospects of regular, organised promotion or growing responsibility within the organisation.

In fact, as a result of their technical, scientific or managerial competence, the *cadres* possess a cultural capital which makes them comparable with the bourgeoisie of the nineteenth century (see chapter 1), although there are also marked differences between the two. *Cadres* exercise decision-making functions in all companies, but this is dependent upon powers being delegated to them from on high, so the power to take decisions is not really that of the *cadre*, but of his employer. The career-pattern of today's *cadre* was unknown to the bourgeois of old, who inherited his father's position (family firm or professional practice) along with his wealth, and stayed in that position all his life. As with the classical bourgeois, the contemporary *cadre* possesses knowledge and culture, but it is clear that these are not the same as before. The culture possessed by the *cadre* is no longer reserved to a bourgeois élite (as during the nineteenth century), but is spread throughout society. It will be argued that the influence of the *cadres* within French society has increased even more rapidly than their numerical expansion, since they have developed a new focal culture which has become the central reference point for virtually the whole of French society.

The emergence of the *cadres* was related to the social and economic transformation of French society during the post-war boom, and the extension and democratisation óf the education system (see chapter 5). As *cadres* are recent products of social and economic change, it is hardly surprising that they are largely recruited from amongst those experiencing either upward social mobility (from the popular classes), or downward mobility (from the old bourgeoisie). France's industrial take-off during the 1950s led to changing demands being placed upon the workforce: more technical and managerial staff were needed to run the new industries, at the expense firstly of farmers, and later of manual workers. However, the spectacular increase in social mobility greatly exceeded that which economic changes objectively demanded, with the result that during the first four post-war decades, France became far less rigidly class bound than it had been on the eve of the Second World War. Nearly all of the social mobility which occurred took place within the middle classes of the central constellation. The behavioural and attitudinal patterns adopted by the middle class act as models for the rest of society to absorb and eventually imitate. In this sense, the middle class exercises a hegemonic influence, imposing its lifestyle and attitudes on other categories of the population.

The typical ritual of this new middle class is the barbecue. This is different in every sense from the bourgeois dinner described in chapter 1. There is no ostentatious hierarchy, nor is there any ritualised division of roles between members present. Everything is reversed: grilled meat replaces roast, the barbecue takes place outside, and the presumption of equality between participants replaces that of highly formalised inequality. Unlike the bourgeois dinner, the barbecue is not a highly ritualised show, designed to confirm publicly the social standing of every member present. But in a more discreet way people are classified and reclassified, as participants continually strive to gain recognition of their social standing, and to climb another rung on the social ladder in the eyes of other participants. The barbecue takes place outside in rustic surroundings, often under a tree. It gives the impression of being highly improvised, although it will almost certainly have been carefully prepared. This impression of spontaneity contrasts with the highly rigid context of the dining room during the bourgeois dinner.

Everybody present at the barbecue will stand up or sit down as he chooses, not feeling constrained to ask the hosts before grilling another kebab, or pouring another glass of wine. The scene is one of apparent disorder, but in fact everything is well organised. Whereas the *maîtresse de maison* dominated the bourgeois dinner, it is now the husband who controls proceedings. It is he who lights the fire, hands out the kebabs, etc. The wife performs a more limited, subordinate role, preparing salads and vegetables in the kitchen. The complicated recipe of the bourgeois dinner is replaced in the barbecue with raw vegetables and uncooked meats for grilling. Because those who eat also prepare their food, there is no longer any distinction between producers and consumers. The process is no longer one in which the bourgeoisie puts on a show for members of the middle and lower classes, and recalls everybody to his social position. Instead, each participant attempts to impress everybody else, which presupposes a greater degree of equality between members.

Although invented by the central constellation, this ritual has become widely diffused throughout the whole of society. There are many variations on the same theme. The barbecue might take place by the pool of a luxurious villa on the Mediterranean, or in the courtyard of the neighbouring farm. The barbecue itself might be expensive, or home made. This illustrates both the universal nature of this ritual throughout society, and the many different ways in which it takes place. The barbecue is in fact a model for the functioning of the new French society: behaviour-patterns and opinions emerge from within the middle classes and are then diffused more widely throughout society. This means that French society is far more difficult to analyse than when traditional simplistic pyramidical or Marxist classifications of the class system prevailed.

THE MORAL ACTIVISTS

Within the central constellation, one group has been especially innovative and has had a considerable impact upon society as a whole. This *innovative core* of the central constellation comprises: the teaching profession, social workers, members of new cultural professions, and service personnel working in the socio-medical field (nurses, physiotherapists). The numbers of the innovative core more than tripled from 1962 to 1975, from approximately 110,000 to 350,000. These workers tend to be young, mainly because their careers have only recently been invented or expanded. Moreover, they are disproportionately feminine, especially within the teaching profession. Because these were largely new professions, their members were recruited mainly as a result of social mobility. They had either experienced upward social mobility, as the sons or daughters of *employés*, or else had descended from the classical bourgeoisie as a result either of choice, or of a failure to obtain adequate qualifications to become a *cadre supérieur*.

Members of the innovative core possess a strong identity, share a series of common attitudes, and perform an original role within the central constellation, and by extension within French society as a whole. Having been involved in the events of May 1968, many of these activists were temperamentally unable to return to normal professions and to accept the place that had been prepared for them within society. Instead, they chose 'pedagogical' professions, which enabled them to help people, rather than concentrate upon their personal advancement. Many of these people subsequently felt bitter because they considered they were being exploited by the authorities in order to control marginal categories of the population: such as the special teachers, for example, who had wanted to help underprivileged children, but who saw themselves transformed into state agents to control the behaviour of young delinquents. Once a part of the innovative core, its members were average in everything (level of education, income), except for the original role they performed within French society.

After May 1968, many members of the innovative core created new associations, self-help groups, or other organisations defending particular causes. The French sociologist Emmanuèle Reynaud has aptly labelled these people 'moral activists', as opposed to political, religious, or trade union activists. These 'moral activists' are concerned above all with the good of others, but rather than attempting to convince people to adopt a pre-ordained set of beliefs, they incite them to assume greater control over their daily lives. The moral activists have developed their own particular ideology which might be labelled cultural liberalism, an ideology which played an important part in shaping the philosophy of the French Socialist Party renovated by François Miterrand during the 1970s. This cultural liberalism, invented by a relatively small core group, has since become accepted far more widely in French society. The new philosophy represented by cultural liberal liberalism has more in common with the left than with the right, but we must be careful not to confuse this philosophy with traditional left-wing ideology. Whereas the left's traditional ideology stresses the importance of quantitative demands (redistribution of wealth, welfare, common ownership of the means of production), cultural liberalism lays greater emphasis on 'quality of life' issues (the right to difference, defence of the environment, participation in decision-making and so on). Indeed, cultural liberalism is best portrayed as a new belief-system, invented by a new combination of social groups – the 'innovative core' of the central constellation – which has subsequently expanded its influence to other groups within French society. It would be inaccurate to portray cultural liberalism as in any sense subversive, since its salient themes are perfectly compatible with the existing order, and many of its ideas are accepted throughout society.

To the extent that they possess both knowledge and culture, the moral activists can be compared with the bourgeoisie of the nineteenth century. Yet their culture is more widely diffused throughout society than that of the old bourgeoisie. It is the 'focal culture', extending its influence up to higher social groups, as well as down to lower groups. This focal culture is relayed to all strata of society through the mass media. Having invented this new focal culture, the moral activists occupy a powerful position within society, along with that of the small group of media professionals who help to diffuse their message.

The impact of cultural liberalism upon people's lifestyles is difficult to overestimate, one of the most spectacular aspects of this being the practice of unmarried couples living together. Such a complete reversal of behaviour-patterns was in itself remarkable, but the great originality of this transformation was that it originated from this particular group within the new middle class, and was subsequently adopted by groups both higher up and lower down the social scale. This broke with the traditional, established model that changes in patterns of social behaviour originated at the top of the social scale and were then imitated by the middle classes. The moral activists were imbued with a strong consciousness of their generation – the May 1968 generation – somewhat like a more traditional class consciousness. This strong generational identity spread to affect other members of the same generation in different social groups. The effect of this generational spirit was to weaken the solidity of more traditional working-class or bourgeois identities.

In summary, it is clear that the 'moral activists' could not be likened with the middle class of the nineteenth century, described above. The old 'middle class' consistently attempted to imitate social models handed down by the bourgeoisie (but lacked the means to do so), as well as attempting to distinguish itself as vigorously as possible from the popular classes. By contrast, the moral activists do not really seek to differentiate themselves from the popular classes. Indeed, forming part of a left-inclining galaxy, they share many of the same ideological beliefs as those prevalent within the popular constellation (beliefs they themselves have been instrumental in influencing). Moreover, they are likely to imitate popular fashions and consider themselves as part of the working class.

By the end of the 1970s, the moral activists had made their appearance on the national political scene. The Socialist victories of 1981 led certain commentators to proclaim that after having assumed social and cultural leadership, the moral activists would in turn become the new political class, replacing the traditionally bourgeois political élites. This has not materialised. The moral activists suffered an historic setback as a result of the failure of the Socialist economic policy from 1981 to 1983, with which they were closely associated. This failure had two main consequences: the moral activists lost, probably for good, their temporary grip over political power, and they were also forced to recognise that top industrialists and civil servants held the real economic power, which remained resolutely outside of their control.

Their inability to capture lasting political control, however, has in no sense lessened the cultural influence of the moral activists, since cultural liberalism has become the norm respected by most other groups within society, especially within the central constellation. Moreover, the moral activists continue to dominate the tissue of associative groups which have proliferated in all spheres of French society. It is true that these activists do not in any sense represent a threat to the existing social order. In fact, it is arguable that they have allowed themselves to become absorbed into the structure of existing society, despite their initial declarations of intent to change it. By becoming more fully integrated into society, however, they have succeeded in transforming many of the beliefs which permeate contemporary France.

Classifications of social groups at a national level can be misleading, since it does not allow us to take the influence of local variations into consideration. It is obvious, for example, that a worker living in a rural area, who cultivates his own garden and mixes with farmers on a daily basis, is likely to view life differently from another worker who lives in a large urban centre, surrounded by a working-class environment which strengthens his sense of class-consciousness. Workers who live in a working-class district are generally more conscious of their class ideology than are those who live in a predominantly bourgeois area. The intensity of class feeling is thus heavily influenced by an individual's surrounding environment. The fact that half of the French population lives in small towns with under 25,000 inhabitants, within which the 'middle-class' mentality predominates, is of considerable importance. Within such towns, representatives of the popular constellation are more likely to conform with the surrounding environment and adopt 'middle-class' attitudes than they are in larger urban communities.

The identity of France's rural communities has been transformed beyond all recognition during the post-war period and they have in their turn become the preserve of the 'middle class' (see chapter 1). The small and medium-sized town is the ideal location for the dynamic core elements of the central constellation to exercise their social influence. In these communities, these new radical middle classes are able to exercise a preponderant influence in local associations, parishes, or political parties, which they are able to shape in their own image. In fact, the cultural influence of the innovative core of the central constellation is such that even in working-class districts, those workers who take on responsibilities in local organisations tend to adopt 'middle-class' attitudes and behaviour-patterns.

The moral activists are thus frequently able to dominate rural and small and medium-sized town communities. It might be argued that they are just as guilty of 'moralising' in relation to the popular classes as bourgeois ladies were during the nineteenth century. In order to ensure that their influence is as pervasive as possible, they have become extremely adept at exploiting local institutions to further their aims and making maximum possible use of collective resources. Their power can thus be found at the micro-level of local associations and pressure groups, rather than at the macro-level, at the summits of the state. However, the importance of these micro-institutions must not be underestimated. In the sphere of cultural or moral identity, the institutions created by the moral activists perform a role of fundamental importance. In order to preserve the power of these micro-institutions, the moral activists are forced continually to come up with new ideas and associations, in order to keep themselves in the public eye. As long as they do conceive new ideas, the moral activists are able to attract the attention of the mass media (their objective allies), which is a means of ensuring that they will exercise influence in the future. The power to attract the attention of the media can itself be seen as a sort of political power.

In any society, those groups in an unstable, uncertain position within the social hierarchy are always the instigators of social change. The dynamism of such groups gives them strength and coherence. To take but one example, agricultural progress in the course of the 1950s came about as a result of the efforts of a generation of young farmers who knew they had either to adapt or to disappear. Another such unstable group in contemporary France is that of university graduates, who feel an endemic sense of instability, on account of the fact that their university degrees, whose prestige has lessened with the expansion of higher education, do not automatically open the doors to prestigious careers, reserved for graduates of the *grandes écoles*. Many ambitious graduates, unable to secure prestigious jobs in the civil service or in industry, have joined unstable, even marginal institutions, or have established their own businesses. In the medium-sized towns, these frustrated careerists come together in professional clubs or political parties, where they hope to obtain a better social recognition of their talents. As with the moral activists, these careerists have been recruited through a high degree of social mobility. They are either from popular backgrounds, or else have descended from the bourgeoisie. The existence of an unstable category of ambitious, partially frustrated graduates is likely to have considerable implications for the future of French society. It is probable that because of their need for social recognition, these French 'yuppies' will themselves invent new ideologies and lifestyles, which will ensure that they perform an important role in the future.

We saw above how the expansion of the middle class in the USA, analysed by Daniel Bell, had been accompanied by a weakening of middle-class identity: once the idea of being middle class was accepted by everybody, the specific class connotations associated with that state were weakened. Bell has illustrated how American society has begun to restratify itself into new 'classes', as a result of the splitting up of the middle class. It is possible that the same process is underway in France in relation to the central constellation. It is easy to imagine, for example, that divisions will increase within the central constellation between higher- and lower-status *cadres*, or between the *cadres* and the new professions. Should this occur, the notion of all these groups belonging to one central constellation, essentially united in relation to fundamental perceptions, might be progressively called into question. In such circumstances, each group would probably develop a greater sense of 'class' identity, tending to withdraw it from other groups within society. This has not yet occurred in relation to the central constellation in France.

The model we have portrayed of a central constellation, which is composed of a broad variety of social groups, and subject to all sorts of different influences, appears better able to explain the transformations of French society than does the pyramidical schematisation, whereby all social change or innovation comes from above. This conception presupposes a high degree of social mobility within French society, which gives observers the impression that this society is forever changing (despite retaining its fundamental structures intact). Within the transient French society of the last quarter of the twentieth century, different social groups have acquired a degree of autonomy from one another, which has enabled them to take their own initiatives and launch their own fashions. The whole dynamic of social change in France today can best be understood by analysing how particular groups interact with each other, and how behaviour-patterns initiated by one group influence other groups within society. For this reason, it is impossible to foresee the evolution of French society merely by pointing to predictions of technical progress, or long-term demographic evolutions, and it is difficult to predict how the structure of French society might change in the next twenty years. Rather than presage future developments, it is preferable to understand how these relations between different social groups can produce social change.

Part II

The de-mystification of the great national institutions

3

The army and the church

The regiment returning triumphantly to town after a military manoeuvre and being enthusiastically greeted by the local population: this image belongs firmly to the past. Under both the monarchy and the republic, the army was the incarnation of the nation itself, and the most sacred duty of every French citizen was to serve in it in defence of his country. Military processions occurred frequently, in order to remind citizens of the fundamental values of patriotism, hierarchy and order. In contemporary France, the flag, the procession and the uniform are symbols of a bygone age, except when they appear on television every 14 July, the date of France's major national celebration.

At the end of the nineteenth century, army officers were recruited from amongst the ranks of the bourgeoisie, or the small provincial nobility. These two groups, especially the latter, often remained loyal to the idea of the monarchy and hostile to that of the republic. However, they did not regard the army in the same light as other republican institutions such as the civil service. Whereas they considered it an honour to serve one's country in the army (which they clearly dissociated from the republic), to serve the republican state directly was regarded as being little short of treachery. This ambivalence helped partly to explain why the army and the republic maintained conflictual relations until the First World War, as epitomised by the anti-republican stance adopted by a large proportion of army officers during the Dreyfus affair at the turn of the century.

An officer's rank did not merely designate his function and occupation, but might be likened to the title of a nobleman, since it was always mentioned whenever he was addressed or referred to. Army officers were educated in two *grandes écoles*: Polytechnique and Saint-Cyr. All officers shared a strong sense of loyalty to their colleagues, devotion to their units and pride in their posts. The officer corps enjoyed considerable prestige amongst the population as a whole.

Military service was in theory obligatory for every French citizen, although during the nineteenth century the sons of the bourgeoisie were frequently able to by-pass this regulation. For the young peasant, it provided his first opportunity to leave the village and to experience what life was like in the towns. In many respects, the army was a more effective school for the peasantry than any other institution. Not only did the peasant learn how to wield arms, but he was also taught the basic duties of being a citizen, such as discipline, respect for the authorities and respect for authority in general. During the nineteenth century many young army recruits would speak only their own patois, or local dialect, so that non-commissioned officers had to act as interpreters between the soldiers and their officers. The First World War was France's last peasant war. The nation's victory at the end of the war was accredited to the endurance and discipline of the peasantry, which con-stituted the vast bulk of the nation's five million dead, as well as to the high quality of its officers. The symbolic importance of this immense collective effort is remembered in the thousands of war-memorials in villages and towns throughout France.

Because national service was obligatory even for the sons of the bour-geoisie, it was grossly unpopular, as the many examples of insubordination and desertion before 1914 testify. The impact of Socialist and pacifist ideas before 1914, especially amongst the workers in the large cities, meant that widespread anti-militaristic sentiments existed, fuelled by memories of the army's bloody suppression of the Paris Commune in 1871. However, anti-militarism was not limited to the towns but was widespread in left-wing rural areas as well (such as Vaucluse in the south-east), and in certain peasant regions such as Brittany which retained a strong sense of regional autonomy. The mutinies which took place in the French army in 1917 reflected the extent of peasant anti-militarism. French military doctrine, which stemmed from the Revolution and Napoleon, was based on the idea that, in the event of aggression, the whole French nation must be armed and ready to defend the national territory against an aggressor. A large, obedient peasantry to man the infantry-battalions was thus an essential precondition of national independence. In order to understand France's social and economic policies during the nineteenth century and indeed until 1958, this fundamental relationship between the existence of a large, stable peasantry and the imperatives of national defence cannot be overstressed. Such military think-ing placed obstacles in the way of rapid industrial development and urban-isation before the Second World War, since this could have occurred only at the expense of weakening the peasantry.

THE PROFESSIONALISATION OF THE ARMY

France's collapse in 1940 and the subsequent history of the Second World War underlined that military victory depended far more upon the sophisticated equipment possessed by an army (aircraft, tanks, rail networks and so on) than it did upon maintaining a large infantry. That realisation came too late to save France in 1940, but it did provide an impetus for the army to modify itself profoundly after the war. Moreover, it enabled French governments to abandon their outdated ideological attachment to preserving a huge peasantry, which facilitated the post-war rural exodus, and stimulated the growth of industrialisation and urbanisation. The traditional army was crushed as a fighting force in 1940. It was gradually replaced by a modern army composed of technicians and more professional soldiers. However, this modernisation intervened only after the end of the Algerian war in 1962; between 1945 and 1962, the French army was engaged in continual combat in its colonies, first in Indo-China, and then in Algeria. After the end of the Algerian war in 1962, no obstacles remained to the full-scale transformation of the French army. This transformation brought in its wake the development of a modern arms industry and the creation of an ambitious nuclear arms programme.

Few traces, if any, remain of the traditional army in modern France. The army has ceased to be a potential counter-power to the republic, as it was during the nineteenth and for much of the twentieth century. It has been firmly subordinated to the civilian authorities since de Gaulle crushed its political power in Algeria from 1958 to 1962. The influence that the army could have on domestic French politics was dramatically underlined between 1954 and 1958, as the Fourth Republic gradually collapsed under the pressures imposed upon it by the Algerian war. The creation of the Fifth Republic in 1958 came about after the French Parliament had voted for the return of the wartime resistance hero General de Gaulle to head the government, under pressure from the French army in Algeria, which threatened to invade mainland France unless de Gaulle took over. Far from maintaining Algeria in French hands, however (as the army had believed he would), de Gaulle began a gradual process of leading the ex-colony to independence. Alongside this, he relied on his overwhelming political support in the nation to reduce the army's capability of intervening in domestic politics in the future.

The reconciliation of the army with the political regime in the Fifth Republic has helped to promote the development of a wide consensus on national defence, which to a large extent cuts across the boundary between left and right. Several indicators testify to this. Anti-militarism has almost disappeared. Moreover, despite fierce initial protests from the left during the 1960s and much of the 1970s against de Gaulle's decision that France should have its own nuclear weapons, there is today a general consensus between the parties on the need to maintain France's independent nuclear deterrent. This stance is justified, with variations according to party, as an essential precondition for France's maintaining its national independence. Although France remains a member of the Atlantic Alliance, de Gaulle took the nation out of the military command structure of NATO in 1966. All successive French Presidents have confirmed this decision, and reasserted (to the occasional irritation of the country's allies) that France is its own master in relation to the nation's nuclear defence.

This consensus over defence contrasts with the situation which exists in most Western European countries, in which nuclear disarmament issues have become seriously divisive. It is of great symbolic importance in illustrating this consensus that the annual defence budget, which was previously the occasion for ferocious ideological and political divisions in the National Assembly, is usually one of the more uncontroversial budgets passed. It is far less controversial, for example, than that of education or agriculture. A less important indicator of the same mood, at least amongst the political class, is the virtual unanimity with which the main parties support the concept of national service. Despite Mitterrand's paying lip-service in the 1981 campaign to the need to reduce national service from one year to six months, his promise was conveniently forgotten once he was in office. All male citizens are supposed to serve one year in the army. Since de Gaulle's reign, however, individual citizens have had the opportunity of escaping from the army by pleading conscientious objection to military service, in which case they spend a longer period performing civil duties instead. Most recruits are too anxious merely to serve out their period in the army to be concerned with insubordination or desertion.

We saw above that France's nuclear weapons are now accepted virtually unanimously within France. The Rainbow Warrior crisis of 1985 illustrated that a large majority of French people agreed on the necessity of retaining nuclear weapons, even if this meant continuing nuclear tests in the Pacific, which have repeatedly brought France into conflict with New Zealand, Australia and other South Pacific nations. Indeed, there was a remarkable contrast between the widespread international condemnation of the French government over the Rainbow Warrior affair, and the French people's consensus. Likewise, pacifist or anti-nuclear protest movements have made little headway in France, unlike in most Northern European nations (West

Germany, Scandinavia, the United Kingdom) and the USA. This can probably be explained by the anti-national, pro-Soviet use that the Communist Party (PCF) made of the idea of pacifism during the cold war of the 1950s. Most French people recognise both the army and the independent nuclear deterrent as a necessary insurance policy against foreign aggression. Military exploits continue to bring political popularity to their instigators. In short, French chauvinism remains very much alive. There is undoubtedly a nationalist undercurrent in the manner in which most French people regard the army. The relative success of France's military exploits in Chad in the 1970s and 1980s and the role French troops played in the international peacekeeping force in Lebanon from 1982 to 1984 both illustrated that whether controlled by the left or right, French governments are willing to resort to the use of arms in regional conflicts to defend the country's interests and prestige.

Despite the public's greater acceptance of the army, it has had to face major difficulties which are inherent in the role it is called to play in modern France. Senior army officers cannot accept being viewed merely as civil servants since it is they who are responsible for defending the nation, and who must if necessary risk their lives for their country. The officer corps continues to distrust civilian politicians, whom it regards as poorly qualified to make defence policy, and upon whom it can usually exercise considerable influence when drawing up defence plans. The military chiefs instinctively feel that *they* should control defence policy, since war and military combat are within their professional sphere of competence.

Since the end of the colonial wars in 1962, the general public has no longer felt itself so concerned by defence issues, partly because the prospect of men being conscripted to fight in a conventional war has considerably receded in the nuclear age. Indeed, defence is the preserve of the military specialists, who are provided with expensive and devastating military equipment and left to get on with the task of defending the nation. The complexity of modern warfare is such that most citizens prefer to place their trust in the army to defend the nation, rather than to consider what individual contribution they might be able to make to national defence. This passive approach is an entirely rational one. In fact, it is difficult to imagine how the average French citizen could realistically assess what his role would be in an actual combat situation, given the devastating power of modern weapons. None the less, such passivity is frequently frowned upon by army chiefs.

Given that modern warfare lies within the sphere of competence of the professional army, why is national service still obligatory in France?

Curiously, the generals are rather indifferent to the future survival of national service. Indeed, many army officers would actively welcome the French army becoming even more of a professional army, along the lines of those in the United Kingdom or the USA. The abolition of military service would make the army far more easy to manage. The reason why there is no great demand for the suppression of national service is that nobody is prepared to abandon an old myth: that by requiring each individual to declare his readiness to shed his blood for his country, military service is a precondition for becoming a full citizen. The suppression of national service would create a severe budgetary problem. An army composed entirely of professional soldiers rather than unpaid conscripts would lead to considerably increased costs having to be met from the defence budget. The military world thus largely escape from the economic constraint of having to meet the market cost for its workforce.

The last time the French army was actively engaged in real war (rather than in limited regional conflicts such as in Chad) was in the Algerian conflict of 1954 to 1962. The vast majority of officers and non-commissioned officers in France's contemporary armed forces have never known a war, the idea of which has a rather mythical character even for them. For that reason, today's professional soldier daily experiences the contradiction between his objective condition as a servant of the state and his professional aspirations of military glory. In spite of his unusual position within society, the modern professional soldier forms an unmistakable part of the central middle-class constellation.

None the less, the constraints of military life do distinguish the professional soldier from his civil counterpart. The modern soldier leads a nomadic life, having frequently to change garrison and to move into new areas. This mobility can have a negative effect on family life, since it might prevent the military family from being able to buy their own house, as well as prohibiting a soldier's wife from finding a stable occupation. In theory, there are no fixed hours of employment for officers and non-commissioned officers, who must always be available for exercises, patrols and military manoeuvres. These constraints incite many military personnel to live together, in army accommodation close to army barracks, and to isolate themselves from civilian society. For this reason, young men who choose the army as a career often come from military families, while young officers frequently marry the daughters of elder officers. The army remains an institution which permits social promotion, but this is in practice reserved to the children of non-commissioned officers and of military policemen (*gendarmes*) who can aspire to become commissioned officers. In fact more than most other professions, the army is tending to become a caste which recruits its successive generations of officers from within its own ranks. The élite schools and colleges managed by the army which prepare young men to become officers tend to institutionalise the extremely narrow recruitment base of the army.

Top-level army officers are more like managers of a huge bureaucracy than military chiefs. The higher an officer rises in the army hierarchy, the less likely he is actually to control military decisions, which become the responsibility of the politicians. This process is a generalised one throughout Western democracies, equally valid in relation to the UK or USA, for example, as with regard to France. Even operational decisions, such as whether the airforce should raid a particular village in Northern Chad, or whether French soldiers in the Lebanon should be able to defend themselves from aggression, were in reality finely tuned political decisions for which the responsibility had to lie with the competent political authorities, the Defence Minister or the President of the Republic and not the officer in command.

Despite its changing role, the French army remains the conservatory of traditional military values, such as honour, patriotism, obedience, and the spirit of sacrifice. It attempts to instil these values throughout the ranks, especially amongst the full-time professionals in the non-commissioned and commissioned officer grades. These values are increasingly alien to civil society. In order to break its isolation, the army has surrounded itself with a series of institutions which share its value system, such as ex-soldiers' associations, the territorial army or para-military associations (for example youth and student groups). The army has traditionally been the model of the large pyramidical organisation, based upon respect for hierarchy and authority. However, this hierarchical model no longer inspires most modern organisations, in which the need to respect authority for authority's sake is no longer recognised as an essential method of organisational behaviour. By contrast, modern organisational theory stresses that decisions must be reached by agreement between higher and lower levels.

Until the 1960s, army officers genuinely believed that they more than anybody else served the country's highest interests, that they incarnated the supreme values which were shared by most French people, and that the army was an exemplary institution which all other institutions should imitate. For that reason, they considered themselves superior to mere civilian servants of the state, and their perception of themselves was widely shared throughout society. No such illusions survive today. Army officers represent only one category of civil servant amongst various categories of equal status and importance. This loss of prestige has been accepted by many officers with bitterness and a sense of deception.

THE DECLINE OF THE CHURCH

Ever since the French Revolution, marked by its strongly anti-clerical character, relations between the Catholic Church and the republic had always been difficult. The church's close association with the monarchy of the *ancien régime* made it into an obvious target of attack for the French revolutionaries, who duly decreed the disestablishment of the Catholic Church in 1795 and confiscated its lands. Church and state reached a new compromise under Napoleon's concordat of 1801, according to which the Catholic religion was recognised as the religion of the 'great majority' of French people. The church provided the backbone of support for the restored monarchies of 1815–30, for the July monarchy of 1830–48 and for Napoleon III's Second Empire of 1852–70. The democratic political system gradually came into existence in France towards the end of the nineteenth century, with the creation and consolidation of the Third Republic from 1870 onwards. However, the restored republic was opposed by the church and the social forces it represented.

At the centre of the ideological conflict that took place between the church on the one hand and the anti-clerical movement and the republic on the other was the question of who would dominate the peasantry. The church was the most important institution within the anti-republican camp, and it united around it all those who wanted to re-establish the *ancien régime*. Relations between church and state degenerated rapidly once the Third Republic had been established. Confrontation came to a head during the Dreyfus affair at the turn of the nineteenth century, when the church sided with the army and anti-Semitic nationalists against the republic. The end-result of this renewed struggle came in 1905 when the Radical-led government of Combes decreed the separation of church and state and the end of the compromise represented by Napoleon's concordat. The Catholic Church was weakened in so far as Catholicism was no longer the official religion. In another sense, however, the attacks of anti-clericals strengthened its legitimacy since by fighting against it, the anti-clericals indirectly recognised the strength of the church, as well as providing an easily identifiable enemy against which the church had to struggle. Despite sporadic conflicts between the church and the republic since 1905, harmony has in general prevailed in relations between the two institutions, and the church has in practice accepted the republic unambiguously since 1945.

Control over the nation's education has continued on occasion to be a source of conflict between church and state (the most recent example of this was in 1984). During the early years of the Third Republic the conflict between the church and the republic was total in relation to which authority should control the values and fundamental beliefs of French people. The church considered that it had a divine duty to control people's souls, that it should be entrusted with their education, and that the state should confine itself to its management of public administration. The state refused this claim since it was determined to inculcate French citizens with republican values. These diverging interests explained the conflict between church and state over education which first appeared during the late nineteenth century, and which has continued down to the present day.

Despite the separation of church and state in 1905, until recently the Catholic Church continued to claim to minister to the spiritual welfare of the overwhelming mass of French people, with the exception of around one million Protestants and several scattered Jewish communities. The bishop was considered to be the spiritual leader of the whole population within his diocese; it was his responsibility to ensure that his flock went to heaven. He enjoyed a status equal to that of the prefect or the general, with whom he shared the official platform during 14 July celebrations. But the legitimacy of the church was strongly contested by a powerful anti-clerical movement, which derived its strength from the war waged against the church by the republic at the turn of the century. Anti-clerical positions were supported by a majority of the population in certain regions in France, and amongst certain social classes (in particular by the new industrial working class of the towns). Whereas the church declared that it had a universal duty to save souls, the anti-clerical movement considered that it had an absolute duty to liberate the French people from an obscurantist and anachronistic religion which was being exploited by the ruling classes to maintain their social ascendancy. Catholicism, with its stress on hierarchy and authority, was the means through which the population was being indoctrinated to accept a social system which served the interests of only one class, the bourgeoisie. On this point, anti-clerical and left-wing political positions tended to converge.

The first doubts that appeared about the extent of religious practice in France, which the church considered to be almost universal, surfaced in 1943 in a study by H. Godin and V. Daniel. Godin and Daniel claimed that while the immense majority of French people were baptised, fewer than one-quarter were regularly practising Catholics, attending mass every Sunday. In certain regions and towns in France, the proportion of regularly practising Catholics fell below 10 per cent. Only in a few deeply pious

Table 4. *A declining religious identity (%)*

	1974	1977	1983	1983/74
Catholics	86.5	81.0	83.0	−3.5
Regularly practising	21.0	17.0	14.0	−7.0
Occasional	18.0	14.0	17.0	1.0
Non-practising	47.5	50.0	52.0	+4.5
Other religion	3.5	4.0	3.0	−0.5
No religion	10.0	15.0	14.0	+4.0
TOTAL	100.0	100.0	100.0	

Source: SOFRES, *Opinion publique* (1984)

regions was there a high, quasi-unanimous level of religious observance: the West (Brittany, west Normandy and the Vendée), the North, the East (especially Alsace-Lorraine), and the south-east Massif Central. Elsewhere, regular attendance at church averaged between 10 and 15 per cent of the population. Indeed, contemporary historians are providing evidence that certain areas in France (for example the Paris Basin, or the north-west Massif Central) never really succumbed to the influence of the Catholic Church, as measured by degree of church attendance.

According to the various studies of religious affiliation in France appearing from the 1940s onwards, the church had previously greatly exaggerated the extent to which most French people regularly practised their nominal religion. In reality, for most people church attendance was of an extremely irregular character. The minimum degree of religious observance was that of celebrating the 'four seasons' of the lifecycle in church: baptism at birth, first communion as an adolescent, marriage at the start of adult life and funeral at the start of the next world. This basic minimal conformism was extended in certain regions to include the celebration of a number of annual festivals in church, namely Christmas, Easter, the Feast of the Assumption, All Saints' Day, Ascension Day and Whit Sunday.

During the nineteenth century there had existed two radically different forms of Catholicism. In those regions where religious observance was practically uniform, as well as in those social classes in which religious practice flourished (the nobility, a part of the bourgeoisie), to be a Catholic was to lead a devout life, and to participate in a counter-culture at odds with the mainstream culture of French society. This counter-culture might be compared with that formed later on by the Communist Party and the industrial working class. For these devout Catholics, everything could be explained in terms of religion, and behaviour-patterns, opinions and values were all intended to conform to a strict Catholic viewpoint. The church itself acted

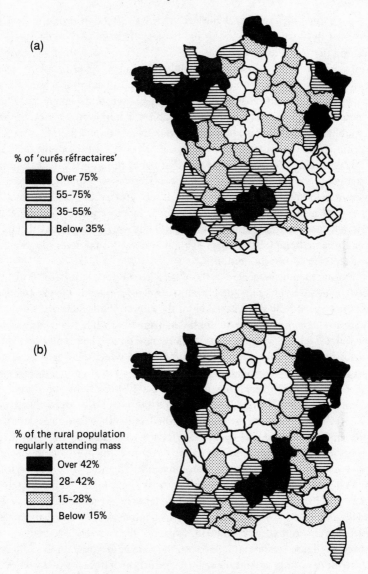

(a)

% of 'curés réfractaires'

Over 75%

55-75%

35-55%

Below 35%

(b)

% of the rural population
regularly attending mass

Over 42%

28-42%

15-28%

Below 15%

Figure 4 The stable geographical distribution of religious
belief. Source: H. Le Bras, *Les Trois France* (Paris, Seuil, 1986)
a: 'Curés réfractaires' (1791). 'Curés réfractaires' were priests
who refused to swear their loyalty to the civil constitution of
the clergy adopted by the Revolution in 1790.
b: Religious practice (1960–70)

as a counter-society. It provided a whole range of institutions which enabled devout Catholics to escape completely from the 'godless' institutions of the republic. Children would be sent to schools run by Catholic nuns or monks, and would be encouraged to train as priests. Access to the priesthood seminary provided a means of upward educational and social mobility for devout Catholics from poorer backgrounds which could be compared with the system of grants for able children in the schools of the republic. Richer Catholics devoted considerable time and money to sponsoring charitable activities and associations in favour of the poor, such as sewing-circles, youth clubs and sporting associations. The organisational strength of the church could be seen most clearly in the agricultural sector, where an impressive network of para-Catholic associations had been established to help Catholic peasants. These included farmers' cooperatives, friendly societies, trade unions and banks. They were so impressive that the republicans attempted to imitate them, in order to win peasant support for the republic against the church.

During the post-war period, this Catholic counter-culture has virtually collapsed, as a result of the rural exodus, the development of the mass media and most especially the weakening of the church itself. Since the Second Vatican Council (1965), the church's doctrine has changed so rapidly as to be scarcely recognisable for today's older generations. The old people of the 1980s had grown up with a Catholic Church which had held out the prospect of hell and damnation for sinners in the 1930s; but such threats are now regarded as superstitious nonsense, even officially by the Catholic Church itself. As God has been transformed into a symbol of love rather than fear, the gravity of sin has greatly diminished: rather than being a prelude to eternal damnation, sin has become an obstacle to leading a truly happy life. Because it is no longer punished by the threat of damnation, sin no longer provokes the same feelings of remorse and guilt. The ritual of confession has relentlessly declined as a consequence. Finally, instead of postponing the pursuit of happiness until they were in heaven, as believers were encouraged to do under the old theology, the Catholic Church now accepts that people have a right to happiness on earth. Far more than merely a relaxation of stricter religious beliefs and practices, the change in the church's official doctrine constitutes a fundamental transformation of its vision of the world. Not surprisingly, many devout Catholics have felt cheated by the watering down of the church's official doctrine, which runs contrary to the religious beliefs they were socialised to accept. By contrast, many activists in para-Catholic associations, as well as in the church, have been encouraged by what they considered as the Catholic Church's adaptation to the modern world.

The decline of the Catholic Church can be largely explained by the disappearance of the peasantry, just as the PCF's decline can be explained by the disappearance of the industrial working class. However, this explanation is insufficient, given that the peasantry was not the only social class strongly imbued with religion, and that peasant attachment to the church varied considerably according to region. The bourgeoisie was also strongly religious during the second half of the nineteenth century, but neither the old nor the new middle classes have proved particularly fruitful territory for the church. This is somewhat surprising, given that the new middle classes of the central constellation have given birth to a large number of new social movements since the 1960s (including some religious ones). What religious activity the new middle classes have displayed, however, has taken place largely on the margins of the Catholic Church, in Bible-reading groups, in the charismatic movement, or in various religious sects. It is even more surprising that the church has paid relatively little attention to attracting the support of the new middle classes, a duty which has been sacrificed to the elusive task of recruiting support from industrial workers (who are largely secular) and the old disappearing bourgeoisie. This might well prove to be shortsighted, since the future health of the Catholic Church depends upon its appealing to the expanding social groups within the population.

The relative lack of attention paid by the church to the new social groups that have emerged in the post-war era is in marked contrast to the intense consideration it gave a variety of different social classes during the inter-war period. After the First World War the church established a series of para-Catholic organisations in an attempt to increase its influence in various different sectors of society. Three groups were initially established to extend the church's appeal amongst workers, peasants and students respectively. They were united under the control of a mother organisation, Catholic Action. Each of these organisations was remarkably successful. The greatest success during the inter-war period was the creation of the Young Christian Farmers (JAC), which attempted to bring back into the fold of the church all those who lived in the countryside. Parallel organisations were subsequently created to cater for young Christian workers (JOC) and young Christian students (JEC). The JAC proved extremely successful – indeed too successful, since it demanded its independence from the church and gradually withdrew itself from its orbit. The more the JAC distanced itself from the church, the more it adopted overtly political stances and transformed its task from that of winning converts to the Catholic faith into that of training Catholic activists to exercise an influence in other professional or political organisations. The creation of JAC was thus ultimately of limited value to the church. JAC activists soon dominated all of the different farmers' organisations, such as FNSEA and CNJA, the main farmers' unions. The only regions which escaped from its influence were those in which anti-clericalism was strong, and those in which traditional Catholics distrusted the independent stances adopted by the JAC. Although the JAC continues to exist, it has abandoned all its religious ambitions, and has also largely lost its inspiration and influence.

The JOC and the JEC were successful to a lesser extent. The student organisation JEC also quarrelled with the church hierarchy and eventually declared itself totally independent of any ecclesiastical influence. Its success can be measured by the fact that many of its student leaders of the 1950s have held prominent positions in government during the 1980s: Michel Rocard (Prime Minister, 1988–), Henri Nallet (Minister of Agriculture), Robert Chapuis (Minister for Technology) etc. The workers' organisation JOC relied on 'worker priests' to attempt to increase the church's influence amongst industrial workers. Under the impetus of the worker priests (many of whom end up by identifying totally with the workers and not the church), the JOC managed to increase the feeling of class consciousness amongst industrial workers, rather than attracting them to the bosom of the church. The formal links between JOC and the Catholic Church did not last for long. The increased involvement of Catholic activists amongst industrial workers also led to the creation by the church in 1919 of a Christian trade union, the CFTC. The CFTC subsequently became independent of the church and split in 1964, when a majority of activists declared themselves in favour of the secularisation of the union, and renamed it the CFDT. A minority of members preferred to form a new explicitly Christian trade union, which kept the old initials CFTC. Although today's CFDT no longer claims to be a Christian union, many of its ideas are tinged with Christianity, and many of its members willingly accept being labelled as left-wing Christian activists. Thus, the various attempts carried out by the church to extend its influence within particular groups within society have more often than not backfired.

The decline of religious belief in France can be measured by the weakening of the church itself as an organisation. The number of men training to be priests began declining at the beginning of the twentieth century, from around 1,500 per annum in 1900 (excluding Alsace-Lorraine), to around 1,000 per annum in 1950 (including Alsace-Lorraine). That figure fell to 500 in 1960, an average of 200 during the 1970s and a mere 100 in the 1980s. Moreover, increasingly large numbers of priests began expressing their dissatisfaction with the role, the function and the institution of the priesthood during the same period (especially in relation to its hierarchical character). The result of this growing disillusionment was that a large number of priests left the church, followed by a catastrophic decline in church attendance from their ex-parishioners. This left a diminished band of ageing priests to glorify the Catholic Church. In 1965 there were 41,000 secular priests in France, 36,000 in 1975, and 30,000 in 1985. By 1995, this figure will have declined to 20,000 unless married men and women are allowed to become priests.

For a period of approximately twenty years (1955–75), a clear contrast could apparently be drawn between the fragile state of the church's organisation (as epitomised by the priesthood) and the continuing loyalty of the mass of faithful churchgoers to the church. Although a decline in religious practice amongst young people could be observed from 1965 onwards, it was only in 1970 that a real drop in the level of declared religious practice was recorded amongst the population in general. The decline in religious observance can be traced in part to the changing nature of the Catholic religion itself: if attending mass on Sunday is no longer portrayed as a strict moral obligation, then it is scarcely surprising that the numbers going to church regularly have fallen. Other factors, such as the drop in the number of priests, the closing of churches and the holding of fewer masses, have all contributed to the decline in religious observance, as measured by church-going. On the other hand, the techniques used for measuring church attendance have changed as well. Whereas in the 1950s, church attendance was measured by priests or sociologists counting the numbers of people present at services, since the 1970s evidence of church attendance has been supplied almost exclusively by opinion polls. By 1988, even the most pious observer could not deny that there had been a serious decline in religious practice. Whereas one-quarter of the population attended mass every Sunday in 1955 (24 per cent), that proportion had declined to little more than one-tenth (12 per cent) in 1988.

The decline in religious practice which has occurred during the post-war period was concealed for a long time for a simple reason. Whereas it was virtually impossible for church attendance to decline in the secular areas, where it had been extremely weak to begin with, it remained at a high level in the most pious regions. That situation has now changed and church congregations have declined even in the most religious regions of France (such as Brittany, the Vendée or Rouergue), although the number of people attending church remains higher there than elsewhere. The decline of the Catholic religion in France can be measured in a number of other ways apart from regular attendance at Sunday mass. To take but two examples, the proportion of children being baptised at birth has declined from 92 per cent in 1958, to 85 per cent in 1970 and 65 per cent in 1983; and the number of church marriages and funerals, which has been steadily declining for a century, especially in the large towns, has fallen dramatically in the last ten years.

Throughout its history, the Catholic Church has been able to preserve and extend its influence because it has given a Christian veneer to what were essentially pagan rituals, practices and beliefs. Popular forms of religion, which predated Christianity, were resurrected in a different form and reinterpreted by the Catholic Church in order to extend and preserve its influence. The Catholic Church thus satisfied the proven religious needs of different communities, even when their origins were not specifically Christian. The church's mission was to Christianise the whole of society, rather than individual citizens; the best means of achieving this was to build upon pre-existing forms of popular religious practice. The notion of Christianising the whole of society had to be reconsidered after the Protestant Reformation of the sixteenth century, however. The Reformation insisted upon the primacy of the direct link between the individual and his creator; religion thus passed from the public sphere to the private. The Counter-Reformation had to accept this reversal, since its objective was to win back people's souls for Catholicism, and this involved accepting the possibility of conversion. The distinction between the public and private spheres was new, totally foreign to the Middle Ages. It concealed a dangerous virus for the institution of the church. Individual spirituality gave an unprecedented degree of free will to the individual, which ultimately weakened the institution of the church as a necessary intermediary between people and their god. The triumph of the individual's relationship with God has had an effect upon popular religion as well. The rituals of popular religion, previously sanctioned by the Catholic Church, have fallen into disuse as a result of the unwillingness of the clergy to continue to perform pagan rites under the guise of Christianity. The diminishing band of priests now insists that parishioners demonstrate their Christian faith before they are willing to administer the holy sacraments. This change has hastened the decline of the church, by emptying it of those who previously attended in order to enjoy religious ceremonies.

There has been little research into surviving forms of popular religion. In Limousin, religious processions have occurred once every seven years since 1519, when the community displays its local religious relics. These ostensions have become highly commercial and are used to attract tourism to the region. Despite this, they still fulfil the function of expressing a local identity. Local religious festivals have become lay occasions (they are no longer controlled by the church), but this does not deprive them of their religious importance. The vitality of these festivals might even suggest a renewed enthusiasm for religious symbolism, which is no longer adequately catered for by the Catholic Church. The demand for religious rites is widespread, expressed by many people's rejection of recent liturgical changes within the Catholic Church, and by the popularity of pilgrimages, religious festivals or cults, such as the *culte des morts*. This renewed religious fervour can be reduced neither to a form of popular religion opposed to the dominant religion represented by the Catholic Church, nor a new version of paganism, hypocritically dressed up in Christian rituals. Rather, it represents the endurance of a profound religious current within contemporary France, whose religious needs are no longer entirely satisfied by the Catholic Church.

Despite the decline in religious practice, religion remains the best variable to explain the great ideological and political cleavages throughout French society. The Catholic belief-system, as it operates in France, places considerable importance on the primacy, wealth and security of the family. Practising Catholics tend also to occupy a higher socio-economic status than non-believers or non-Catholics, and are more likely to be home-owners. For these reasons, a strong religious belief is the best indicator of an individual's likely predisposition to vote for a right-wing political party in France. Until François Mitterrand took over the presidency in 1981, previous French Presidents had always made a point of being photographed coming out of mass on a Sunday, especially during election periods. Despite falling church attendances, there is ample evidence to suggest that a substantial proportion of French people remain imbued with a fundamentally Catholic mentality. Indeed, there is a striking contradiction between the decline in church attendance and the flourishing state of other symbols of religious belief, such as the religious press and church schools. The press that falls within the Catholic orbit is immensely important: *Le Pèlerin* has more than two million readers weekly, as many as the *Nouvel Observateur* or *Le Point*; *La Vie (catholique)* can boast 1,700,000 readers. Catholic publishing companies are also enjoying a boom. These signs all suggest the survival of a powerful religious current within French society.

A RETURN TO RELIGION?

The Roman Catholic Church has long been torn apart by disputes over the attitude it should adopt towards modernity and change. For the traditionalists the church must remain faithful to its origins, and reject 'modernistic' values, which are of a transient nature and will ultimately fade away, leaving a divinely inspired, infallible and universal church. For modernisers, however, the church must recognise the existence of modernity and social change and attempt to bring them within its orbit. Only by controlling new developments within society can the church hope to survive.

Indeed, the modern history of the Roman Catholic Church, from the Syllabus of 1864 up to John-Paul II, has been dominated by attempts to recapture the church's old influence over Western civilisation. In spite of appearances, all attempts to bring the church into line with modern society have in fact been based upon a rejection of modern values and a strong will to recover the church's social influence. This might explain why the genuinely modern Catholic organisations in France such as Catholic Action, the JEC, the JOC and the JAC have invariably run up against the church's intransigence and its refusal to compromise with modern society. Indeed, even the famous Second Vatican Council was an attempt to stem the tide of modern society. The church's refusal to adapt is epitomised in the present Pope, John-Paul II, who never ceases reiterating the church's traditional doctrines, especially in relation to the corruption of modern society. The success of his message relates to the fact that modern societies are themselves in the throes of a lasting moral crisis. When John-Paul II limits himself to condemning modern society in general terms, opinion polls suggest that the vast bulk of French people (83 per cent) agree with him, or find him a sympathetic figure. However, once he begins speaking of people's personal problems and intrudes into their private lives, for example by attempting to dictate codes of sexual morality, his message is far less popular: in one opinion poll, 52 per cent of all French practising Catholics refused to recognise that the Pope has a right to interfere in their personal problems.

In fact, John-Paul II is calling into question the individual's moral autonomy, which the Second Vatican Council conceded. According to the Second Vatican Council, each individual had to be free to make his own moral choices, as long as he was prepared to assume the consequences of these. There was a direct link between the individual and his god; religion was a matter of the private individual relationship between people and God. By admitting that religion fell into the private rather than the public sphere, the church no longer claimed a right to interfere in politics. Paradoxically, having denied itself any right to intervene in the public sphere (for example in politics, or economic, social or cultural policy), the Catholic Church has had to intensify its action within the private sphere to recover its influence. However, it is precisely in the private domain that many believers today refute the Catholic Church's right to interfere. The Pope is today given a far more favourable reception when he intervenes in public affairs (as long as he defends the individual against the state), than in strictly private ones. For that reason, he can evoke virtually unanimous support amongst French people (as elsewhere) when he praises the spirit of Polish resistance against bureaucratic Communist rule, but meets with a lukewarm response when he condemns abortion or divorce.

The church's successful defence of its own schools in 1984 against the Socialist government's attempts to incorporate them within the state education system illustrated the continuing strengths of the Catholic Church as an organisation. In response to the government's reform plans, the church did not hesitate to intervene in defence of liberty. The opinion polls suggested three-quarters of the French people backed the church's right to retain its independent schools, despite the fact that practising Catholics represented at most 15 per cent of the population, and only one-tenth of French families sent their children to private schools. The overwhelming majority considered that the right to choose their children's education was one of the fundamental principles of democracy. By opposing the proposed reform the church showed itself to be an extremely powerful organisation, which proved to be the spokesman for a wide range of diverse pressure groups. The combination of the church, of a burgeoning pressure-group movement and of overwhelming opposition from public opinion was sufficient to force the left-wing government to abandon its planned reform in July 1984. The church schools conflict reversed those values traditionally associated with left and right: the church defended the principle of liberty, whereas the left-wing parties and the lay teachers' union, the FEN, called upon the need for authority to be respected. The majority of French people felt that in order to defend its positions of power, the left had abandoned its traditional principles of liberty and equality for all citizens. One of the great myths of the nineteenth century had been shattered overnight.

The reaction against modernity expressed by many of those activists who had experienced May 1968 ought to have been conducive to a religious revival. These activists rejected both economic rationality and bureaucratic political power. Instead, they emphasised the importance of the emotional side of life and of a return to nature. Many religious communities were formed after 1968, composed of individuals in search of a superior spiritual logic to which to subordinate themselves. Individuals joining these religious communities would become well integrated to the extent that they were able to find answers to their personal needs for self-development and realisation. To enter one of these 'emotional communities', it was not necessary to have become converted in the formal sense (although this often did occur); a personal commitment was, however, demanded in terms of an engagement to seek personal spiritual satisfaction. Individuals would regularly be called upon to relate their spiritual experiences to other members of the group. Membership of one of these groups demanded merely a personal commitment to the community, and individuals could leave at any time. The rituals which prevailed within these religious communities testified to a strong strand of anti-intellectualism; they were intended to stimulate 'emotional convergence' between members, for example by means of expressive body movements during prayers. Because they were anti-intellectual, the post-1968 religious communities distrusted abstract theologians, as well as established clerics. Their creation was one sign of a religious revival which took place outside of the existing churches.

Evidence exists in France, as well as in many Protestant countries, that a return to religion is taking place. Within the USA, growing religious fervour has been a characteristic of the 1980s, and all the indices point to levels of religious observance returning to their 1960 rate, whether amongst Catholics or Protestants. In many ways, a new ecumenical form of Christianity is being invented, which can be shared by Catholics and the various Protestant creeds alike. Another sign of renewed religious fervour in France is that of recruitment to the monasteries, which have once again become attractive to certain young people for the first time in over fifty years. The development of the charismatic movement is a further signal of renewed religious fervour expressing itself on the margins of the traditional churches.

The charismatic movement, particularly strong amongst Protestants but also amongst certain Catholics, insists upon the direct personal relationship between God and the individual, and encourages the development of personal forms of religious ecstasy. Anti-intellectualism and a search for emotional liberation lead the movement to reject the intellectualisation of religious beliefs represented by the churches, as well as the institutionalisation of established rituals. Finally, even if marginal groups are excluded, the renewed strength of religious sects of all sorts testifies to a definite religious revival in Western societies, at least amongst certain sections of the population. It is difficult to predict, however, whether these seeds of renewed spiritual life will have a broader impact on the general public in the future, especially on the new middle-class groups of the central constellation.

Contemporary French religious beliefs are characterised by a great diversity, although France remains nominally at least an overwhelmingly Catholic country. There are four main quadrants of Catholic belief. That of stability consists of those who are Catholics as a matter of ritual. These people are Catholics in order to conform with everybody else. The 'exiled' are those who consider themselves as Catholic, but who no longer practise their beliefs as they used to when they were younger. There are those who are indifferent towards religion. This group is composed of two sub-cultures: the 'culturals', who are Catholic because it is part of French culture and the 'indifferents' who are more or less inclined towards unbelief. Finally there is a diminishing group of devout believers, who unquestioningly accept all the positions adopted by the Catholic Church.

The decline of the Catholic Church as a total universe is indicative of longer-term trends in French society towards the weakening of traditionally powerful institutions, and the control they exercise over members of society. French people are freer than ever before to believe what they want, to behave in a manner they deem suitable and to espouse the values which they consider correct, irrespective of their social background. At first sight there appears to be little connection between an individual's social origins, whether or not he practises religion and, if so, the extent of his religious practice. Of course, the son of an industrial worker from the anti-clerical department of Creuse is likely to be indifferent towards religion, although that is by no means a foregone conclusion. Likewise, although the disciples of the fundamentalist Catholic rebel, Archbishop Monsignor Lefebvre, are more likely to come from the traditionalist bourgeoisie than from other social groups, this is not necessarily so. Religious believers in France are far too diversified a group to be limited to any one social group or region, although elderly people are more likely to be devout than the young, and certain areas such as Brittany retain a more Catholic character than elsewhere.

The Catholic Church is certainly no longer the majestic institution that it used to be which spoke by general consent in the name of God. It can no longer claim to reign undivided over the spiritual life of the French nation, but it remains a powerful organisation. It has become the centre of a network of influence which extends well beyond the formal ranks of the church and encompasses a large variety of groups and activists. Although the church can no longer claim to be able to dictate a code of conduct even to the faithful, it continues to represent a certain idea of the world that around one-half of French people share.

The Catholic Church has had to face up to the competition offered with increasing fervour by alternative religions. The second most important religion in France today is Islam. The third is Judaism, which has grown considerably in importance, not least because of the Jewish faith of many of the *pied-noirs* who came back from North Africa to live in France during the 1950s and 1960s. The strengthening of the Jewish community has led to the growth of anti-Semitism, which has in turn reinforced the Jewish identity. These developments have relegated Protestantism to France's fourth religion. Those who are confirmed non-believers represent around 15 per cent of the population. A majority of French people remain nominally Catholic, although church attendance will usually be limited to a few symbolic occasions. The Catholic Church has been transformed from a potentially totalitarian institution which claimed to derive its authority from divine will and which used to be a formidable rival to the state into only one major institution amongst others within society. France is no longer the eldest daughter of the Catholic Church. Like the USA, it has become pluriconfessional. Those with a religious faith will belong to one of four different confessions (Catholicism, Islam, Judaism or Protestantism), or to any of a multitude of religious sects. Others might decide that no religion corresponds to their philosophical beliefs, or else that their religious attachment is purely nominal.

4

Working-class institutions

In opposition to the great bourgeois or peasant institutions of the nineteenth century, the working class developed two twentieth-century institutions of its own, the Communist Party (PCF) and the trade unions. These institutions gave working-class people a degree of organisation, defence and above all identity, by way of a revolutionary message and the perspective of conquering power for their class. The historical role of the proletariat was to replace the bourgeoisie in power and to replace capitalism with Socialism, and eventually Communism. Unlike most of its European counterparts (except in Italy), the French working class thus took refuge in myth. Because heavy industry has given way to the electronics and chemical industries and to the service sector, and because the working class has become richer and better educated, this myth has lost its credibility. The growth of trade unions followed the development of heavy industry, which brought in its wake high concentrations of workers. The decline of trade union recruitment in every West European country is obviously connected with the decline of this type of heavy industry and the reduction in the number of poorly qualified and poorly educated people that it used to employ.

THE DECLINE OF THE FRENCH COMMUNIST PARTY

If it is true that the French Communist Party is 'the church for those without a church' (A. Kriegel), then it is scarcely surprising that the PCF, like the Roman Catholic Church, should be in decline. The PCF was formed in 1920 as the result of a split in the old unified Socialist Party, Section Française de l'Internationale Ouvrière (SFIO), founded in 1905. The PCF's formation responded to Lenin's call for pro-Soviet Communist parties to form themselves out of the older Socialist parties, to join the Third International and to pledge absolute loyalty to the Soviet Union, the motherland of the Revolution. The 1920 split had a profound impact on the future development of the left in France, which was henceforth divided by two rival parties, the PCF and the SFIO, the Socialist rump that remained after 1920. During the Third Republic (1920–40), the latter party established its clear ascendancy as the leading party of the left. This pattern changed dramatically in the Fourth Republic (1945–58), as the PCF exploited the prestige it had gained as one of France's main resistance forces to establish itself as without question the main force on the left. During the Fifth Republic, the PCF has never fully recovered from the serious loss of support it suffered in 1958 for opposing de Gaulle's return to power. Since the mid 1970s its leading position has been completely overhauled by François Mitterrand's Socialist Party (PS), a new political force whose genealogy can be traced to the SFIO. By contrast, the PCF has suffered successive electoral setbacks. The parties of the French left (Communist and Socialist) have been renowned for alternating long periods of disunity and internecine 'fraternal' rivalries with far shorter periods of left-wing unity, during which the parties have been able temporarily to overcome their differences and pursue common objectives: 1934–8, 1944–7, 1972–7 and 1981–4. On these occasions, the discipline and unity of the left could be considerable, although it was always short-lived.

The PCF has been unquestioningly loyal to the USSR for most of its existence, and has taken its orders from the Soviet Union at least until the late 1960s. Despite liberalising its doctrine and its image in the 1970s and adopting a measured distance from the USSR, the PCF remains associated in the public eye with the defence of Soviet positions. By the end of the 1980s, the paradox of the situation was that a defensive Communist leadership in France was amongst the least favourable of West European Communist Parties to Gorbachev's reforms, which indirectly threatened the existence of the ossified PCF leadership, and directly challenged many of the preconceptions upon which the party had traditionally based its political activity.

From being a mass organisation, the PCF is becoming a party of dedicated activists. In the aftermath of the Second World War, over one-quarter of French voters supported the Communist Party (28.3 per cent in the November 1946 legislative election); by the late 1980s, that figure oscillated around or under 10 per cent (9.8 per cent in 1986, and 11.2 per cent in 1988). The traditional electoral geography of the PCF vote showed that the party's areas of strength coincided with areas in which the Catholic Church was weak, just as the party was weak where the church was strong. A perfect illustration is the Massif Central. In the profoundly secular north-west of the Massif Central, the PCF used to gain most votes in this region of small peasants. Thus, in Creuse in 1956, the party polled over 50 per cent of the vote, whereas in the south-east of the Massif Central a high level of religious practice coincided with the weakest level of PCF support in the region. Throughout France as a whole, the strongest pro-Communist areas were the rural anti-clerical South-west, and the industrial suburbs of large cities, especially in the Paris 'red belt', the huge suburbs of north, east and south-east Paris. On the other hand, the secularised *départements* to the east of the Paris Basin tended to vote for parties of the right. Only in the north of France did a strong degree of religious practice coexist with a heavy Communist presence (which itself had to contend with a long-established tradition of anti-Communist working-class Socialism). There were virtually no Communists in the overwhelmingly Christian west and east of France. Except in the North, the Communist and Catholic Churches did not compete against each other in the same areas.

The modernisation of agriculture in the post-war period has led to a massive exodus of small, anti-clerical peasants from the traditional rural bastions of the PCF. Similarly, the modernisation of industry has reduced the size of the industrial working class in the traditional heavy industries. The two main social constituencies of the PCF have thus been progressively reduced in size. Despite this the PCF has on the whole remained faithful to its narrow interpretation of what the working class consists of and has largely abstained from recruiting support in other social categories (unlike the Italian Communist Party). During the 1960s, various sociologists emphasised the emergence of a new, rapidly expanding working class, composed of technicians, workers in new industries, and clerical workers in the tertiary sector. However, the party has never really accepted the notion of a 'new working class'. In the late 1960s, one prominent Communist leader at least, Roger Garaudy, used these studies to support his conclusion that 'the working class is continuing to expand, by integrating increasingly important strata of intellectual workers'.

That idea was strongly contested by Georges Marchais at the 19th party congress in 1970. He argued, with remarkable intellectual vigour, that the Marxist notion of class must not be watered down and subverted by enlarging it to such an extent that it lost its precise significance. Marchais defined the working class as 'the proletarians of the factories, the mines, the building-sites and the fields'; if absolutely necessary, he accepted adding 'workers in transport and communications, factory technicians and draughtsmen in large companies'. On the other hand, it was impermissible to label as working class non-manual workers in the civil service, nationalised industries or local government; office or shopworkers; members of the intellectual classes such as engineers, managers, technicians, teachers or researchers, or even the bulk of manual workers in small factories. All of these strata could ally with the proletariat, but could never become part of it. Such doctrinal orthodoxy recalled that of the priests who refused to put themselves at the service of popular religion.

In the 1970s, this narrow ideological definition of the proletariat went alongside a narrow strategic vision of left-wing unity, based on the idea of the PCF as the revolutionary party of the working class, in alliance with the Socialist Party (PS), an essentially reformist, social democratic representative of the middle classes. According to the PCF leadership, the policy of the Union of the Left, consecrated by the signing of the common programme of government with the PS in 1972, ought to have enabled the PCF to dominate the left-wing alliance thanks to its firm hold over the industrial and rural working masses. Although the PCF leadership gambled that the PCF–PS alliance would benefit the Communists, the left union progressively favoured their Socialist rivals. Despite warnings from Moscow of the dangers of the left union strategy, it was welcomed enthusiastically by PCF activists. The PCF did eventually call a halt to the left union experience in 1977, but by then it was too late: it had lost control of the left to its Socialist rivals. The 1977 PCF–PS split was the single most important event which accelerated the long-term movement of disavowal of the PCF by its previous sympathisers, a movement which had been gathering pace since 1974. The bulk of Communist activists and sympathisers could neither accept nor follow this sudden reversal of strategy by the PCF leadership, especially in an era when both the Soviet Union and Marxism were losing their sacrosanct appeal, even amongst many Communists. The contrast between the PCF and the PS in the 1970s was striking, as the PS profoundly restructured itself to attract support from the new classes created by social change: technicians, middle-ranking clerical workers in new industries, teachers and professionals, as well as representatives from the burgeoning associative movement. These categories flocked to the PS in the 1970s, and provided the party with many experienced activists who entered local government after the left's 1977 municipal election triumph and Parliament in 1981.

The electoral audience of the PCF is only one indicator of its strength. The number of party activists and the state of its organisation is another. The party is an organisation composed of members, activists and paid party workers. For members two major annual events are organised: the yearly membership renewal campaign and the *fête de l'Humanité*, the annual Communist celebration in September. For the activists, party duties are more demanding: weekly meetings of the PCF cell, and various party activities such as selling *L'Humanité Dimanche*, the Sunday newspaper, participating in other party meetings and making the PCF's presence felt in those organisations close to the party, of which the CGT, the Communist trade union, is the most important. Finally, those local councils which have been controlled by the PCF for a long time prefer to recruit their workforce from party members, who thus become paid party workers. Although no more than 1,000 party workers are directly employed by PCF, around 15,000 depend indirectly for their employment on the party through its control of local government.

According to G. Marchais's report at the PCF's 16th congress in 1961 (when the party organisation was at its strongest), the Communists claimed 100,000 party office-holders: '30,000 leaders of party cells, 25,000 leaders of sections, 3,300 federal leaders. With our 1,400 mayors, our 21,000 municipal councillors, our 150 general councillors, and our tens of thousands of other Communist officials, we easily have 100,000 party office holders.' This figure was greatly exaggerated, not least because the same people might have two or three different roles – for example a mayor might also be a *conseiller général*. If the number of activists has until recently remained relatively stable, the number of ordinary party members has varied considerably. Every year, the PCF has a vigorous recruitment campaign to persuade existing party members to renew their membership and to sign up new members to replace those who leave. Although the precise evolution of party membership is difficult to quantify during the past thirty years, there has undoubtedly been a massive decline, admitted by party leaders and political commentators alike. Communist party membership has suffered from the fact that the party has ignored the expanding social groups of the central constellation, and even the *employés*, who have been considered at best as allies of the industrial proletariat. PCF membership reached a high in 1978, when the party claimed 632,000 members. Although this figure was in reality nearer to 450,000, it was considerably higher than that of a decade later (no more than 250,000).

The PCF has traditionally attempted to provide a complete counter-society for its activists, able to control every aspect of their lives, as the church used to in a Breton village. If they want to, Communist activists can live entirely among other Communists, read only the party press or books published by the party, participate in party festivals, receive health-care from clinics run by party activists, go on party-organised holidays to eastern Europe, and so on. For the Communist activist, non-Communists are pagans to be converted to the faith, to be shown the way to human dignity. The really committed activist ends up living for and by the party. To leave the party would mean breaking off all his social ties and losing the world within which he has become accustomed to living. Numerous ex-Communists have testified to the emotional ordeal involved in breaking with the party.

The intellectual, ideological and emotional universe represented by the

PCF is extremely coherent and thus very satisfying for its members. The party explains to its members how the world, society and its injustices function and provides answers to every question. For its voters, the PCF is above all the only party which really wants to change society, and which shows its genuine hatred of social injustices. The party's political discourse is entirely preoccupied with injustice, fed by endless examples of the misfortunes suffered by the poor everywhere, in France as in the Third World. Every injustice is imputable to capitalism and imperialism. Only Socialism can provide a means of escaping from today's desperate hardships to a better life. But only the *party* is capable of achieving Socialism. Consequently, even if the party occasionally makes mistakes, to disagree with the party is by far the most serious crime that an activist can commit, far more serious than any error committed by the party leadership itself.

In its heyday the party was the new tribune of the common people. In carrying out its tribune function, the PCF was the spokesman for all exploited members of society. These *mécontents* have traditionally called into question the value of indirect parliamentary representation, because they consider all representation to be partly synonymous with treason, unless the representatives remain constantly under the control of the people. This suspicion of politicians is deeply rooted in the French consciousness, which regards only direct democracy as being truly legitimate, as we saw above. When it is adequately fulfilling its tribune function, the party ensures that the people's elected representatives are called to account for their actions by the people. Should this tribune function be unsatisfactorily fulfilled in the eyes of the voters (a logical consequence of the PCF's decline), other forces exist to fulfil it. That message has been understood by Jean Marie Le Pen, leader of the extreme right-wing Front National who has skilfully addressed himself to some of those protest voters who used to vote Communist by voicing a number of populist themes aimed against politicians in general.

The PCF has classically associated itself with four great mobilising themes for the popular electorate: peace, national independence, anti-fascism and defence of republican (public-sector) schools. Only the latter theme remained a mobilising one for the masses, and even that has recently become devalued. Moral indignation continues to underpin the party's political discourse, even though popular mobilising issues for such anger are becoming increasingly rare. Such moral indignation asserts that the people are honest, but that their governments are corrupt. This can be illustrated by citing from a document presented at the PCF's 22nd congress in 1976. This document, entitled 'What the Communists want for France', solemnly declared: 'We Communists say that all that goes to show how rotten the system is, how decadent the world is. We are fighting for a new world. We are fighting against violence, hatred and immorality.'

The final problem for the PCF is that Marxism is no longer considered as an established scientific truth (if it ever was), or as the only genuine science. After exercising a dogmatic attraction on a large number of intellectuals in the course of the 1960s and 1970s, it is generally considered in the same circles today as merely a theory, sometimes useful and sometimes outdated, but totally anachronistic as a doctrine for political action. Amongst the public, Marxism was always accepted by at best a minority, and today it is rejected by an overwhelming majority.

The brutal ideological U-turn of the left-wing intelligentsia is as surprising for the external observer as its blindness to reality in the 1950s and 1960s. How could these intellectuals have been so blinded by Marxism that they refused to recognise the existence of Soviet labour camps, or the reality of the Soviet police state? How could they have been so naive as to proclaim Stalin the man they most loved in the world? The ideological straitjacket of Marxism prevented left-wing intellectuals in France from being honest with themselves and recognising the true nature of the Soviet Union, especially under Stalin. By the end of the 1970s, reverence towards the USSR had given way to serious criticisms. In particular, the dramatic crisis of conscience created by Solzhenitsyn's revelations in 1975 forced a re-evaluation of the USSR. It seems certain that the May 1968 movement, by illustrating that the PCF could be outflanked on its left, opened the way to the USSR's fall from grace, and ensured that Solzhenitsyn was listened to by those left-wing intellectuals who would have rejected him ten years earlier as another Kravchenko. Once a gap appeared in the worldview of Marxism, the whole ideological edifice collapsed, at least as it had until then been applied to the USSR.

Moreover, the 'scientific' basis of Marxism in France – as elsewhere – was also collapsing. The PCF's moral indignation seemed incongruous to the public, which was becoming increasingly tolerant and hedonistic. The party's great mobilising themes were losing their attraction. It could no longer pretend to be the only legitimate representative of the working class, given its dramatic decline of influence within that class. Indeed, the party's traditional discourse of injustice and misery seemed out of step with a society which had enriched itself so rapidly. In response to these developments, the PCF has had to aim its message at the new paupers, from which the traditional industrial workers want to differentiate themselves and the poorest class. Moreover, the Soviet Union can no longer serve as an exemplary model of Socialism since the Gulag, the KGB, Afghanistan and Poland have given it so deplorable a reputation. Like the other trade unions but more so, the CGT is losing its mobilising power and its activists. All around it, the PCF's strongholds are collapsing, and it finds itself forced to rely on its core of paid party workers and dedicated activists, who could not live or breathe outside the party. To develop the analogy between French Communism and Catholicism, the PCF is constantly becoming a sect and openly fighting the world outside it which derives its strength and unity from this struggle. Like any other sect, it must protect its members from the perverting influences of the outside world. By denouncing this perversion, the PCF still manages to find an audience, but it is an increasingly limited one, and the party incarnates fewer and fewer hopes for social change.

THE DECLINE OF TRADE UNION ACTIVISM

Throughout Western nations, trade unions are in decline, both in their number and in the members they attract. Moreover, public opinion everywhere is becoming less and less favourable to the unions. This does not necessarily mean, however, that they have lost their influence at all levels of society. This can clearly be seen in relation to the transformation of the role of trade union leaders in France, which is in marked contrast with the situation in the UK. French union leaders have gained respectability and legitimacy and consequently enjoy increased access to those in power, as well as to the public. The importance they are given on television illustrates this: the leaders of the three main unions, H. Krasucki (CGT), E. Maire (CFDT) and A. Bergeron (FO), are treated as personalities who are almost as important as ministers, whereas their predecessors were certainly not. It was only in 1967 that IFOP, one of the leading opinion poll organisations, started asking questions about the image of unions in its surveys, the results of which were published for the first time in the periodical *Sondages* in 1968. Indeed, polling organisations had traditionally ignored trade unions, undoubtedly considered as less glamorous than other objects of their attention. Although questions about strikes have been asked since 1953, it is only since 1979 that the popularity of the different unions has been regularly measured in opinion polls.

Even in their heyday, trade unions in France never enrolled more than one-fifth of the workforce as card-carrying members. Within this average, considerable differences have always existed. In small companies with fewer than 100 employees and especially in those with fewer than 50, trade union membership is extremely rare. At the other extreme, the great public service organisations and nationalised industries have a strong trade union presence:

for example, virtually every state-school teacher is in a union. In traditional heavy industries also, such as mining, the chemical industry, textiles and iron and steel, trade union membership is dense. Membership is much less so in other industrial sectors. In fact, the four million or so union members can largely be found in companies which employ seven or eight million workers. In half of French companies, the rate of union membership varies between 40 per cent and 50 per cent, whereas in the other half the unions have always been extremely weak. Since 1979, the number of union members has declined in each of the major trade union federations, especially in the pro-Communist CGT, the largest trade union. Only the pragmatic, apolitical Force Ouvrière has been able to resist this trend.

French trade unions have traditionally been divided along ideological and political lines, a factor which has considerably weakened their overall effectiveness. Ideological divisions explained why early this century no one unified trade union movement emerged to back a single political party on the left, as in the social democratic tradition prevalent in Germany, Britain or the Scandinavian countries. There are three major and two minor trade union federations in France which compete for members and support in professional elections. The largest union is the Confédération générale du travail (CGT). The CGT was formed in 1902 as an organisation committed to the doctrine of syndicalism: the conquest of power by the working class through the weapon of the general strike. The early CGT vigorously opposed the first unified Socialist Party (SFIO), which it accused of betraying working-class interests by fighting parliamentary elections. A tradition of working-class self-sufficiency and direct action developed, according to which the liberation of the workers would result only from the direct efforts of the workers themselves, and parties and Parliament were distrusted. Although never more than a small minority of workers were attracted to the CGT or to syndicalist ideas, which went out of fashion after the First World War, the legacy of 'workerism' remained powerful and later on was given new expression by the PCF. The CGT split in 1918 into two rival federations, the larger pro-Socialist CGT and the small pro-Communist CGTU; they reunited in 1936 under the impetus of the left's Popular Front alliance. The modern CGT dates from 1947, when the PCF captured control of the federation from its previous Socialist leadership. From 1947 onwards, the CGT has been dominated by the PCF, providing the party with a strong base in the industrial working class. None the less, although the CGT retains its status as the strongest union, its influence has been reduced within the past twenty years. This testifies both to the decline of the PCF and to the implausibility of revolutionary ideas amongst today's workers. Moreover, the CGT has been particularly struck by increased unemployment in the traditional industries where its support was strongest, such as iron and steel, mining and shipbuilding.

The second largest French union is the Confédération française démocratique du travail (CFDT). The CFDT was formed in 1964, when a majority of members of the older Christian union, the CFTC, decided to establish themselves as a secular union. From its origins, the CFDT associated itself with new ideas, especially with *autogestion* (workers' control of factories), which came into vogue after May 1968. The CFDT has always declared itself to be independent of any political party, but its sympathies are broadly Socialist and pro-PS. The third largest French union is Force ouvrière (CGT–FO). Force ouvrière was formed in 1947 out of the minority of the old CGT who refused the new Communist leadership. From the start, Force ouvrière has declared itself a 'moderate', pragmatic union, and resolutely rejects such utopian ideas as *autogestion*, or revolution. There are two other union federations. The Confédération française des travailleurs chrétiens (CFTC) was formed in 1919 as a Christian trade union, which sought to promote Christianity and largely rejected the confrontational style of unionism represented by the CGT. Since 1964, the CFTC has continued to exist as a small national union, but with little influence. The Confédération générale des cadres (CGC), as its name implies, concentrates on recruiting managerial, technical and office staff. Its support amongst this category of workers is today in decline, partly because the other unions now take the recruitment of *cadres* seriously.

The decline in trade union membership has affected all of the major union confederations. The central issue is whether this decline is merely a conjuncture, or whether it represents a major transformation of the trade union movement. The second hypothesis is the more plausible. Indeed history has shown that in periods of economic crisis and unemployment, workers have a tendency to abandon their trade unions, from which they know that they stand little chance of gaining any improvements in living conditions. In such circumstances, union activism might cause problems for individual workers, notably the prospect of unemployment if they are fired by their employers for their union activities. The downturn in workers joining trade unions has been noticeable since 1973, but a spectacular decline can be registered from 1979 onwards. The causes of this decline are varied: the restructuralisation of the French economy, leading to reductions in the workforce in traditional heavy industries with strong union traditions; the expansion of the service sector and new industries where unionisation is difficult; fundamental transformations in the labour market and the emergence of unemployment. The massive entry of women into the labour-force surprised the trade unions, who were initially ill-prepared to

cater for their demands, and to mobilise them behind their banner. The seg-
mentation of the labour market means that the unions' fortunes vary
according to the type of job or industrial sector concerned. For while certain
workers are guaranteed stability of tenure, and others in expanding sectors
are indirectly secure in their jobs because of labour shortages, unemployment has had a dramatic effect on union recruitment in less stable sectors of
the economy. Around one-half of the workforce can depend on a stable job
which is likely to remain so, but the other half lives in conditions of increasing job insecurity. If unemployment was calculated only in relation to those
sectors where workers have little job security, the unemployment rate
would have to be doubled, as 10–20 per cent of this population are
unemployed.

Faced with these profound transformations in the world of work, the
trade unions are looking for a new beginning. The union is a relatively
young institution which celebrated its centenary in 1984, 100 years after the
1884 law legalised trade unions. Trade unionism developed along with
heavy industry, and has always been influenced by the industrial structures,
the mentalities and the balance of power of the early industrial era. During
the fifty-year period from 1884 to 1936, trade unionism grew up in a world
of liberal capitalism, where job insecurity was the norm, where the 'boss'
was well known and often to be seen, and where trade union struggles
formed part of a more general class struggle. The traditional organisation of
trade unions around crafts and then around industrial sectors has produced
trade union organisations in which professional federations are more
important than local structures, a development which has favoured the
regulation of conflicts and negotiations at a national level.

The major advances in trade union history have occurred through
national rather than local agreements. The Matignon agreements of 1936
concluded between the state, the trade unions and the employers, closely
followed by wide-ranging collective agreements reached at the level of
national industrial sectors, confirmed this vertical, centralised structure of
collective bargaining. This procedure was repeated with the Grenelle
agreements, at the height of the May 1968 events. The state played a decisive
role on both occasions in negotiations between trade unions and employers;
everybody concerned naturally looked to national-level negotiations to
secure a resolution of conflicts. The trade unions, the employers' associations and the government have thus become a functional triad, since each
partner must strengthen the others in order that all will remain credible
bargaining-partners. Obviously, the trade unions have benefited most from
this process, since it has accorded them a representative status that the
workers themselves have often refused. Government recognition, clearly

an instrument of state power, is highly valued by the unions, who are anxious not to jeopardise their status by excessive intransigence in representing the workers' interests. Such recognition has also given the unions an aura of legitimacy in relation to the public.

French working-class culture developed during the nineteenth century from the exercise of crafts, by workers organised in craft unions. This counter-culture was strengthened as a result of the social exclusion imposed on the workers by the dominant bourgeois culture, against which working-class values asserted themselves. The will for self-development and improvement has always been a strong aspiration of working-class élites in France. The sociologist Renaud Sainsaulieu has distinguished between four great workers' cultures corresponding to different groups of workers and types of companies:

The *unanimity culture* brings together the mass of unskilled workers with neither responsibility nor chances of promotion, whose only opportunity of an improvement in conditions lies in mass collective action. Relationships within this group are highly emotional. Decisions must be taken unanimously. The authoritarian or charismatic leader maintains the cohesion of the group. This culture is the traditional one which prevailed during the nineteenth century.

The *withdrawal culture*, born with Taylorism, is that which prevails in the small, traditional factory, as well as in the great bureaucracies. It is in these spheres that the most marginalised workers predominate (unorganised unskilled workers, women, immigrants). These workers are often in a precarious economic position, refuse collective action and seek solace by concentrating upon their lives outside the workplace. The 'boss' alone decides how work is to be organised.

The *separatist culture* can be found mainly in those categories undergoing upward professional mobility, especially in those modern sectors where new technologies have had the most impact, or in research institutions. This culture is especially prevalent amongst workers with good promotion prospects. Relationships are formed, but are confined to small selective groups. Collective action is rare. The boss decides upon promotion.

The *negotiation culture* prevails amongst professional people and the *cadres*, whose expertise is widely recognised. Relations at work are based on everybody's recognition of everybody else's varied skills and competence. The group has a high profile, and is ready for confrontation if necessary. For that reason, the negotiation culture has a high sense of its own self-sufficiency and is unwilling to accept leaders imposed from above. Authority patterns must therefore be liberal.

The 'unanimity culture', that of the working-class masses produced by the Industrial Revolution, is now anachronistic: it is to be found only in those industrial sectors in decline. The 'withdrawal culture' prevailed during the industrial growth of the 1950s and 1960s; it remains in evidence in small factories in the more marginal industrial sectors, where its effects are offset by the paternalism of the small employer. The effect of withdrawal is also experienced by those marginalised by unemployment. On the other hand, the two latter cultures are developing in the new expanding sectors of the economy. Their development seems likely to transform the trade union organisations. A new working-class culture is developing upon these new bases. Influenced by these new cultural references, it seems likely that the French working class will be less predisposed in the future to engage in the heroic class struggles of the past and more favourably inclined to participating in a greater variety of activities and institutions such as neighbourhood committees, friends, family, holiday, and so on.

From the beginning, the trade union movement used the strike as its main weapon, as a means of struggle which gave experience to union activists and as a means of recruiting new members. Strikes were originally seen by the trade union movement either as skirmishes, or as well-ordered battles which foreshadowed the final battle, that of the general strike which would guarantee the proletariat's conquest of power. While this historic event was awaited, punctual local strikes were useful: strike action reminded workers that the bosses were class enemies, enabled activists to strengthen the union's identity and reinforced the cohesion of the group of workers concerned. The longer strikes lasted, the more they were felt to root the trade union and the strike weapon itself in the workers' consciousness as indispensable and to mobilise sympathisers to support the strikers. The great national stoppages would last for a shorter period of time, but had a major symbolic effect, which made them into important events in working-class life. During these strikes, all the workers would feel that they belonged to an homogeneous social class, with the same interests and aspirations.

The number and extent of strikes have been declining since the mid 1970s. Conflicts are becoming more localised, but also longer and increasingly bitter. Whereas 35,000 factories were affected by strikes in 1973, only 4,000 were affected in 1982. The number of days lost because of strikes was cut by half during this period, and the numbers of strikers in 1982 was five times smaller than in 1973. These localised conflicts often concern only one workshop within a factory, or one category of workers, for example

Table 5. *Erosion of public confidence in trade unions*

'Do you place your confidence in trade unions to defend your interests: always, usually, infrequently, or not at all?'

	Percentage of salaried working population	
	Always/usually	Infrequently/not at all
October 1979	57	36
December 1982	44	48
October 1983	46	45
September 1985	37	59
December 1986	49	43
October 1987	47	46

'Do you consider that the trade unions articulate and put forward the demands of the workers: very well, fairly well, not very well, or not at all well?'

	Percentage of salaried working population	
	Very/fairly well	Not very/ not at all well
October 1983	45	49
December 1986	44	51
October 1987	35	60

Source: SOFRES, *L'état de l'opinion* (1989)

unskilled workers, women, or immigrants. This creates categorical solidarity which makes the trade unions' task more difficult, since the sympathy of all the workers for a particular action will not necessarily be forthcoming. By representing one category of workers (immigrants, for example) the union might alienate another (such as native-born unskilled workers). Often a workshop or a particular category of workers will decide upon a spontaneous, wildcat strike, which takes little account of the trade union or of other workers. The trade union is no longer the driving force behind such strikes, but as often as not will attempt to control them (giving support and advice where necessary). The role of the trade union activists has correspondingly been transformed: they are no longer ringleaders of industrial protests so much as advisers and organisers. This evolution will undoubtedly be strengthened by the growing diversification of working conditions, by the development of more autonomous 'teams' of workers, and above all by the workers' higher average level of education and cultural awareness, which combine to increase their capacity for autonomy and their critical approach.

Parallel to this, the trade unions are now increasingly losing the confi-

Table 6. *Public perceptions of trade union power (%)*

	November 1967	March 1969	November 1969	March 1982
Trade unions are too important	11	21	24	42
Trade unions are not important enough	41	29	28	20
Trade unions are sufficiently important	28	28	36	27

Source: O. Duhamel and J.-L. Parodi, 'Images syndicales', *Pouvoirs*, no. 26 (1983)

dence of the general public that they had managed to reconcile during the last twenty years. Until the 1960s, the trade unions had been seen by a majority of the population in the same light in which they considered themselves: as instruments of workers' defence and as revolutionary forces. Consequently, they were perceived as enemies of the established order and as trouble-makers. Since that earlier period, the unions had managed to acquire respectability and legitimacy as representatives of the people, who defended the interests of all wage-earners (very broadly defined) and who represented 85 per cent of the working population. Public opinion polls clearly illustrated the transformation of the public's image of the unions' role and representative status.

However, the trade unions have been losing their good image for several years amongst all sections of society, and have shared in the general declining public confidence which has recently afflicted all national institutions. Although virtually nobody wants to ban trade unions, and a clear majority considers that their abolition would be bad for democracy, this same majority accords them no more confidence as national institutions than political parties or politicians, both notoriously unpopular. They come well behind the police in the public's favour. Indeed, they have lost their aura of untouchable virtue, as have the republic, the church and the army.

THE RENEWAL OF TRADE UNIONS

Public signs of disaffection with the trade unions (such as loss of members and diminishing public confidence) have led many commentators to conclude that the trade unions are in certain decline. But nothing can be less certain. Although the unions have lost members and public confidence, in certain respects their social role has been strengthened.

The economic crisis has restrained the unions' margins of manoeuvre in wage negotiations and has reduced wage-confrontations between workers and employers. As a consequence, the unions have sought new areas in which they can put their demands forward (such as work-practices and the rules of organisation in the workplace). The progressive disappearance of the Taylorian organisation of companies, along with its military-style chain of command, will undoubtedly continue to increase practices of negotiation and dialogue between management and the shopfloor. New methods of work organisation, based on autonomous teams of workers, new technologies, the rise of Japanese-style 'quality circles' or the discourse valorising the 'enterprise culture', are all signs of the transformation of the firm, encouraging more worker–management dialogue. The growing diversity of working conditions now forces each particular group of workers to spell out its own objectives and strategies. Those matters which affect workers most – working conditions, hours, flexible working, relationships with the company hierarchy – are increasingly subject to negotiation. All analyses which have been undertaken of experiences of workplace participation have shown that where failure occurs, this is largely because of the weakness of the organisations concerned (employers, white-collar staff, trade unions), whereas success depends upon their strength and their capacity for innovation.

Any negotiation demands competent negotiators, and it is usually only the trade unions which can train and supply them. Employers and *cadres* are anxious to deal with delegates who are genuinely representative of the workers, without which deals reached through negotiation risk being permanently challenged by the grass roots. There is a major paradox here. Employers openly express their satisfaction if trade unions lose members and sympathisers, since that lessens their power. However, when such developments do occur, employers complain of no longer knowing with whom they should be talking.

It is thus hardly surprising that the left-wing government multiplied the opportunities given to the workers to elect their representatives. By so doing, the left seemed to be weakening the trade unions, but at the same time these measures gave the unions a new legitimacy, based more on representing workers in negotiations with employers, and less on grass-roots militancy and strikes. Traditionally, the trade union used to be the only institution which opened itself to working-class activists, except for the political parties (in practice, the PCF). Today, the worker can get himself elected to a number of different representative bodies, although he needs the support of the trade union to do this. Under the Socialist-led government from 1981 to 1984, the Auroux, Roudy and Rigout laws increased the functions of the workplace committees, composed of worker and management delegates, which have existed in all French firms with more than fifty employees since 1945. These committees enable regular consultation to occur between management and the workers, although their decisions are not binding upon management. Socialist legislation gave the workplace committees new areas of responsibility, one consequence of which has been that these committees have often split up into a series of specialised sub-committees. The training sub-committees (*commissions de formation*) are particularly important because of their efforts to define and put into operation training policies in the firm. The budgets of certain workplace committees are considerable, and their numerous social and cultural activities can definitely improve the standard of living of those workers who are able to benefit from them. Elections to the workplace committees have become a barometer of the influence of the various trade union federations. Candidates for election are usually but not always supported by one of the major trade union federations. These elections illustrate that between 1974/5 and 1982/3, the influence of the pro-Communist CGT declined sharply, whereas the other main federations all increased their support: during this period the CGT declined from 40.7 per cent to 30.7 per cent, whereas the CFDT increased from 19.1 per cent to 22.4 per cent, and FO from 8.4 per cent to 11.5 per cent. Non-union candidates increased from 16.5 per cent to 20.4 per cent.

Elections outside the firm have become more and more frequent, especially for worker representation on industrial tribunals (*conseils de prud'hommes*) and for the governing bodies administering France's social security system. Social security elections have shown similar results to those of the workplace committees. All of these different elections are major contests for the trade union federations, which see their relative strengths reinforced or diminished. In addition, since 1973 SOFRES opinion polls enable us to follow the popularity of the different trade unions within public opinion in general and to register the dramatic decline of the CGT.

A genuine socio-professional democracy has come into existence in the last ten years. It has given the trade unions a new basis to their legitimacy, new functions to fulfil and new tasks for their members to carry out. Trade union members are no longer highly politicised but usually impotent activists, as their predecessors generally were. They have become elected representatives and managers, rather than ringleaders of industrial protest. In order to prepare for and win elections, trade unions now find themselves in a situation which is analogous to that of the political parties: they must be attentive to the demands of their clientele, keep their supporters motivated by newspapers and meetings and organise support through a network of committed activists. The trade unions are only beginning to recognise the dimension of their new tasks and to get used to their new position within society.

From the moment of their election, trade union officials are weighed down by countless responsibilities, since at least one union representative is needed to sit on the management committee of all the firm's various employee-orientated institutions: educational, medical, medico-social, cultural, sport, leisure and so on. Moreover, various committees or other bodies proliferate at the national, regional, *département* and local levels: economic negotiating bodies, and committees dealing with such varied issues as social protection, employment, training, energy, housing, the environment and so on. At least 100,000 activists from different trade union federations assume responsibilities in these various spheres. The existence of such an extensive number and range of committees and other bodies poses the threat to the trade union movement that activists are deflected from specifically union activities within the firm. Set against this, such activities give the trade unions a far larger audience, create additional sources of support for their existence (they are vital bargaining partners) and link them more closely with other institutions in society.

This institutionalisation of the trade unions has helped to legitimise them and to integrate them into the rest of society to a far greater extent than before. For that reason, the crisis of membership recruitment which has afflicted the trade unions is regretted chiefly because it symbolises the passing of an era (that of heroic struggles and devotion to noble causes), rather than a loss of influence. Those trade unionists who are able to forget the unions' past 'heroic' history and concentrate on their new institutionalised role are likely to derive the most satisfaction from recent changes affecting the French labour movement. The economic power of the American and British trade unions should serve as examples to the French unions. In France, the FEN (National Education Federation, representing teachers and other workers in the state education system) has learnt the lesson of this evolution and created a whole series of affiliated institutions to serve its members' various interests (medical, financial, social) and extend its influence. Supporting itself upon these affiliated institutions, FEN is able to provide a more complete service for its members, whose interests it defends efficiently in its dealings with the education ministry. Putting forward a trade union of civil servants as a model for the workers' unions might seem paradoxical, or even scandalous, but it is probable that its example will be emulated.

5

The national education system

Universal primary education in France was introduced by the founding fathers of the Third Republic. The Ferry Laws of 1881, named after the famous republican education minister, imposed an obligation on parents for the first time to send their children to primary school until the age of eleven; such education was to be universal, obligatory and free. The main goal of the founding fathers was to transform backward conservative peasants into educated citizens, dedicated to the defence of the republic. Education was a form of social engineering, since a national education system would be a tool for disseminating democratic ideas within the traditionally conservative villages, as well as a means of breaking the grip of traditional conservative notables over the local peasantry. These educational reforms were to create a new, rival network of influence within the villages, whereby the local schoolteacher competed with the landlord and the priest in order to influence the peasantry. The republicans did eventually succeed in their objective of imposing a single unified republican culture, but this took longer than expected. The spread of national education gradually broke down the older regional barriers, which had prevailed over much of France throughout the nineteenth century. It helped create a uniform, centralised nation, in which national identity overrode separate regional sentiment. However, the speed with which this process occurred must not be exaggerated. Until the First World War, Breton peasants in fact remained more Breton than French, even though they often aspired to become imbued with the national culture and language. Learning French was regarded by peasants as a means of improving their socio-economic position, and as an indispensable precondition for any upward social mobility. If the school gradually succeeded in instilling French culture and language in all regions of France, this owed as much to the demands of peasant parents (convinced that a knowledge of French would help their children) as it did to the positive efforts in this direction of the central government.

Primary-school teachers concentrated on transmitting the basic elements of a rudimentary education to their pupils: reading, writing, mathematics, French history and geography. They were also responsible for inculcating basic moral values, as well as stressing the need to respect discipline and social hierarchy. Schoolteachers were thus responsible not only for teaching their pupils, but also for educating them in broader social norms. After leaving school, young people from the popular classes would return to the farm or the family workshop, where they would forget most of what they had learnt. However, they rarely forgot the social attitudes (respect for hierarchy and order) instilled at school, and such attitudes were reinforced by youth clubs, sporting teams, and then for boys by military service. These values triumphed as much in Catholic schools (around one-third of the total) as they did in state schools. Victory in the First World War was due partly to the sense of discipline and patriotism instilled in the children of the peasantry by the primary-school system.

Children from bourgeois families did not follow the same educational route as those from the lower social classes. From the start of their education, young bourgeois children attended separate primary schools (some state, others private), and were thus kept apart from children from peasant or working-class families. After primary education, boys from bourgeois families usually progressed to the secondary school (*lycée*), alongside a small number of the brightest boys from peasant or working-class families who received grants to continue their education at secondary school (*lycée*). At the *lycée*, pupils would study for the *baccalauréat*, the wide-ranging examination created by Napoleon. Girls' *lycées* were first established in 1880, but initially had a limited syllabus and did not prepare their pupils for the *baccalauréat*, which was a symbol of culture and education which opened the path to university, or to one of the élite *grandes écoles*, and guaranteed future career success. The *grandes écoles* catered only for a small, predominantly male, bourgeois élite, which would be called upon to form a ruling class and govern the country (see pp. 104–6 below).

It was hardly an economic catastrophe if a boy from a bourgeois family failed his *baccalauréat*, since he would be able to live off the family's wealth, and would inherit his father's firm or professional practice. Secondary-school teachers laid great stress on the humanities, Latin and Greek, in order to promote an appreciation of classical culture amongst their pupils. This was felt to set them apart from the lower classes in society, and to befit the dominant role they were being prepared to perform within society. After the *baccalauréat*, young men would go on to study at university in Paris or a provincial capital, where life was a leisurely, hedonistic type of existence, in which cafés and girls were as important for young students as study. Once a university degree had been obtained, the young graduate would return to the family home and get married.

These two different patterns of education – popular and bourgeois – were poles apart and taught each generation the place it was supposed to occupy in society. There was a third type of school created between the two wars, catering for primary technical education: in technical schools pupils were prepared for skilled manual occupations. It must be stressed that specifically technical education has never really been regarded as a legitimate exercise by governments in France. Indeed, French opinion in general has usually been that technical expertise could be learnt on the job, either in the fields or in the workshop. It is only for the élite personnel, such as engineers, that the idea of a technical culture has been accepted (as opposed to technical training following the acquisition of a more general culture). The general belief, amongst the popular classes in particular, was that the best technical apprenticeship was a father teaching his son the tools of the trade.

From around 1950 onwards, it was apparent that if France was to modernise itself, it was essential to create a greater equality of opportunity across the boundaries of social class, and to use the education system as the main means of achieving this. It was also recognised that more technical education was necessary to train the technicians needed in an expanding industrial sector. The post-war baby-boom made this a superhuman task, since schools now had to welcome an increasing number of children and teach them for a longer period (the minimum school-leaving age was raised from fourteen to sixteen in 1959, operative from 1967 onwards). The schools were constrained to adopt new pedagogical methods in order to be able to respond to the challenge created by the expanding birth rate, and new economic imperatives. These various objectives were not all fulfilled to the same extent. One of the great triumphs of post-war education policy has been that all children now receive full-time education between the ages of three and sixteen. In contrast to certain other countries, this has been achieved without fundamentally overhauling the basic structure of the education system: infant school from three to six, primary school from six to eleven, intermediary school (*collège*) from eleven to fifteen, and secondary school from fifteen to eighteen. The French education system remains generalist in content, and technical education continues to be looked down upon by teachers and pupils alike. Economic rivals such as Germany or Japan have adapted their education systems far more effectively than France to provide technical training to respond to the needs of industry.

The enormous growth in the schools and universities in France can be illustrated by several figures, which indicate that the French national education ministry manages more staff than any other institution in the world, except the Red Army! In 1986/7, the education ministry employed 1,125,000 people, the vast majority as primary- and secondary-school teachers.

THE CHANGING ROLE OF THE TEACHER

The primary-school teacher performed an essential political, ideological and administrative role during the Third Republic. He used often to act as the local mayor's secretary, as well as leading a network of local associations, often in competition with those offered by the priest. Indeed, critics of the Third Republic mocked the 'Republic of School Teachers' that they claimed the regime had been transformed into. It was undoubtedly true that the teaching profession supplied a large proportion of the republic's politicians. In the large cities, a secondary-school teacher would usually be a highly respected figure in the local community. Of course, there were fierce rivalries between the state's *collèges* and *lycées*, and their equivalents in the private, mainly Catholic, sector, but these rivalries only served to reinforce the prestige of teachers in both public- and private-sector education. In fact, because of the importance society bestowed on the transmission of knowledge and cultural values, the state schools – *collèges* and *lycées* – were primordial institutions in French life. This could be illustrated by the importance attached by parents and the local community to the distribution of school prizes and prize-giving ceremonies.

The role performed by schoolteachers in politics remains extremely important in contemporary France, but their position in the social hierarchy has declined considerably. In addition, the schools as institutions have lost a good deal of their prestige, a development which can be explained by the fact that everybody now has access to secondary education. For this reason, it is impossible to compare like with like when looking at how schools have evolved since the beginning of the twentieth century: today's *collèges* and *lycées*, to which everybody has access, have nothing in common with the élitist establishments of the beginning of the century. The expansion of education and the growth in the number of schools has inevitably lessened their prestige within society and at the heart of the local community. Moreover, the fact that small primary schools serving one village have been regrouped into larger institutions serving small towns has had an important social effect, since primary-school teachers are no longer easily identified with the local village, which has lowered their standing within the local community. In addition, the old practice whereby the primary-school teacher would act as secretary to the local mayor has fallen into disuse.

Notwithstanding the diminishing prestige of the school as a social institution, in many small and medium-sized towns schoolteachers have taken on new functions in various local political, administrative and cultural institutions. Indeed, many schoolteachers have become elected as town councillors or become mayors, especially since the 1977 municipal elections. The high instance of political participation amongst teachers is hardly surprising, given that they have more spare time than those working in most other professions, which they are able to devote to party political or voluntary-group activity. Because their position in the social hierarchy has declined, some teachers are inclined to attempt to regain lost social prestige by succeeding in politics, especially by becoming local *notables*. In general, primary and secondary schools continue to play an important part in local cultural life, and are anxious to provide their services for the benefit of local councils and other institutions. The schools also perform an important economic role since the salaries of teachers and auxiliary staff employed by the school can represent a considerable sum. In fact, in many small towns the local economy would be seriously affected without the economic support provided by the education ministry.

The 1981 general election in France, following the victory of the Socialist Mitterrand in the presidential election earlier that year, witnessed the entry *en masse* of teachers into the National Assembly. The republic had once again become a 'republic of schoolteachers', although the new breed of teacher-deputy was no longer the highly respected secondary-school (*lycée*) classics master of the Third Republic, but the primary (*instituteur*) and intermediary school (*collège*) teachers who had rejoined the Socialist Party in the course of the 1970s. The best example of one of the new breed of teacher-deputies was Pierre Mauroy, President Mitterrand's first Prime Minister (1981–4). Mauroy, the son of a primary-school teacher, was himself by profession a teacher in a secondary technical school, as well as being leader of an important national association of youth clubs (*clubs Léo-Lagrange*).

This transformation of the position of teachers within French society has been accompanied by a transformation of the relationship between school and family. In the traditional pattern of relations between family and school, the two institutions were complementary: the family taught children the need to respect authority, while it was at school that they developed friendships with other children of the same age and obtained a basic knowledge. Within the family and at school, the child was taught of the need for obedience, respect for authority, and correct patterns of behaviour. Such standards of behaviour were preached relentlessly to children of bourgeois parents, although they were relaxed somewhat amongst children from upper-bourgeois origins, and were far laxer amongst the children of working-class and peasant origins. These strict moral codes have largely disappeared within both the school and the home in the course of the last twenty years, and more rapidly within the home. This has created numerous problems within the schools; the chief one is lack of respect for the authority of teachers.

The moral evolution underpinning the changes in teaching methods seems to have started during the inter-war period and to have come to fruition after the war. In substance, at the heart of this evolution lay a loosening of the constraints which ruled the life of the child, permitting a freer development of the young individual at the expense of received codes of behaviour. The events of May 1968 (see chapter 13) were symbolic of the triumph of youth, and also of a new teaching style which had taught the individual to expand his own personality, rather than to conform to pre-scribed rules. The importance attached to these new methods naturally scandalised the advocates of more traditional methods, who had failed to realise how times had changed.

By the 1980s, the transformation of the relationship between parents and children had become complete. The family is no longer primarily an auth-oritarian structure where correct modes of behaviour are instilled into the young child; today's typical French family is a far more flexible structure which permits the child to develop his own identity. The nursery schools have understood this transformation well. The creation of universal nursery education between the ages of three and six is one of the great triumphs of post-war education. French children start school at an earlier age than those in any other major industrial country: in 1982/3, 91 per cent of three-year-olds were attending nursery school. Within the nursery school, the young child is encouraged primarily to develop his own personality rather than to respect excessive discipline. Such freedom, however, is far more difficult in primary and secondary schools, where a minimum of discipline must be maintained and collective rules respected for the system of function efficiently.

Schools receive children who have little notion of traditional discipline, or of the need to respect collective rules. Within the classroom, such chil-dren are likely to rebel against teaching-methods which appear designed to suppress individual spontaneity and identity. To a large extent, the diffi-culties faced by the teaching profession today arise from the fact that chil-dren are encouraged to develop their personalities within the family, and this has meant that their expectations of school have changed dramatically. Moreover, the advent of an age of mass communication has further compli-cated the traditional role performed by the school. Television acts as a sort of 'parallel school', an alternative source of information to that provided by the schoolteacher. In order to remain in step with their pupils, schoolteachers today are constrained to keep up with television programmes, and must be ready to provide a commentary on programmes of educational value. It is clear that the role of the teacher in the modern school is no longer to tell the 'truth' to attentive pupils, but to explain the many complicated aspects of a particular reality. The dilution of the schoolteacher's role (competition from television, parents) has weakened the status of the teaching profession within society, and strengthened the role of the family unit as a source of education, to some extent in competition with the school.

Finally, it must be stressed that the value system underpinning French society has diversified with extreme rapidity since the early 1960s (see part IV). One consequence of this is that schoolteachers are uncertain which moral values they ought to be transmitting. Parents are able to overcome the difficulties of communication between generations by the emotional warmth of family life and by the feeling of security and identity that is bestowed by the family. Schoolteachers do not possess such emotional resources. In fact, schoolteachers are no longer concerned with instilling the correct moral values, but with allowing children to develop their capacities of analysis and criticism. Such subject-matter is by definition more difficult to teach. Whereas traditional disciplines such as classical literature helped to transmit moral values from one generation to the next, it might be argued that the study of history and sociology are more suitable to the demands of contemporary society, which values the individual's capacity for critical thought.

DEMOCRACY AND MERITOCRACY

After numerous reforms and counter-reforms, the dual system of the nineteenth century outlined above (primary education for the popular classes; secondary school for the bourgeoisie) gave way to a single unified national education system, albeit one which coexists alongside a private sector subject to substantially the same rules concerning qualifications. This unified system of national education was introduced gradually in a series of post-war reforms in 1959, 1963 and 1965.

In principle each child now has to follow the same core curriculum from the beginning of infant school (ages three to six) until the end of *collège* (ages eleven to fifteen). During the post-war period, the objectives underpinning the education system have been radically transformed. The duty of teachers is no longer to teach children from different social classes the role they were expected to perform in adult society. Instead, teachers have a duty to fight against inequalities of all sorts, especially the inequality of opportunity which used to be directly attributable to the education system. With the idea that national education can be used to promote equality of opportunity, the contemporary French education system claims to educate all French children in the same way. In theory at least, each child must have the same chances of reaching the summit of the social hierarchy, whatever his social class of origin. In practice, varieties within the state system are considerable. There is an enormous difference between the prestigious Parisian *lycée* and the run-down inner-city school.

In relation to education, the ideas of meritocracy and of family choice are obviously at two opposing ends of the (ideological) spectrum. Almost by definition, the family seeks to transmit wealth and social status to succeeding generations, and thereby to perpetuate existing inequalities within society. Those families highest up the social scale are best placed to perpetuate this state of affairs. For this reason, those who argue that parents must have prime responsibility for deciding what type of education their children receive, indeed for educating their children themselves (a stance strongly supported by the church), can usually be classed on the right. The idea of meritocracy, by contrast, presupposes an equality of opportunity, if not an equality of outcome. It is in the name of creating equality of opportunity that the left has traditionally declared itself favourable to educating every child in the same state schools.

If the role of the school is merely to transmit knowledge (the right's traditional argument), the real process of education, the transmission of values, must be confided to the family. This results in perpetuating social differences, a position supported by the right either in terms of defence of the family or of natural social inequality. Ideally, the process of education would be entrusted to the family itself, but in the absence of this the school must limit itself to transmitting knowledge, and must not attempt to pass on values, the domain of the family. Those on the left have adopted a radically different viewpoint: the state school must transmit not only knowledge, but republican values as well, in addition to promoting the greatest possible equality of opportunity. For this reason, state schools must be in charge of every child's education from the earliest possible age. This was one reason for the creation of nursery schools to look after very young children from the ages of three to six before they started attending primary school; another reason was the widespread demand amongst young mothers to go back to work as early as possible after having their children.

In spite of the improvements in national education in France, the system has failed in many respects. Sporting activities and artistic education are practically non-existent and remain largely confined to the sphere of the family. Both sport and art remain symbolic of social division. The plastic arts, for example, are limited to children coming from educated middle-class families and are practised only at the university level. In fact, the education system has succeeded in diffusing an intellectual culture far more effectively than it has in spreading artistic culture.

It is certainly surprising that there is such a small place for sport in the schools. The French state school system provides for two hours of gymnastics per week, but this is hardly sufficient to give pupils a taste for sporting activities. The responsibility for providing training has been left to sports clubs and local councils, and each social class passes on its own sporting preferences to its children. It is obvious that football and horse-riding do not attract young people from the same social classes, and only a minority of sports, such as swimming and cycling, are enjoyed across the boundaries of social class. Against this, it must be pointed out that certain traditional middle-class sports, such as skiing and tennis, are enjoyed by a wide cross-section of the French public, as a result of the provision of more accessible training facilities and courses.

The transformation of the school system in France can be illustrated by several figures. As a result both of the post-war baby-boom and of the raising of the minimum school-leaving age from fourteen to sixteen in 1967, the number of children at school doubled from 6,000,000 to 13,000,000 between 1959 and 1980. In 1958, only 50 per cent of French children started school at the age of six, while 30 per cent left at fourteen. In the early 1980s,

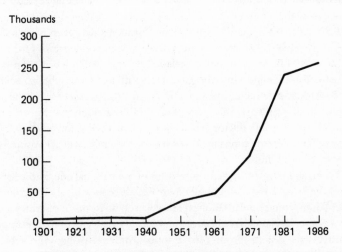

Figure 5 Growth in the annual number of school-leavers
obtaining the *baccalauréat*. Source: Ministère de l'éducation
nationale

the vast majority of children started school at the age of three and left at sixteen. Nearly 50 per cent decided to remain at school until they were eighteen.

Despite the apparent uniformity of the national education system in France, there exist a considerable number of differences between rival schools. These differences are recognised and institutionalised in the examination results published by each school. Those parents who are aware of a school's record attach great importance to the number of pupils who receive the *baccalauréat* each year. Other parents take less notice of a school's performance, since they consider that because France has one national state education system, any *lycée* must be like any other. However, the parents' ability to choose the right school for their children and to live near to a good *lycée* can be decisive for the children's future. Indeed, some parents even decide where to live simply on the basis of the quality of the local schools, and others are willing to send their children to schools a long distance from home if they consider it to be in their best interest. Parental choice is enlarged still further by the possibility of sending their children to private schools.

The ages at which pupils progress through the school system can be of fundamental importance in determining their future. The annual performance of each pupil has to be approved before he can progress to the next school year: those who fail must repeat the year, so that it becomes less likely that they will be able to pass their *baccalauréat* at the average age of eighteen. Moreover, the prestigious *grandes écoles* operate an age-limit for entry, which makes it imperative that potential students pass every year before they can even be considered for the special examinations necessary for entry to these schools. This constraint explains why the small minority of potential candidates for entry into the *grandes écoles* attempt to pass the *baccalauréat* at the earliest possible age of sixteen. To pass the *baccalauréat* at sixteen is regarded as a matter of family glory, the logical consequence of the stiff competition for entry into the top *grandes écoles*. To succeed academically as early as possible is thus the surest means of securing a superior social position for the rest of one's life.

Taken as a whole, the various reforms of the national education system since the 1950s have undoubtedly increased the educational opportunities of children from popular families. However, new forms of discrimination between social classes have become increasingly visible within the comprehensive state system. From 1967 onwards, differences between subjects studied began to replace those between different types of school as the best indicators in explaining the uneven educational performance of the different social classes within the school. Children from working-class backgrounds are more likely than middle-class children to be channelled into the lower-status vocational or 'pre-professional' streams during the last two years of the *collège*. Moreover, working-class children are far more likely to have to repeat a year than their middle-class counterparts. The increase in numbers of school pupils having to resit a year suggests that selection and assessment procedures have been strengthened over time.

Under the present system, a pupil has the 'right' to repeat one year, without this affecting his choice of subjects; should he be required to repeat a second time, however, he is invariably 'orientated' in the direction chosen by the school. In practice, should a pupil have to repeat more than one year, he will in reality be downgraded by his school in three different ways. Firstly, he is downgraded in relation to his age (since he is older than most of his class mates); secondly, he is placed in one of the lower-status 'practical' streams; and thirdly, his future social status will be lower as a consequence.

It can thus be seen that the age of a pupil at a given level of education can be decisive in assessing his future career chances: a pupil who has had to repeat even one year before taking his *baccalauréat* might be regarded as having 'failed', creating a negative impression upon employers. We saw above how the age at which a pupil passed his *baccalauréat* was previously of exaggerated importance for bourgeois families. Under the present system the importance of age has been extended to the whole of society, since any hiccup in the 'natural' progression to the *baccalauréat* is likely to reflect negatively on the pupil. It might be argued that age is a more objective criterion than any other of assessing a pupil's performance, but it is not

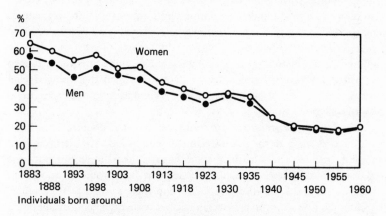

Figure 6 Proportion of a generation leaving school without any qualifications. Source: C. Baudelot and R. Establet, *Le Niveau monte* (Paris, Le Seuil, 1989)

neutral. Children from popular and even modest middle-class families tend to take longer to progress through the school system than do those from educated middle-class backgrounds, who receive more stimulus from the family environment.

The high degree of selection, as well as the practice of 'orientation' of the weaker pupils, creates great pressures on French schoolchildren. They are called upon to succeed at the right age, and are subjected to tough annual pressure to pass assessed course work, at which failure rates are often high. Pupils who fail more than once are certain to be 'orientated' into second-rate subjects preparing them for low-status work once they leave school. At the end of each year, pupils are classed hierarchically for the attention of society as a whole: those who have performed poorly carry with them the stigma of failure, an unfortunate predicament in a society where failure is frowned upon. Those who under-perform are forced by the system to believe that what has happened to them is their fault, which can destroy young people's confidence in an age of high unemployment. In fact, most schoolchildren who fail to pass the *baccalauréat* leave school with a sense of failure. By contrast, a small successful élite (which achieves the right mark at the right age) feels vindicated on two levels: by its educational success, and by its social origins (usually bourgeois). Those who leave school with a sense of failure attempt to compensate for this at other levels, such as excelling in sport, or raising a family.

The French secondary-school system has thus developed into an enormous bureaucratic machine during the last thirty years. The essential function of this machine is to group young people into categories, to select an élite to go on to higher education and positions of authority, and to condemn the rest to occupy the lower and intermediary positions within society. That the élite which emerges from the school system tends to be composed of children of the existing social élite underlines the extent to which the reforms of the 1950s and 1960s failed in their objective of increasing the educational opportunities of children from less privileged social backgrounds.

The French school system continues to maintain a separate technical sector, distinct from the mainstream general schools. The persistence of separate technical schools in France illustrates the shortcomings of the general school system. It might be argued that there would be no need to separate technical schools if the *collèges* and *lycées* paid more attention to technical training within the overall syllabus, rather than concentrating on abstract, formal learning. This explains the lack of good technicians and engineers at an intermediary level in French industry.

Around one-fifth of schoolchildren leave school at the age of sixteen without any educational qualifications. The importance of this is far greater than used to be the case, since no qualifications were previously needed to work on the family farm, or to help in the family business. The decline of agriculture and small artisan-style businesses has closed off one avenue of employment for children from 'popular' families which did not necessitate educational qualifications. In the expanding economy of the pre-1974 period of full employment, when unskilled work was plentiful and unskilled workers could be trained on the job, it was easy for young unqualified school leavers to find work. Since the mid 1970s, however, the situation has changed: with the growth of unemployment, employers are asking for educational qualifications at all levels of the work hierarchy. Young, unqualified school leavers often face a desperate situation, which increases the pressure on pupils to succeed at school. Unemployment thus imposes new, urgent duties on the schools. The economic climate has brought into sharp focus the extent to which the school system fails the less talented pupils, who are left with a bleak economic future.

Of course, teachers have complained since time immemorial that educational standards are falling. The evidence available suggests that standards have fallen in some subjects (French and Latin, for example), but have risen in other (mathematics). Compared with other countries, France performs well: one survey illustrates that the standard of education received in French schools is better than in most other countries. This judgement is to the credit of the post-war secondary-school education system in France. Secondary schools are educating five times more pupils today than a generation ago, and are issuing ten times as many educational qualifications without any serious lowering of standards in them. The continuing transformation of the French educational system is likely to make the difference between schools and subjects studied more important than ever in the future. In these circumstances, it seems probable that most families will start being more selective about which school they send their children to, adopting a strategy which was previously limited to bourgeois families.

THE SELECTION OF ÉLITES

The higher education system in France is not directly comparable to that of the nation's major European partners. In most European countries, the universities constitute either the sole or the main institutions of higher education. It is through them, especially the top four or five, that the selection of the nation's élites occurs. There may well be competition for students from polytechnics (in Britain), or *Fachhochschulen* (in Germany), but these institutions do not have the prestige of the universities, for which selection procedures are rigorous. In France, by contrast, the universities do not comprise the top tier of institutions of higher learning: this position is occupied by the *grandes écoles.*

Entry into the *grandes écoles* takes place after an extremely intensive two-year course at the *lycée* after the *baccalauréat.* At the end of this preparatory course, there is a highly competitive examination. Successful candidates secure a place at one of the élite schools (Polytechnique, Fondation nationale des sciences politiques, Ecole normale supérieure (ENS), Hautes études commerciales (HEC) etc.); unsuccessful candidates have to settle for university. The most famous *grande école* is probably Polytechnique, founded during the Revolution in 1793. Today it concentrates on training engineers, who assume top positions in industry after graduating. The other schools specialise in a whole variety of disciplines and professions. Of particular importance are the Ecole normale supérieure (teacher training), the Hautes études commerciales (top business school), the Institut d'études politiques (breeding-ground for future politicians), the Ecole nationale d'administration (training future top civil servants) and the Ecole centrale des arts et manufactures (training managers for industry). These élite Parisian schools are copied by provincial versions at the regional level, as the numerous business schools testify.

In order to be accepted into Polytechnique, as well as most of the other schools, it used to be necessary to have studied Greek intensively. Greek was taught only to the top classes in the *lycées*; selection to form part of the educated élite thus took place by way of the classical humanities. This has changed in the last twenty years or so, as mathematics has supplanted classical studies as the essential element in entrance examinations to most of the *grandes écoles.* The top classes in France's *lycées* therefore now devote considerable time to studying mathematics. A high standard in mathematics has become an indispensable precondition of entry into most of the *grandes écoles.*

The recruitment and replacement of social élites traditionally used to occur by a son following the same career path as his father. In a relatively static society, with little mobility between social classes, the replacement of élites was a fairly straightforward process. In the private sector, sons would usually inherit their legal or commercial practices from their fathers; educational qualifications would be superfluous in this context. The role performed by the *grandes écoles* had to be placed in context, to the extent that it was not necessary to have studied at a *grande école* to form part of the élite, except in the civil service, where graduation from one of these schools was vital. In contemporary France, the *grandes écoles* have expanded in number and in importance. To achieve high status in industry, for example, it is no longer usually sufficient to inherit a comfortable position, but necessary to obtain a qualification from one of the élite business schools. The increased importance placed on qualifications has made entry into the élite more of a formal process, based essentially on succeeding at one of the prestigious schools.

Alongside the *grandes écoles* there exist around seventy universities, to which all students who have passed the *baccalauréat* have the right to enter without taking an examination. In reality, an unofficial form of selection operates for the more prestigious universities, such as the Parisian ones, as well as for acceptance on the most popular courses. Despite a tradition dating back to the twelfth century, the university in France has never performed the same functions as in most comparable countries such as Germany, the UK or the USA (at least not since the Revolution and since Napoleon created the system of *grandes écoles*). Its prestige has suffered because the best students are to be found in the *grandes écoles*, and because insufficient resources are devoted to scientific research within the universities. During the nineteenth century, there was a clear division within the universities between those departments which prepared students for a career (law and medicine) and those which taught a general culture which did not lead directly to any employment except teaching (arts and science departments). This distinction is still more or less operative today.

The paucity of scientific research in the university sector in France has a long history. Prior to the twentieth century, scientific research was limited to a handful of institutions such as the Collège de France (founded in the sixteenth century by François I), the Ecole pratique des hautes études (founded in the mid nineteenth century in an attempt to imitate the German universities) and several of the more prestigious Parisian university departments. In 1936, a new development came with the creation of the National Centre for Scientific Research (CNRS). The CNRS operates independently of the universities, and is financed from the research budget of the education ministry. However, its researchers work within the context of the universities, and this has helped to raise the research profile of these institutions. It is important to underline that although the *grandes écoles* might produce leaders, they do not produce research on the lines of universities in other countries such as the UK, Germany or the USA. It is for this reason that the CNRS performs an essential role in coordinating research through the universities in France.

Despite the role performed by the CNRS, French governments tend not to pay too much attention to the universities in France, except when forced to by student agitation as in May 1968 or November 1986. This lack of attention, and failure to consider the universities as an area of major political interest undoubtedly stem from the fact that the top civil servants and most politicians were educated at one of the *grandes écoles* and tend to look down on mere universities. The rapid post-war boom in the numbers being educated at university in France has been impressive, as has the increase in the sheer number of the universities themselves. However, these developments have led to a decrease in the prestige of university degrees and, in an age of high unemployment, provoked a feeling of bitterness that even a university degree is no longer a guarantee that an individual will find work. In order to cope with the massive influx of students, universities have recruited a very large number of university lecturers, with the result that the quality of lecturers varies considerably from one institution to the next.

The career paths of the Fifth Republic's most prominent politicians showed a near-uniform preference for the *grandes écoles* over the universities. President Pompidou was a graduate of the Ecole normale supérieure; his successor Giscard d'Estaing went one better by graduating from the Ecole nationale de l'administration after having first attended Polytechnique. President Mitterrand, who studied law at university, proved to be the exception amongst recent Presidents. Numerous high-ranking politicians are graduates of the Parisian *grandes écoles*, especially the prestigious ENA. The narrow background of most of France's politicians is undoubtedly an unhealthy sign. For it is clear that however brilliant they are, two graduates of ENA will have been moulded by the same system, and will probably share a number of broad preconceptions about how society should be organised. A genuinely dynamic élite needs to be produced from various competing centres of excellence, which permits members of this élite to confront their contradictory point of view on the main contemporary political, economic and social issues.

In order to ensure France's intellectual, scientific and cultural future, it is vital that the university sector of the higher education system is expanded. The essential point is that without this, French culture will suffer drastically, and France is bound to lose its historical position as the cultural capital of the world, a position which is already being lost. If French culture disappears, the West will be left with only one language and one source of culture (Anglo-Saxon): should this happen, the West as a whole will lose the stimulation that the existence of different cultures provides and will undoubtedly decline as a result.

6

The new national consensus

Ever since 1789 the legitimacy of the republic's institutions has been periodically called into question by the extreme right as well as by the extreme left. For the most traditionally inclined right wing, which remained faithful to monarchistic and religious principles until recently, legitimate political power could only emanate from God, and there was thus a divine basis for political legitimacy. The idea of universal suffrage was scorned as a vulgar joke, since the masses were incapable of exercising any informed political judgement. The rallying of the Catholic Church to the republic during the 1890s was a tactical manoeuvre, to preserve the church's best interests under the republican regime. It did not represent a fundamental compromise with the theological foundations of Roman Catholicism, which continued to refute the legitimacy of the republican form of government until after the Second World War. Likewise, the extreme left considered the advent of parliamentary democracy during the latter part of the nineteenth century as a trick of the bourgeoisie, which was intended to allow the ruling class to secure its power over the industrial working class, the peasantry and the petite bourgeoisie. According to the Marxist tradition, which existed in a distorted form in the early Socialist movement (especially after 1920 within the Communist Party (Parti communiste français – PCF)), the primary objective of the industrial working class was to work towards revolution, rather than peaceful parliamentary change. Other early manifestations of antiparliamentarianism on the extreme left flourished during the late nineteenth and early twentieth centuries, such as anarchism, syndicalism, and various doctrines of direct action and violence.

THE LEGITIMACY OF THE REPUBLIC

This double rejection of the republic on the extreme right and the extreme left has now disappeared. There remain only a handful of monarchists nostalgic for a return to the *ancien régime*, and these are divided into various rival orthodoxies. At the other extreme, the PCF has formally renounced its attachment to the dictatorship of the proletariat (at its 1976 congress) and has in practice fought elections and made alliances like any other party since 1962. Despite its theoretical opposition to the 'personal power' it accuses the presidential system of promoting, the PCF has in reality accepted working within the institutions of the Fifth Republic, rather than attempting to bring about a revolution. That was confirmed by the attitude it adopted in May 1968, when the PCF attempted to control the mass strikes which brought the country to a standstill, rather than exploiting them as a launching-pad for a revolutionary uprising. It was also reflected in its strategy of the union of the left, and its drive for an alliance with the Socialist Party (Parti socialiste – PS).

In fact, it is undeniable that a profound consensus exists in France today in favour of the political regime. According to the French opinion poll organisation SOFRES (1988), two-thirds of French people consider that the republic is neither a left-wing nor a right-wing notion, but a fundamental reference-point shared by left and right alike. Above all, the voters' traditionally enthusiastic participation in elections has been taken to demonstrate that French democracy is in good health: 80–90 per cent of those on the electoral register vote in presidential elections, a somewhat lower proportion (70–85 per cent) in legislative elections, slightly fewer in municipal elections (but still a remarkably high 70–80 per cent) and fewer still in cantonal elections (50–70 per cent). Although a tendency to abstain grew in the second half of the 1980s, such participation rates compared favourably with those in the USA or Switzerland, where an average of half the electorate generally abstain from voting in general elections. These comparatively high rates of electoral participation must be tempered by the fact that, for a variety of reasons, around 10 per cent of potential voters are regularly left off the register.

The existence of a regime which, it is generally recognised, enjoys a high degree of political legitimacy and acceptance by left and right is an unprecedented development in republican France. Neither the Third Republic (1870–1940) nor the Fourth Republic (1944–58) could boast such an underlying consensus. This development has had an important effect on the strategies adopted by the main political parties: no serious party can accuse its rivals of being fundamentally opposed to the existing political regime. For that reason, no one party or coalition can seriously identify itself with democracy and the republic at the expense of other parties, as it could during the Third and Fourth Republics. Any party which attempted to do this in the 1980s would lack credibility. Although certain parties (PS, Union for French Democracy – Union pour la démocratie française (UDF), Rally for

the Republic – Rassemblement pour la République (RPR)) can more successfully portray themselves as representing the political mainstream than
others (PCF; National Front (Front national – FN)). In short, the republic
is no longer in danger and is accepted with a greater or lesser degree of con-
viction by all the main political parties.

Such convergences notwithstanding, politicians in France frequently
speak of the necessity of unifying the French nation, as if it suffered from
being in a chronic state of division. This theme of national unity was
inherent in the title of the organisation created by General de Gaulle in 1947
– Rally of the French People (Rassemblement du peuple français) – and de
Gaulle faithfully interpreted his mission as being that of unifying the French
people. The General's RPF was imitated in 1976 by the formation of
J. Chirac's Rally for the Republic out of the second Gaullist Party,which,
despite undergoing numerous name changes, had originally been created
in 1958 to support de Gaulle and the Fifth Republic. Both de Gaulle's RPF
and Chirac's RPR declared that their intention was to fight against division,
against antinational parties (the PCF), and for national unity. The threat
of the dismemberment of the nation has been constantly repeated by
politicians in France, especially by those on the right. However, the spectre
of division or civil war appears to have haunted ambitious politicians far
more than it has the average French citizen.

During the Fifth Republic, French electors have generally divided their
votes between the two main political camps of left and right in roughly
equal proportions. This has led to alarmist commentaries at successive elections according to which France is irreconcilably divided between two
mutually hostile left- and right-wing blocs. In reality, however, this bipolar
division of electoral support between the left (dominated by a centre-left
Socialist Party) and the moderate right (committed to democracy and the
republic) is the norm in most Western democracies. What is regarded as the
usual state of affairs during periods of calm in England (Labour versus Conservative), in the USA (Democrat versus Republican), or in West Germany
(Social Democrats versus Christian Democrats) is considered in France as
proof that centrifugal political forces are determined to destroy the nation's
cohesion and fragile unity. Such interpretations of elections in France are
dismissed by opinion pollsters, who point out that elections are won
amongst floating voters in the centre, and that the bulk of left-wing and
right-wing voters share the same presuppositions about what type of political regime is desirable in France. It is undoubtedly true that while the French
people have a fond image of themselves as a turbulent race divided by conflicting passions, this image is far from the reality.

The direct election of the President of the Republic, which has existed since de Gaulle's successful referendum in October 1962, lies at the forefront of this consensus. The French President serves for a period of seven years, longer than any other mandate in a comparable democratic nation. Direct election has consolidated the power of the President of the Republic as the *de facto* head of the executive. Another factor strengthening presidential power, at least during the 1960s, was the use of referendums, which were used by de Gaulle to create a direct relationship between the providential ruler and the people. That de Gaulle, a general in the French army, was able to introduce the direct election of the President and resort to referendums but not be suspected of transgressing the rules of democracy and the republic, underlined the extent to which the traditional republican fear of strong executive government and powerful rulers had diminished during the Fifth Republic. The legendary figure of Napoleon III, the self-styled French emperor who ruled from 1852 to 1870 after subverting the short-lived Second Republic (1848–52), is now largely forgotten.

President de Gaulle (1958–69) was the first modern French politician to recognise the crucial importance of the role performed by the mass media in modern societies, and especially that of television in reinforcing the presidential function. Successive French Presidents (Pompidou, 1969–74, Giscard d'Estaing, 1974–81, Mitterrand, 1981–8, re-elected in 1988) have followed in de Gaulle's footsteps and used their presidential powers in a decisive manner which would have been inconceivable under the Third or Fourth Republics. Until 1981, many political commentators demanded whether the institutions of the Fifth Republic were in fact consensual, considering that the left (PS and PCF) continued to regard the *principle* (albeit not the practice) of direct elections as suspect. However, François Mitterrand's election as the first Socialist President of the Republic in 1981 and his exercise of full presidential powers until the 1986 general election (when the right returned to office) confirmed that the left now accepted the legitimacy of the presidential institution.

The central role of the presidency in the French political system appeared to have weakened during the period of 'cohabitation' between the Socialist President Mitterrand and the Conservative government led by Chirac (March 1986 to May 1988). During the period of 'cohabitation', executive power was concentrated in the hands of right-wing Prime Minister Chirac, who was invested with the democratic legitimacy of having won the latest election in 1986. Although it played a more restrained part, the institution of the presidency proved its popularity; temporarily deprived of his executive authority, the French President became more of a 'republican monarch' above the political fray than ever before. Mitterrand's re-election in May 1988 (and the return of a relative Socialist majority in June) essentially re-established past patterns of presidential supremacy, despite several modifications of form. It appears likely that the French President will continue to exercise considerable powers in normal circumstances, far more in comparative terms than his American counterpart.

Since the Revolution, the French polity has been characterised by a strong belief in the virtues of direct democracy, and a distrust of elected politicians (see below). This might explain the unpopularity of Parliament as an institution, and why the mayoralty is the most popular political office in France. The success of the French Presidency during the Fifth Republic can be explained by the President's status as the Mayor of the Nation. Direct election creates a situation whereby, through using the medium of television, each serious presidential candidate is known personally to the electors, just as the mayor is known personally to the inhabitants of a small commune. Like the mayor, the President can be called directly to account for his actions. The success of the presidency as an institution thus reflects the continuing preference for direct democracy over remote government by parliamentary assembly.

Democracy in France has classically been permeated by a belief in the legitimacy of the revolutionary tradition. The idea that French citizens have the right to overturn an unjust government, if its institutions are an affront to the ideas of the republic and democracy, has been considered axiomatic. The bulk of French citizens would agree that the 1830 Revolution re-established the people's will against the abuses of the restored Bourbon monarchy of Charles X. In calmer times, this tradition has stressed that the people must constantly be vigilant to ensure that its representatives are carrying out its will. However, the French revolutionary tradition is neither monolithic nor accepted by everybody. Left and right continue to argue, for example, over whether the 1848 revolution or the Paris commune of 1871 were justified expressions of rebellion against unjust authority or not, just as they used to conflict bitterly over the legitimacy of the French Revolution (which is celebrated by practically everyone today). The May 1968 events were the latest genuine manifestation of the French revolutionary tradition. They were successful, at least in so far as de Gaulle resigned one year later.

The French revolutionary tradition has become a somewhat mythical aspect of French democracy. Its origins lie in the legacy of the political philosophy of the eighteenth-century Enlightenment and the French Revolution. Once elected, the deputy is no longer the representative of his electors alone, but incarnates the general will of the nation as a whole. Thus he acquires a personal legitimacy, which in theory owes nothing to his electors. The deputy incarnates power, but in the French republican tradition (as classically formulated), power is always suspected of being abused and of leading to corruption. For that reason, the deputy has often been as distrusted by his grassroots constituents as the central government is; in turn, the deputies have traditionally distrusted the central government for potentially abusing power. According to this tradition, the French citizen only really has confidence in direct local democracy at the level of the village, where the people's representatives can be tightly controlled. By contrast, representative democracy is always suspected of being illegitimate. The government in Paris, whether it be monarchist or republican, is by definition withdrawn and believes itself to be all-powerful, which leads inevitably to misuses of power. The duty of the local community is to guard itself against these misuses as best it can. However, even the most honest and conscientious of local politicians is likely to be corrupted by the influence of Paris once he becomes a deputy.

The French 'revolutionary tradition' stressed that there is strong agreement amongst French citizens upon several fundamental values which no government must attempt to deny, as well as several fundamental rules that it must not transgress. Should a government deny these values, or transgress these rules, according to the revolutionary tradition, the citizens have no option but to take their protests to the streets. This tradition is not primarily a justification for actual insurrection (although it has motivated insurrection in the past) as much as a means of ensuring that governments respect the foundations of the republic and that there is a balance of power between governors and governed. The political culture (originally represented by the revolutionary tradition) which fundamentally distrusts representative democracy is widely disseminated within French people's consciousness, especially in relation to how they regard and distrust the politicians who govern them. Within the Fifth Republic new mechanisms of control have emerged which allow the electorate to exercise a far more regular supervision over their elected representatives than during previous republics: the multiplication of elections, the use of referendums and the advent of opinion polls. De Gaulle was able to channel the revolutionary tradition to his benefit during the early years of the Fifth Republic (1958–62) by appealing directly to the people for support in referendums aimed against the parties and politicians of the Fourth Republic. This procedure eventually backfired in 1969, when the General was forced to resign after having been disavowed in a referendum. These factors maintain a constant pressure on governments and ensure that regular communication occurs between electors, deputies, the government and the President.

What remains of this revolutionary tradition in contemporary France, where the vast majority of citizens appear to agree on the basics of the political system? It is clear that until recently the main left-wing parties (PCF and PS) continued to refer to the French revolutionary tradition in order to justify their over-ideological political discourse, as well as to distinguish themselves from the right. In this vein, the Socialists attempted to portray their victory in 1981 as more like a change of regime than a mere change of government. However, these illusions did not last for long, as the Socialists had to set about the daily business of governing the country and managing the economy. Henceforth, street demonstrations from dissatisfied groups have been open attempts to press for concessions from the government, rather than insurrections aimed at overthrowing the government. This can be clearly illustrated by the mass demonstration of one million people in 1984 against the Socialist government's proposed reforms of church schools and the education system: the demonstrators' objective was to force the government to shelve its bill, rather than to abdicate (see chapter 5). Likewise, the student demonstrations which took place in November and December 1986 were indicative of this new public spirit. The demonstrations initially took on all the appearances of a classical 'insurrectionary' movement, especially the many violent confrontations between students and police along the lines of May 1968. However, unlike their counterparts in May 1968, the young demonstrators never called into question the government's right to govern. All they wanted was the suppression of the proposed university reform, and they succeeded in their objective.

The Fifth Republic has witnessed a relative harmonisation of voting trends between different regions in the country. During the Third Republic there was a complete contrast between certain regions which were overwhelmingly right wing and others which were just as overwhelmingly left wing. In Brittany, for example, the real political competition occurred between the right and the extreme right, whereas Socialism was non-existent and social Catholicism attracted a mere handful of activists. In contrast, in the north of the Massif Central or in Limousin, the main political conflict took place between Communists and Socialists; even the Radicals were marginalised. This regional fragmentation of electoral competition undoubtedly explained why there were no real national parties in France before the Fifth Republic (except the PCF). This situation has radically changed in contemporary France, and the left–right cleavage has become the central one in all regions (although predominantly left-wing or mainly right-wing *départements* have not disappeared). The political scientist F. Goguel has compared the elections of 1902, 1946, 1974 and 1978 in order to determine the variations over time in the number of *départements* which voted overwhelmingly for or against parties of the right (which he labelled the 'established Order'). His results are presented in table 7.

Table 7. *Right-wing départements in 1902, 1946, 1974 and 1978*

Year	Over 55%	45–55%	Under 45%
1902	20	26	42
1946	35	36	20
1974	21	54	16
1978	22	58	11

Source: F. Goguel, 'Culture politique et comportement électoral' in H. Mendras (ed.), *La Sagesse et le désordre* (Paris, Gallimard, 1980)

From table 7, we can see that the number of 'average' *départements* more than doubled, whereas those which were overwhelmingly on the left declined from 42 to 11. In 1902, the right polled more than 85 per cent in three departments, whereas there were none in this category in 1978, and only nine where it obtained between 60 and 70 per cent. In 1902 the gap between the most right-wing and the most left-wing *départements* (Manche and Creuse respectively) was 80 per cent, a figure that had fallen to 30 per cent in 1974 (Bas-Rhin and Ariège).

Goguel explained these changes in 'Culture politique' by referring to the left's profound transformation during the twentieth century:

In 1902, the left preoccupied itself essentially with political reforms and ignored the social and economic sphere. Left-wing values were overwhelmingly political ones: the secularisation of society, and the reduction or suppression of the Catholic Church's influence. The only left-wing parties which proposed profound social and economic reforms in the 1902 campaign were the two Socialist parties, the 'reformist' party of Jean Jaurès and the 'revolutionary' party of Jules Guesde: the former polled 6.09 per cent and the latter only 4.27 per cent. On the other hand, the numerous Radical–Socialist candidates spoke of the need for tax reform, but this was mainly for the form and nothing was done to achieve this during the ensuing Radical-led government. In short, the left's victory in no way threatened the economic structure of French society. In the later elections this was no longer the case. In 1946, 1974 and 1978 the left no longer defined itself merely in terms of political and ideological objectives. Rather . . . it proposed to introduce irreversible revolutionary changes in the social and economic sphere. In short, in the later elections a social and economic left replaced the political left of 1902.

This 'nationalisation' of politics has extended to municipal and cantonal elections in France, during which the candidates define themselves primarily in relation to national parties, and on the basis of the central left–right cleavage which predominates at the national level. Consequently, local elections have been regarded as important tests of national opinion and serve to reveal the strengths of the competing parties in between parliamentary and presidential elections. Cantonal by-elections provide another regular source of information about the performance of the main parties. By-elections for seats in Parliament in the Fifth Republic are considerably rarer, in part because of the substitute (*suppléant*) system, whereby a deputy is elected along with a substitute during a general election, and the latter takes over the seat should the former be named as a minister, or resign. The few parliamentary by-elections that do occur provoke intense media attention and can have an impact on the government's confidence. Other forms of election exist which testify to the French people's sense of civic duty. Elections within the trade union movement regularly give an indication of the strength of the various unions. Finally, European and regional elections have recently been added to the numerous other occasions on which the French people are invited to vote.

POLITICAL CULTURE AND POLITICAL COMMUNICATION

In 1988 French opinion polls celebrated their fiftieth anniversary: the first was back in 1938 over the French public's reaction to the Munich agreement. The frequency with which opinion polls have been conducted has increased so rapidly that virtually no day goes by without the publication of a poll on some aspect of current affairs. Indeed, some 600 polls were published in 1987, an average of two per working day – far more than in most of France's neighbours. Opinion polls measure the state not only of the parties, but also of the leading politicians, who can be delighted or destroyed by them. President de Gaulle used to treat the polls with the utmost consideration and would always consult IFOP, one of the leading opinion poll organisations, before making important political decisions. The first direct presidential election in 1965 helped to make IFOP's fortune as an opinion poll organisation, since it predicted that de Gaulle would be forced to a second ballot, against the judgement of most commentators.

Opinion polls used to be commissioned mainly by companies to test products, or by parties and governments to test the popularity of their policies. However, in the last ten years, the mass media themselves have become major clients of the opinion poll organisations, as television, radio and newspapers attempt to win the circulation or ratings battles against their rivals. This increased demand for opinion polls has opened their results up to a national audience. The electorate is kept informed of the slightest developments in public opinion by the constant stream of polls which are quoted in the media. In fact, the development of polls and the mass media has meant that the circulation of information about politics and current affairs has increased enormously, and extended to all strata of society.

Undoubtedly the public is better informed about politics today than in the pre-mass media age, and this has helped the electorate to make intelligent political choices when voting.

Opinion polls influence not only governments and parties, but also pressure groups and certain categories of citizens. The case of the May 1968 demonstrators might be taken as a good example of how public opinion polls affected the strategies adopted respectively by the rebellious students and the government. At the beginning of the May 1968 events, a majority of the electorate declared itself favourable to the students' demands and continued to support the wider social movement that the student protest sparked, until the workers rejected the compromise package of social reforms negotiated between the unions, the employers and the state in the Grenelle agreements. From then onwards, the balance of public opinion turned against the strikers, which enabled de Gaulle to retaliate by dissolving the National Assembly and organising the mass Gaullist demonstration of 30 May on the Champs-Elysées. More recently the mass demonstrations of 1984 against the Socialist government's education reforms and of 1986 against the Conservative government's plans to reform French universities both forced the incumbent administrations to back down and abandon their plans for reform. The knowledge that in both cases a majority of public opinion was in favour of the demonstrators and against the government had a salutary impact in influencing the latter's decision to withdraw.

The development of modern means of political communication in France has taken place against the background of a wide consensus over the way in which society and the world should be viewed. Indeed agreement over general principles and values might be said to constitute a common ideology shared by the overwhelming majority of French people, who also agree on the institutions which incarnate these values. Even the most violent ideological conflicts in France take place within the context of an agreement over the rules upon which society is based and upon its fundamental values. The notion of consensus has recently acquired a strong ideological flavour, as synonymous with a desire to maintain the status quo. None the less, I propose to retain the word consensus and use it in a more neutral sense to analyse those areas in which there is virtually no disagreement amongst French people. My concern is to illustrate that the consensus is not merely a political one but permeates all areas of French society.

A basic consensual social agreement underpins specific political disagreements between different groups within modern France. The main political, social and economic institutions in contemporary France form part of this overall consensus. The family is considered as an institution of the highest importance by 92 per cent of the French, and work is positively rated almost as highly (84 per cent). The nation is less universally valued (67 per cent), but it is making progress. Indeed, as many on the left as on the right value the importance of the nation, although older people are inclined to attach greater importance to it than younger people. The idea of civic duty is widely felt within French society, since 87 per cent consider that it is important to be a 'good citizen'. The right to own property is not seriously called into question by anybody, nor is the right to inherit wealth, which illustrates the strengths of the two related values of family and property. Those reformers who have sought to tamper with the right to inherit wealth, as the Socialists did in 1981, have rapidly discovered that it is too strongly rooted within French society and have had to back off. Nature is another highly valued concept that the French are anxious to safeguard against the dangers of technology. The fundamental values of liberty and equality are shared cultural references for most French people, although those on the left prefer equality whereas those on the right prefer liberty. Finally, security has always been a major preoccupation of the French. The need for security and the desire for equal treatment combine to explain why the social security system is more highly valued than any other institution: 97 per cent of French people consider that the abolition of the social security system would be dangerous.

The influence of television probably reinforces this cultural homogeneity. It is important, however, not to overestimate its influence: ever since the 1950s, studies (especially in the USA) have shown that television has a selective impact on people, and that messages diffused on television are only assimilated by the viewer if he agrees with their content. Television messages might reinforce a viewer's pre-established convictions, especially if they concur with the beliefs of a wider circle of friends. None the less, it would be false to assert that television itself creates beliefs. Research carried out in France has generally been concordant with that of the USA in reaching this conclusion.

The quality of life is one of the essential themes of this consensus. Every French citizen considers that he has a right to a certain standard of living, without which he is not really recognised as a part of the national community. It is in this sense that poor people are often labelled as 'excluded' from the national community. Of course, the models to which different groups aspire to satisfy their desire for a good standard of living vary, but are not inherently contradictory. Each social group considers that it has the right to a greater or lesser amount of goods, services and social protection. Economic prosperity is obviously a necessary condition for this common objective. Whereas before 1945 France's political debate used to be centred around the conflict of competing moral values, it has been transformed since then into one of competing economic policies. The growth of the nation's GNP is taken as a standard of success by all of the political parties and has been transformed by them into a moral imperative. Almost everybody accepts the need for industries to be profitable and for the economy itself to operate at a profit if people's standards of living are to be maintained. The great innovation of the Fifth Republic is that all of the main social forces have come to share the same economic language, even though they propose different economic policies. This is an additional proof of the fact that a basic consensual agreement underpins specific disagreements.

The transformation of public opinion has been particularly marked in relation to attitudes taken towards industry, and towards the economy in general. The traditional image of the French used to be that of a nation which distrusted industry and which regarded profit as immoral. This well-ingrained pre-capitalist sentiment was not limited to the Marxist left, but was very much in evidence amongst old-style Conservatives as well. It seems totally archaic today. The great majority of French people are now convinced of the necessity for the country to be economically successful. Along with this transformation has come a fundamental change in the manner in which businessmen are regarded: far from being the greedy sharks of old, they have become respectable, even admired citizens.

This ideological U-turn can be explained in part by the continuing process of economic education which French people have undergone during the past twenty years. Politicians and journalists appear on television every day to explain how the economy works, why inflation is an economic menace, why the franc has been devalued and why unemployment is likely to be a lasting feature. This effort at economic education through the media has proved successful, and few people today believe in the possibility of an alternative economic policy to that which has been led by Conservative and Socialist governments alike since the mid 1970s. The failure of the Socialists' attempts to relaunch the economy by using Keynesian-style demand techniques during 1981/2 and the return to a tough anti-inflationary policy in 1983 only confirmed that the economic rules governing France's position in the international economy could not be ignored. France could not pursue a reflationary economic policy which was at odds with that being carried out by its main trading partners. The Socialists' economic turnaround was necessary in order to convince a considerable fraction of their electorate that economic rules had to be respected. Only the left could have driven home this lesson. It proved that this was not merely an argument employed by the right to safeguard its privileges. Finally, the 1983 change of direction illustrated that the need to respect economic constraints overrode whatever ideological objections the left might have had to pursuing an economic policy which was largely indistinguishable from that of its right-wing predecessors.

The 1983 U-turn can also be linked to the ideological discredit of Marxism and of certain of the more traditional of left-wing values. According to the opinion polls, nearly all French people have a negative reaction towards the word Marxism. Until recently, the left dominated the ideological debate in France, whereas Conservative and traditional values remained largely unexpressed. This began to change with the revelations made by Solzhenitsyn in the 1970s of conditions in the Soviet Union. Suddenly the left lost confidence in many of its traditional ideas, at the same time as it gained power in 1981 for the first time for twenty-five years. The left's coming to power coincided with the strong re-emergence of the right, both politically and ideologically. Indeed, Conservative values and ideas enjoyed a new popularity, not just in France but throughout most of the developed world. This forced the Socialists away from the older maximalist ideological presuppositions they had voiced before 1981 towards sharing many of the ideas that have been traditionally associated with the right, especially concerning the economy.

Voting behaviour is more strongly influenced by the importance of a person's *patrimoine* (property, stocks and bonds, shares in private companies, other unearned income) than it is by his earned income. Amongst people with high incomes, those who possess no *patrimoine* are more likely to vote for a left-wing party than are others. Indeed, the possession of a *patrimoine* tends to be more important amongst people who vote for the two main right-wing parties, the UDF and the RPR, than does the actual level of their earned income. Amongst the category of 'poor property-owners', who are predominantly older people living in the countryside, by far the most important group (73 per cent) is that which votes for either the RPR or the UDF, the two main right-wing parties. In contrast, the Communist electorate is overwhelmingly composed of those who possess no *patrimoine*; even within the poorest categories of the population, the PCF performs weakly amongst those who can boast some form of *patrimoine*. Thus it can be clearly seen that the possession or not of unearned wealth or property is one factor which distinguishes between members of the same socioprofessional category, although it does not call into question the overall consensus which underpins French society.

The development of the profound social consensus which unites the French has been accompanied by a decline in ideology. However, the decline of ideology is not the inevitable consequence of increased consensus, and it is possible that ideological conflict could re-emerge without actually harming the fundamental agreement on the essentials that exists amongst French people. In fact, it is difficult to imagine a society without any conflicts of ideology or interests, or clash of rival identities. Such a society would not be a society at all, but an amorphous mess without spirit, ambitions or plans. The consensus of which politicians speak is not the same as that which I mentioned above. When the politician talks of consensus, it is with the intention of securing his adversaries' agreement to his own projects and ambitions. A society which was devoid of political conflict, and the competition of competing political parties, would not in reality be a democratic polity at all. Indeed, it might be argued that political conflict itself forms part of the new consensus, once the main parties all abide by the rules of the game and function within the political system. Moreover, it is often only through conflict that important political decisions can be taken, since political issues are brought to the forefront of the public's attention by disagreement: areas in which there is complete agreement are often also areas in which no policy evolves.

Once the great cleavages which developed in the nineteenth century began to disappear, especially during the latter half of the twentieth century, the institutions which had symbolically represented these cleavages inevitably began to change their character. The church, the army, the school and the republic have become accepted by everybody, and consequently no longer perform the function of instruments of identification and differentiation amongst French people. They have lost their old divisive character and all form part of the profound consensus which underpins modern French society. Indeed, despite the breaking down of traditional institutions, the French people have never been more proud to be French, and their national unity has never been as solid.

The breaking up of the old social classes and the weakening of previously great national institutions are obviously two developments in the same direction. In the past, the pressures towards national unity were as strong as they were precisely because France was divided into antagonistic social classes and vastly different regions: only by promoting the central state could the nation itself be safeguarded. This tradition stems from the centralising kings of the *ancien régime* from the seventeenth century onwards, and especially from the dominant strand of the French Revolution. This undoubtedly explains why calls for *rassemblement* and national unity have been favourite themes in the speeches of politicians, who have pretended to discern the danger of civil war in order to promote their own causes. However, the weakening of traditional institutions and the breaking down of old barriers mean that such political discourse is less convincing in the France of the 1980s. Faced with this transformation of the framework of social relationships, pessimists speak of a divided society which has lost its bearings and is progressively falling to pieces. The analyses presented here lead us to adopt exactly the opposite conclusion. The great variety of social allegiances and of codes of behaviour, as well as of ideologies and value systems, that exist within contemporary France do not operate within a vacuum. They form part of an essential consensus over the fundamental values which govern French society. This is the most profound transformation that the nation has experienced in the post-war decades.

7

A village democracy

French people are generally proud of their nation's diversity. They like to think of France as a nation with an inexhaustible variety of scenery, customs, architecture, ethnic groups and gastronomic traditions. And yet France is no more diversified than Italy and Spain, or even Germany and the United Kingdom. In fact, references made to the diversity of French society have to be set against the efforts of political regimes in France, since well before the French Revolution, to promote national unity and to reinforce the power of central government over the provinces.

There are various ways of portraying the divisions which have traditionally separated different regions of France. The most famous internal border was that which historically divided the *langue d'oïl* from the *langue d'oc*. The *langue d'oïl* corresponded approximately to those areas to the north of the Loire which were governed by customary law; the *langue d'oc* was composed of regions to the south of the Loire which were governed by written law, inherited from Roman law. The northern regions of the *langue d'oïl* tended to be more inclined towards Conservative parties and ideas, mainly because peasants were tenant-farmers (rather than freeholders) and usually felt obliged to follow their Conservative landowners. In contrast, in the southern regions of the *langue d'oc* the peasants were freeholders, possessing their own farms, and were able to exercise their political rights in a less constrained fashion: this was one reason for their greater inclination for left-wing parties and ideas. This model was not watertight, however, since the political behaviour of both tenant-farmers and peasant freeholders varied greatly according to region.

Another traditional internal border in France was that which separated the areas to the north and south of a line running from Caen to Geneva. During the nineteenth century, the areas to the north of this line began a process of industrialisation which soon differentiated them from areas further to the south, which remained overwhelmingly rural until 1945. Widespread urbanisation and industrialisation during the post-war period, along with the dramatic decline of the peasantry, have diminished the importance of this second internal boundary. The decline of the peasantry can be illustrated by the changing composition of the workforce during the past century in France's ninety-six mainland *départements*. In the mid nineteenth century, the peasantry represented more than 50 per cent of the working population in the vast bulk of *départements*, excluding a dozen or so to the north of Paris. By 1891, *départements* with peasant majorities had been so pushed back to the southern two-thirds of the country (south of an imaginary line from Le Havre to Belfort), a movement which had been greatly accentuated by 1911 (south of a line from St Malo to Geneva). By 1954 only a dozen *départements* retained a peasant majority, concentrated in the south-west and west. By 1982, not a single *département* retained a peasant majority. The counterpart to the decline of the peasantry as a proportion of

Figure 7 Linguistic boundaries. Source: R. Rémond, *Atlas historique de la France contemporaine, 1800–1965* (Paris, A. Colin, 1966)

the working population has been the increase in the proportion of the workforce engaged in industry. Industry originally dominated a handful of *départements* in the north, but gradually spread its influence towards the east and centre, eventually covering the whole country. By 1982, no *département* employed less than 20 per cent of its population in industry, although the number with more than 40 per cent of their population engaged in industry declined from 35 to 15 between 1975 and 1982. The proportion of tertiary-sector workers has similarly experienced an upward curve in virtually all *départements* since 1954 (the second post-war census); this has been especially noticeable in the south and in Brittany. To summarise these developments: the proportion of the population involved in *agriculture* no longer comprises the majority of the working population in any *département*; *industry* has progressed in all areas of France during the last decades, even in the most rural *départements*, although it is now starting to decline; the *tertiary sector* has also grown rapidly, especially in areas of recent industrialisation.

The opposing characteristics of different regions in France have often seemed so well entrenched that sociologists and historians have sought ever more complex explanations for why this should be the case. However, no single satisfactory explanation has emerged for the roots of regional divisions in France: the further back researchers look for explanations, the more difficult it becomes to distinguish between competing hypotheses. This can be illustrated by considering the extent to which French regions have become 'de-christianised'. Whenever the idea of de-christianisation is put forward, the underlying presupposition is that French regions were all initially converted to Christianity, and that the intensity of religious belief was the same in all areas. But an opposing hypothesis is equally plausible: that certain regions were more open to the influence of Christianity than others. What is less obvious is whether the degree of piety shown by particular regions can be related to the effectiveness of Christian missionaries, or whether different social structures (or traditions) made certain areas more receptive to Christianity than others.

There were numerous differences in peasant mentality throughout France, and hypothetical evidence would strongly suggest that these were linked to the underlying feudal social structure. In those areas where the feudal economic system was dominated by a powerful nobility, which maintained distant relations with the peasantry, peasant communities developed a strong sense of group solidarity and self-defence, in order to defend their interests against the misuse of power by the nobility and its agents. This pattern was not, in general, repeated where the nobility was less powerful and where relations between a less powerful noble and the peasantry were warmer: in the west, for example, peasants respectfully subordinated themselves to their feudal masters to whom they felt close.

THE VITALITY OF LOCAL GOVERNMENT IN FRANCE

Rural France has probably the smallest local politico-administrative structure of any country – the municipal council based on the commune. There are some 36,000 communes in France, of which 34,000 are in the countryside, or in small towns with fewer than 15,000 inhabitants. The modern commune is based on the parishes drawn up by the church between the tenth and twelfth centuries. Communal boundaries were redrawn during the French Revolution, but they usually respected the older parish boundaries. The size and character of communes can vary considerably. Vast disparities in the size of communes can exist within traditionally rural areas, as well as between rural and urban areas. Thus communes in Brittany are large, whereas those in neighbouring Normandy tend to be tiny. Communes are far from being an anachronism; most French citizens identify with their commune, and attempts to reform local government by regrouping communes into larger units have invariably been met by intense hostility. Whatever the reasons for their creation and for the boundaries drawn between them, the communes are valued by most French people as institutions expressing the identity and independence of France's many thousands of local communities.

The attachment of French citizens to their communes can be illustrated by the consistently high turn-out at the six-yearly municipal elections, which elect France's 36,000 municipal councils. Their frequently tiny size, however, has occasionally laid communes open to the charge of being wasteful and inefficient. During the 1960s, French governments shared the anxiety of their counterparts in certain other European countries that local government should be run as efficiently as possible (especially given that control of local expenditure figures prominently in national economic policy). Governments were determined to secure the most efficient possible management of local government resources, as well as the viability of local investment projects. This led to various plans being drafted for the regrouping of the often tiny communes into larger units of local government. The most straightforward of these proposals was to make the canton, the next smallest unit of local government after the commune, into the lowest tier of local government. Small communes would have been reduced to sub-sections of the canton. This would have produced a similar local government structure in France, with its 3,600 cantons, to that of Italy, which has 3,500 local authorities.

Plans to reform local government ran up against the fierce attachment of most French people to their communes. For whereas the commune is identified with by virtually every French citizen, the canton is a far more artificial institution, which often regroups communes with diverging interests and different socio-economic compositions. That politicians faced such opposition to tampering with local government illustrated the strong attachment felt by French people to the idea of direct democracy, as epitomised by the commune. It is interesting to contrast the treatment of local government by France and Britain during the 1970s. In Britain's great local government reform of 1972 (which became operational in 1974) parishes were regrouped into district or county councils by a simple Act of Parliament. French politicians eventually backed away from introducing any such radical scheme to rationalise local government, since they were aware of their people's attachment to local communes. The country most renowned for self-government (Britain) did not hesitate to reduce the powers of local government by a simple Act of Parliament, whereas the most centralised European nation refused to do this. One reason for this is undoubtedly that local government in France has far greater significance as a stepping-stone to national political careers than in the UK. For a French deputy or senator to challenge local government would be tantamount to weakening his own power-base, since virtually all deputies or senators are simultaneously mayors of their communes, whereas a British MP virtually never holds local office as well.

For many French people, the direct democracy embodied by the local commune is the only truly legitimate form of democracy. It is a powerful strand of the French democratic tradition that the real meaning of democracy is the ability to elect someone to office who is well known locally and whose exercise of power can be closely surveyed. National political careers in France have traditionally been built upon strong local roots, although this was more true of the Third and Fourth Republics than it is of the Fifth. In electing their deputies, French voters have usually shown a preference for local personalities, who can be expected to forward the interests of the constituency in Paris. This undoubtedly explains why France's electoral system for elections to the National Assembly has traditionally been based on small single-member constituencies, which allows the local deputy to be called to account for his actions at regular intervals. The popularity of the local commune and the electors' preference for local politicians as their national representatives both stem from a deeply rooted attachment to direct democracy, and a traditional distrust of representative institutions.

In order to understand the French people's attachment to direct democracy, it is necessary to go back to the beginning of the seventeenth century, before the French monarchy began its ruthless centralising crusade against local provincial autonomy. At that time, the village was often a genuine 'community of inhabitants', in which power resided with the heads of family meeting together in the market-place or the church. These heads of family would elect a council, in the presence of a representative of the local lord. In this way, the opposition between the local community and the local noble (or later the king) was visible to everybody. Everyone understood that public matters would be settled by a form of bargaining between these rival centres of power. In certain regions (such as the Pyrenees), the power of the noble was largely nominal and the council would genuinely control the community's local affairs: the leader of the council – the syndic – would be the most important local personality. In other areas, the noble's representative held all real power, and the local community had no option except to obey him or attempt to stall him. Small local lords often complicated this pattern of local relations: they could either be recognised as allies by the peasants, who relied on them to defend their interests against the lord and king, or else be equated with the external authorities and be rejected as tax-collectors and recruiting sergeants.

Research has revealed that the variations in the forms of local government which have existed in France since the seventeenth century are endless: a treatise on comparative government could be written on the basis of these enquiries. Variations have depended mainly upon the social structures and traditions of each region; to a certain extent the regional variations outlined below continue to exist today. The diversity of local authority structures in France can be illustrated by looking at five different regional models.

The *Mediterranean oligarchy*, found throughout south-eastern Mediterranean France, was the modern inheritor of the oldest municipal traditions, dating back at least as far as Roman times. Each village or small town was governed by a council of local *notables*, composed of the wealthiest local men and representatives of the oldest local families. In previous times, the council elected a syndic from amongst its members who would act as its spokesman, a function today performed by the mayor (who is similarly elected). But the council retained the real power, discussed everything and left no room at all for anybody's personal initiatives. Electoral lists were composed entirely of well-known local personalities. There were in effect two categories of citizens: the passive mass of electors and the active élite of potential decision-makers. The average voter could only ratify the choices made by the active minority, the only *real* citizens.

The *mountain democracy* was prevalent in the Jura range of mountains in eastern France and in the northern Alps. The fundamental principle of the 'mountain democracy' was equality, or even egalitarianism. The local political system was construed so as to favour the poorer members of the community, and preserve their communal rights: a rich farmer would rarely be elected to the council, and never to the position of mayor. Political power was refused to the wealthier members of the community in order to prevent them from gaining control over the commonly owned lands and forests. In this way, the community retained its collective control over pastures and forests and protected the economic well-being of its poorer members.

In other regions of France (Limousin, Rouergue), the traditional form of local government could best be labelled a *federal* one, based upon recognising the legitimacy of a base unit comprising either a household or a hamlet. The municipal council would be composed of representatives of the various hamlets or households which existed within the commune. It was the function of the council to ensure that no one hamlet or household received preferential treatment over another. This federalism was either egalitarian in character (as in the poor mountainous regions of central France) or oligarchical (as in the south-west, where each hamlet would elect a representative of a powerful household to the council rather than of an uninfluential one). The mayor would be chosen on account of his ability to act as an efficient intermediary with the outside authorities; he would usually be a prominent local *notable* who was on good terms with central government. At municipal elections, the squire-mayor expected to be endorsed massively by his electorate. Should he fail to secure an overwhelming majority, he would resign immediately as mayor, considering that he no longer enjoyed the confidence of his local community. The role of the municipal councillors was to advise and warn the mayor – as the court would advise and warn a king. But they had little direct input into decision-making, which was the responsibility of the mayor alone.

The *elected princedom*, which existed mainly in the East, could be compared in many respects with the hereditary monarchy and the mountain democracy analysed above. As with the hereditary monarch, the elected 'prince' ran the local community alone, and was responsible for taking all important decisions. The council was reduced to listening to his speeches. As long as he preserved the confidence of his electors, the mayor would govern the commune alone and no one would question his decisions. Should the electorate become dissatisfied with his leadership, however, the mayor would not be re-elected at the next election. His princedom was thus subject to re-election. Because both poor management and frequent changes of municipal stewardship were bad for the commune, it was important to choose a good mayor and to allow him to govern for as long as possible. A good mayor would remain in charge for twenty to thirty years.

These various customary forms of local government were all perfectly compatible with the rules governing municipal elections in France. The legal rules were the same everywhere, but the particular shape of local government depended upon regional traditions and upon the social forces which interacted within a given commune. The same conclusion remains valid. The diversity of customs, the vitality of municipal government and the sense of local and personal identity that it inspires amongst French citizens are remarkable. One of the great paradoxes of modern France is that it is simultaneously one of the most decentralised and one of the most centralised nations in Western Europe. A belief in direct democracy coexists with complaints from all quarters about the centralisation of decision-making, and the excessive power of the French state. Despite legendary French centralisation, the perennial influence of the rural commune responds to a fundamental demand for direct democracy. When French politicians speak of creating neighbourhood committees in their cities, they should look to the rural communes as an example and abandon any thought of allowing them to perish.

This schematic portrayal of the diversity of local government explains the extraordinary vitality of the rural communes, even the smallest ones. Three-quarters of France's 36,000 communes have fewer than 1,000 inhabitants, and their budgets are scarcely enough to pay the salary of one local worker, or to maintain local roads and buildings in a state of good repair. However, even the smallest communes can partially overcome the problems relating to their size by forming themselves into syndicates with other similar communes, which ensure basic municipal services such as waste disposal and provision of water. Moreover, communes have at least one major trumpcard in their dealings with outside authorities, or private-sector interests: they manage the territory over which they preside, which comprises a total of 90 per cent of national territory. This enables them to agree to or withhold planning permission for public- or private-sector developments. Such an advantage is becoming more and more important as the demand for development land intensifies.

Finally, the small commune remains a fundamentally important institution in so far as the identity of the local community is concerned. The intensity with which municipal elections are fought testifies to this. The contestants in municipal elections in these small communes are not primarily interested in satisfying a lust for power, since the small commune is largely devoid of any. The real stake involved is to give local *notables* an opportunity to test their prestige and popularity within the local community, or to attempt to gain public recognition. At each municipal election, the French village puts itself on show. The redistribution of local roles, which always change to some small degree, takes place at election time, and this brings alive the histories of the different families, their quarrels with each other and their present successes or failures. The important changes in the composition of rural communities which have occurred since the war (rapid depopulation, followed by a recovery) have meant that 'outsiders' are often anxious to secure recognition and acceptance by the local community by standing for the council in municipal elections. The extraordinary vitality of small-scale democracy in France is illustrated by the observation that France's 36,000 communes boast 550,000 local councillors, almost 500,000 of whom represent rural communes with fewer than 1,500 inhabitants. Indeed, rural France is the country with the highest number of local councillors per head in the world, higher even than in Switzerland, reputed to be a model of local democracy.

LOCAL INITIATIVES

All this explains why each local community enjoys a considerable degree of freedom to invent the particular style of local society which best corresponds to its financial resources and the character of its people. This can be illustrated by briefly citing two contrasting examples.

The first is of a village in the Vendée *département* in traditionally conservative western France. This village, which was the object of a survey in 1960, seemed to me to have changed very little since the nineteenth century. The squire was also the mayor, thus combining political and economic influence over the local community. The village was characterised by a strong degree of religious observance; the Catholic Church had a profound impact on most people's lives, especially in relation to the codes of moral behaviour they should follow. Following the moral lead given by the church (refusal of contraception, importance placed on procreation), the village had a naturally high birth rate, leading to obvious local overpopulation. Given the existence of such overpopulation, as well as its precarious agrarian economy, it appeared that there were two obvious directions in which the village could develop. Firstly, the local authorities could encourage a rural exodus, which would leave the remaining population in a more secure position: this idea was fiercely opposed by the local priest. The second solution was to allow a degree of industrial development by permitting a local industry to establish a factory in the village (opposed by the mayor); or alternatively, by adopting intensive poultry-farming. The latter solution appeared more practicable, since there were already two broiler-houses in the commune. The village in the Vendée in 1960 had been miraculously preserved in its natural state, largely unchanged for centuries, oblivious to the social transformations taking place all around it.

The same village was the object of a follow-up survey some twenty years later. The local squire was no longer mayor as well, which signified the weakening of the political and economic hold over the village exercised by the traditional *notable*. Instead a new municipal council had encouraged a firm to set up a shoe factory employing 200 people, mainly women. The prediction that the village would turn to intensive hen-farming was inaccurate, mainly because farmers (strongly imbued with rural traditions) were unwilling to subordinate themselves to the orders of an industrial capitalist. Moreover, the village did not suffer from a rural exodus, as might have been feared. The opening of the shoe factory provided a valuable source of employment for local women, and the growth of nearby Angers, the *département*'s largest city, enabled part of the local population (mainly men) to commute to work in the city and remain living in the village. Through a combination of these factors, the village was prosperous in 1980. Despite its material prosperity, many aspects of the village had not changed, notably its ideological conservatism and its attachment to the Catholic religion (which remained real despite a drop in church attendance). The village's salient moral values were passed on from generation to generation, despite the social changes which had taken place. Thus the village chose between several options which would enable it to preserve its traditional character.

An alternative course was adopted by a small village in Morbihan (Brittany), the subject of a survey in 1970. In the course of this first survey, the French sociologist H. Lamarche predicted that, because of the decline of agriculture as an economic activity, around one-third of the farmers would be forced to abandon their farms, and to leave the village in order to look for work elsewhere. In a second survey fifteen years later, Lamarche was surprised to discover that his prediction had proved to be false: all of the farmers he had said would leave fifteen years earlier were still working on their farms and living in the village. Faced with the prospect of adapting their livelihoods or moving away, the Breton villagers accepted the creation of industry within and around the village that the Vendéens had refused. They combined work on their farms with part-time jobs within local industries. Moreover, their wives contributed to the family budget either by working in an outlying slaughter-house, or else by clerical work in the nearest large city (Vannes). The growth of unemployment in the city made it unlikely that the men could find work there, even if they had wanted to. Their decision not to leave was of fundamental importance for the life of the local village, especially since they were able to devote their spare time to cultural and sporting activities which helped to reinforce the village's identity.

In both of these cases, it seemed as if a collective decision had been taken by all the farmers, indeed by the village as a whole. These examples testified to a local community's capacity for autonomous decision-making: the Vendéens refused industrial development, but the Bretons accepted it. Economic change is, of course, of considerable importance in setting the framework for the range of possible options that might be adopted by a local community. None the less, even when economic and social change forces a local community to adapt (or else perish), various choices are open as to exactly how the community decides to respond to these constraints. The examples cited form part of a more general pattern applying to threatened village communities (especially rural ones). In most cases, it is the social group most threatened with marginalisation (farmers) which acts as the driving-force for the adaptation and revitalisation of the local village; the effects of this are subsequently extended to the rest of the local population.

CIVIL SERVANTS AND *NOTABLES*

The central figure in French small-town and rural society is the mayor, who is both an elected official and a servant of the state. It is the mayor who acts as the link between the rural commune and the outside administrative authorities, whether at departmental or national level. Being mayor, even of a tiny rural commune, confers a special authority in French civic life, which goes way beyond the ceremonial function performed by the mayor in the UK. The explanation for this lies in the perfect legitimacy of the municipal election as an exercise in direct democracy. It is the unanimous belief of France's 36,000-strong élite club of mayors that the municipal election confers a status of equality on all of them, from the mayor of Paris to the mayor of the smallest rural commune. Each mayor is the representative of his people, and this status gives him a dignity which does not depend on the number of his electors.

The decentralisation legislation of 1982/3 (see below) has increased the powers of the mayor. The mayor has always had responsibility for drawing up the commune's budget and executing the decisions of the municipal council, but traditionally this power depended upon creating a *modus vivendi* with the prefect (or sub-prefect for mayors of smaller communes), who could exercise his veto over mayoral decisions. Since the 1982/3 legislation, the prefect can no longer veto the mayor's decisions, which must be implemented. He retains the right to challenge their legality or financial probity in the administrative courts or regional Courts of Accounts (*Cours des Comptes*), but this control is exercised *a posteriori*. The mayor's powers have been reinforced in numerous spheres: for example town planning, municipal housing, employment and local economic policy. As a result of

Table 8. *Local government in France (mainland France only)*

Elected officials	Central nominee
President of regional council Regional councillors Regional council (Region (22)	Regional prefect
President of *conseil général* (departmental council) *Département* (96)	Prefect
Conseillers généraux (Departmental councillors) Canton (3,600)	Prefect/sub-prefect
Mayor Municipal council (36,000) Commune (36,000)	Prefect (large towns) Sub-prefect (smaller communes)

these changes, it is more difficult for a mayor to blame central interventionism for the inadequacies of his municipal stewardship.

The symbolic importance of the mayor in the French political system is such that even Prime Ministers have claimed that they would give up all their elective offices if necessary, but never that of mayor. However small the number of electors, a minister's national legitimacy is felt to be called into question should he be disavowed in a municipal election. At least one minister has resigned after being defeated in a municipal election, because he felt he had been disavowed by the local people who knew him personally. This attitude appears extraordinary to foreign observers for whom the national election must by definition be more important than the local one because of the considerably larger number of voters involved. Such assessments are erroneous, however, because they do not take into consideration the French people's preference for direct over representative democracy.

The role of the second chamber, the Senate, is equally difficult to understand unless we admit that this 'grand council of the small communes of France' draws its authority from the legitimacy of direct democracy and municipal election. The Senate is elected by a small electorate of 'grand' electors, composed of elected officials who are, for the most part, representatives of local communes. Each commune is thus indirectly represented in the second chamber. Senators are elected for a period of six years; half of them come up for re-election at three-yearly intervals. While it would be accurate to argue that the Senate is unfairly chosen in respect to representative, national democracy, it has to be admitted that it perfectly reflects

France's rich local democracy, to the extent of over-representing rural communes at the expense of urban ones.

Above the mayor in the local hierarchy is the *conseiller général* (departmental councillor), who represents one of France's 3,600 cantons. Whereas the mayor of a small rural commune will usually deal with the sub-prefect, the *conseiller général* has access to the *département*'s prefect, as well as to the heads of the *département*'s most important permanent administrative services. The *conseiller général* also has the right of access to the President of the *conseil général* (departmental council), who has been the fount of executive authority within the *département* since the 1982 decentralisation legislation, supplanting the prefect in that role (see below). Because the President himself will usually be a *conseiller général* of a rural canton, the two can relate to each other as equals. The President of the *conseil général* is nearly always a national political figure as well and will usually 'deal directly with ministers (and through ministers with the great ministries of the state) to further the interests of his *département*. The importance placed by politicians in France on holding local mandates is considerable, as we discovered above in relation to the mayor. A politician who succeeds in becoming President of his *conseil général* will have succeeded in confirming the strength of his local political base. It was not beyond the defeated President of the Republic, V. Giscard d'Estaing, to bid successfully to become the President of the Puy-de-Dôme *conseil général* in 1982.

The Socialist government's (1981–6) decentralisation legislation, passed in 1982/3, devolved far greater powers to the *départements* than they had previously possessed, as well as creating a new series of twenty-two regional assemblies. Since 1982 the President of the *conseil général* has been legally recognised as the fount of executive power within the *département*, replacing the centrally nominated prefect (see below). In 1982 the President of the *conseil général* also gained considerable administrative assistance, since some of the civil servants who worked for the prefect were transferred to the *conseil général*. The prefect has had his authority curtailed, especially in so far as he can no longer veto proposed expenditure forwarded by the *conseil général*, or municipal council. None the less, he retains considerable powers, including the possibility of referring all local legislation to regional administrative tribunals to ensure its legality, as well as to the new regional Courts of Accounts, which ensure that local authorities are not financially profligate or irregular. The prefect retains his traditional control over law and order and over the operation of ministerial field services within the department, and has acquired certain new powers in relation to economic planning. But considerable power has been devolved to the *départements* and regions. One example of this is that direct central control over the expenditure incurred by local authorities has been replaced since 1982 by *a posteriori* control exercised by the twenty-two regional Courts of Accounts. This applies to the new regional assemblies as well.

The main innovation of the 1982/3 legislation was the creation of a new tier of twenty-two regional authorities, directly elected for the first time in 1986. The President of the regional authority is invested with the executive power over regional policy in a specified number of areas, such as economic development, housing, or training. As with the other layers of sub-central government, the regional prefect has lost his executive power to the President of the regional council, elected by his peers at the first council meeting. Since the Napoleonic era, the prefect has symbolised the centralisation of the French state. The creation of the office of prefect was an attempt to impose a uniform centralised structure dictated from Paris upon a multiform, diversified and rebellious society. The prefect was the representative of central government within the *départements* of mainland France and the DOM–TOM (Départements d'outre-mer – Overseas *départements* – and Territoires d'outre-mer – Overseas Territories). Directly appointed by the Minister of the Interior, the prefect was able to exercise a considerable degree of supervisory control – *la tutelle* – over local authorities (*conseils généraux* and municipal councils): he had the right to veto council proposals, to reject council budgets, even to dismiss a council. He was responsible for coordinating the work of the ministerial field-services within the *département*, and had an important influence in regional planning. These powers were stronger in theory than in practice, however: the exercise of the prefect's influence depended not only upon support from Paris, but also upon agreeing compromises with mayors, Presidents of *conseils généraux* and other local *notables*. The prefect would often become a strong advocate for the *département*'s cause in Paris, having been exposed daily to departmental grievances. The prefectorial influence was more obvious in small communes (where central finance could be promised for capital investment projects) than in large cities governed by a powerful national politician with a degree of financial autonomy from central government. The powers of the prefect have been somewhat weakened since the 1982/3 legislation (see above), but they remain considerable.

At all levels of political decision-making in France (local, departmental, regional and national), two parallel hierarchies exist: that of politicians representing their voters, and that of civil servants representing the state. Politicians and civil servants are continually engaged in a complex system of bargaining at all levels of decision-making which has the effect that national laws and rules are applied with a great deal of flexibility at local level. The classic model, of this bargaining process between the technocrat and the political *notable* is that which compels the prefect and the mayor – from radically different backgrounds – to work together in the interests of the local community. Both prefect and mayor are subject to pressures which each attempts to minimise: the prefect is anxious to isolate himself from Paris, in order to increase his autonomy and lessen central interference; the mayor attempts to conceal his activities from his constituents in order to give himself as free a hand as possible in negotiations. Despite their rivalry, the prefect and the mayor share an objective interest in agreeing with each other and presenting a united face to their respective constituencies (the prefect's Parisian masters; the mayor's local electors). Even before the recent decentralisation legislation, central control from Paris was never imposed as simply or as directly as it appeared to be, and central regulations were in practice administered differently according to regional and local traditions. The 1982/3 legislation has further strengthened the impact of local and regional influences.

In the past, the local French *notable* was a landowner, whose authority at the head of his village was undisputed, and it was he who represented the village to the outside world. His possession of land meant that in one way or another he also ruled local society, and controlled its communications with the outside world. But only the most powerful *notables* would base their power on their outside connections, as opposed to their control over the local community. The powerful squire, for example, would be a member of an extended national kinship group, and would limit his relationships with the people of the village to those based on the exercise of his authority and patronage. The mayor, in contrast, would belong to a local kinship group and would be recognised as the valid representative of the local community. This position has been reversed in contemporary France. The power of today's genuine *notable* (mayor of a large city. President of a *conseil général*) usually stems from the position he occupies in national politics, rather than the tight control he is able to exercise over his local community. It is his national stature which enables the *notable* to attract government resources to his particular town or district. The higher a politician rises in the hierarchy of national politics, the more useful he will be to his local community. Because central government intervenes so extensively in the daily life of local authorities, it is essential that the local *notable* knows how to deal with it, and attempts to ensure that national resources are channelled to his locality. To be successful, this implies that he must occupy a powerful position within the national political hierarchy, whether in government or opposition. The more national resources the *notable* manages to attract to his locality, however, the more national oversight and control over these resources he will be forced to accept.

By creating directly elected regional assemblies and a new category of regional councillors, the 1982/3 legislation opened up an entirely new area within which the appetites of political *notables* could be satisfied. The first direct elections for the new regional assemblies took place in 1986, and witnessed the emergence of a new generation of elected officials. These new officials differed markedly from the more traditional political *notables*. The traditional political *notable* used frequently to hold several elected posts simultaneously, but had few, if any, official responsibilities within his party. Members of the younger generation of the 1986 regional election intake are far more likely to hold only one elective office (40 per cent), but are also more likely to have exercised official functions within their political party. Indeed, many of them (32 per cent) have also acted as advisers either to a mayor, to the President of the *conseil général*, or to a minister. The directly elected regional councils have produced a new younger type of political *notable*. He is far more likely to be a professional politician and party man than the traditional *notable*, who frequently maintained a haughty distance from his party, and whose legitimacy stemmed above all from the special relationship he had developed with his constituents. These new *notables* are certain to make politics more of a profession in France than it has ever been. Their careers depend far more upon loyalty to party than loyalty to electors. Moreover, the number of elected officials is bound to increase, through recent legislation limiting the number of elected offices an individual can hold simultaneously (see below), as well as on account of the sheer increase in the number of elected posts brought about by the new regional councils. All these factors are pushing in the direction of a greater professionalism dominating French politics.

It was partly in order to mount a challenge to the classic political *notables* (most, but by no means all, on the centre or right of the political spectrum) that the Socialist government of 1981–6 passed a law limiting the number of 'significant' elective offices that any individual could hold to two. The halfhearted nature of this reform reflected the strength of opposition to it from political *notables* of all complexions. 'Significant' offices included deputy, senator, Member of the European Parliament, mayor of towns with over 20,000 inhabitants, regional councillor, and *conseiller général*. Political *notables* could continue in theory to combine any two 'significant' offices with the less important elective positions, such as mayor of a small town or rural commune.

The shortcomings of the old system were obvious. The same person could be a mayor, a *conseiller général*, President of the *conseil général*, a member of the National Assembly or Senate, a Member of the European Parliament and a regional councillor. This was without counting the various presidencies of professional, cultural or civic associations that an individual might hold. That they were unable to fulfil all the duties involved with these offices did not worry most *élus*: the crucial consideration was to prevent a political opponent from gaining ground within any one of their fiefs. According to the French Constitution, a minister is not allowed to retain his seat as a member of the National Assembly or Senate, and upon his nomination as minister, he has to resign his parliamentary seat. This constitutional stipulation has not prevented ministers from acquiring other elective offices, especially those of *conseiller général* and mayor.

Despite certain abuses, the practice of *cumul des mandats* (the holding of two or more elective offices) is an essential mechanism for enabling the smooth functioning of France's politico-administrative system. This is because every government department, local authority or political chamber, and, indeed, any other organisation which can claim to be representative, tends to become an inward-looking and closed society, which jealously defends itself against interference and intrusion from outside bodies. The work of the French sociologist M. Crozier has illustrated the extent to which the inward-looking character of its different institutions is one of the major shortcomings of French society. In this context, the practice of *cumul des mandats* performs a positive role, since it enables individual politicians to participate in a variety of different institutions and build bridges between them. This can be illustrated by two different examples. The *conseiller général*, who is also a mayor, will usually become a spokesman for all of the mayors within his canton, and make sure that their interests are defended in the *conseil général*, as well as in relation to the prefect and the administrative field services. The deputy (member of the National Assembly) who is also the mayor of a large town will have access to ministers who might be able and willing to lend support in relation to a particular dossier affecting the town of which he is mayor. It can be argued with confidence, therefore, that it would be a mistake to suppress the practice of *cumul des mandats*, even if the increase in the number of elective offices which exist in France has made some serious attempt at regulation necessary.

In contemporary France, the local process of bargaining and mediating between different interests is performed less at the level of the rural commune (as in the day of the landowner *notable*) than at the level of the canton, of the *arrondissement* (which roughly corresponds to the size of a parliamentary constituency), or of the department. The local *notables* of the 1980s are no longer the landowners of old, but a new mix of elected and unelected people: *conseiller général*, the mayors of small towns, deputies, important local businesspeople, trade union leaders and representatives of powerful local interest groups. These are the people who fill the various committees which exist at every level of decision-making (such as the intercommunal syndicates, economic action committees, or district advisory bodies). They are the new *notables*, who can court the prefect and his permanent staff, and they are beginning to form a specific social group. Indeed, it is these new local *notables* whom the rural senator feels he represents in the Senate, and to whom the mayors of small rural communities usually address themselves when attempting to secure favours for their communes.

Local authorities have become much more adventurous during the last twenty years. Local government finance is composed of a mixture of various local taxes, central government grants and borrowing. For years, mayors limited their horizons to maintaining services by using local tax revenues and central government grants in the best way possible. In many communes there has been a transformation during the last twenty years: today's mayors govern in a far more enterprising and forward-looking manner, which involves them applying for grants or contracting loans in order to equip schools, or provide sporting or cultural facilities. Today these services are the sign of good administration, on the strength of which the incumbent mayor hopes to get re-elected. After years of lethargy, many of today's small towns are now showing signs of a new dynamism and a new willingness to deal with economic matters. The strengthening of the position of the mayor in the 1982/3 decentralisation legislation has reinforced this aspect of local government: the municipal council can now support firms with public money, for example, or even take over fledgling companies.

The local mayor is the only person who can coordinate the activities of the different administrative agencies, and, indeed, must successfully do this if local services are to operate efficiently, or if new projects are to be undertaken. In fact, at the level of the *département*, the scope and diversity of the state's activities is continually increasing, with the result that these activities are often incoherent and contradictory. Thus, the primary, paradoxical role of the local elected official (mayor, departmental councillor, now regional councillor) is to limit the incoherence of the administration. Reciprocally, the administration (the prefect, ministerial field services) has to coordinate and arbitrate between the activities of the different professional interest groups and local elected bodies. For example the farmer's representative represents farmers' interests, and the representative of the chamber of commerce promotes commercial interests. Each representative speaks for his interests and it is the role of the local administration to adjust and arbitrate between the different demands voiced by these interests.

Despite many similarities, there are considerable differences between the smallest and the larger communes. Municipal councils with more than

5,000 inhabitants control budgets of some importance and are responsible for managing numerous public services and organisations which affect their constituents' daily lives. In small- or medium-sized towns, the municipal council is usually the largest employer in the commune. This important fact becomes even more relevant in a period of high unemployment, and it can lead to a deplorable politicisation of local recruitment. Such criticisms have often been levelled at Communist local authorities, but can be extended to include those governed by all political groups.

Apart from the special exception of Paris, the same municipal laws have traditionally regulated local government in large cities as in small rural communes. Until 1977, Paris did not have a mayor, but a prefect and a prefect of police named by the central government; in 1977 the direct election of the mayor of Paris occurred for the first time, transforming the office into a major national political prize: no government can henceforth ignore the Paris town hall, which has been transformed into a *contre-pouvoir* under its present incumbent, J. Chirac. Special regimes were also introduced for Lyons and Marseilles in 1983. Until then, all other towns outside of Paris (none of which had more than 250,000 inhabitants in 1945) were governed in the same way as the rural communes. Thus municipal law, which was developed for the rural communes, became applied to communes of all sizes. As a result of the rapid urbanisation of the last thirty years, an entirely new situation has arisen, and this structure has revealed itself to be inadequate. Around ten metropolitan cities have developed rapidly, and can now boast over 500,000 inhabitants, but except in Paris, Lyons and Marseilles, no new political or administrative structures have emerged to cope with this expansion. The contrast between the mayor and the municipal councillors of a small town of between 1,000 and 10,000 inhabitants and the mayor of a vast metropolitan city is striking. Whereas the former personally or indirectly knows all of the town's citizens, the latter has to administer local services and institutions for hundreds of thousands of inhabitants. Rather than direct contact, the relationship between the big city mayor and his electors is based on indirect networks (associations, council services), which are usually impersonal and always functional.

After centuries of introversion and distrust of others, the French people have become converts to the merits of voluntary associative groups. The local association is of crucial importance in helping to coordinate relations between the town hall and prominent local interests. Numerous associations have developed during the last twenty years. Some of these have been created at the local authority's initiative, and they serve as a sort of external department of the council. In contrast, other associations are formed by various shades of activists who are often opposed to the local authority's policies. The relationship which is established between the authority and a local association can be extremely ambiguous: the local authority claims to represent the general interest, whereas the association can only claim to represent a section of the population. To communicate effectively, however, the town hall needs a network of associations in all the different spheres of local society and is willing to provide a measure of financial aid for such associations in order to get its message across. Even if it is opposed to it, if a voluntary association is to be effective it needs to be recognised by the local authority before it can receive the authority's indispensable financial aid. Both the local authority and the voluntary association are thus forced into a degree of dependence upon each other.

Many of these associations are defensive in character, formed to defend particular local interests, or to oppose unwelcome development planned by the local authority. In so far as these associations frequently reflect a grassroots demand for social change and a distrust of government organisation at any level, they often come to be seen as a threat by the local authority, determined to thwart the plans of the elected body. Membership of associations and interest groups constitutes a fundamental aspect of civic democracy. One French person in two claimed to belong to an association in the mid 1980s, compared with 28 per cent in 1967; such voluntary groups were springing up at a rate of over 40,000 per annum in the 1980s, compared with one-tenth of this figure thirty years earlier. Those who are active in associations generally belong to the central constellation, whereas the participation of members of the popular constellation is far weaker.

Apart from all his other functions, a mayor can no longer afford to be uninterested in his town's economy, especially since around 1975, as a process of industrial restructuring and streamlining has increasingly closed down factories and aggravated unemployment. More and more frequently, the mayor will attempt to find solutions to economic and industrial problems, will pose as arbiter between conflicting interests, and will pressurise the central authorities, the *conseil général* or the regional council to save firms in difficulty, and to attract new economic investment to the area. In extreme cases, the town council might even take over threatened companies itself, as has occurred in the past in Le Havre, Marseilles and Saint-Etienne. Defferre's 1982 decentralisation legislation has given a legal basis to these practices by authorising local authorities to take shares in companies.

The mayors of the largest cities have become top-level personalities in the nation's political life. Many of them have held high-ranking ministerial office, or are likely to in the future. A handful of them might even become Prime Minister. The most important mayors usually have direct access to government departments at the highest levels. Where this is the case, the mayor will ignore the formal administrative hierarchy, and the departmental prefect will find himself in a subordinate position.

The vitality of local government and civic participation at the micro-level of public affairs is one of the salient features of contemporary France. The importance of such micro-participation can be seen in all areas of French life. It can be compared with the disillusionment felt by many French people towards France's great national institutions. It can also be contrasted with the decline in activism in virtually all other areas of public and civic life. The great social movements which emerged after May 1968, such as feminism, the ecological movement and regionalism, have all declined in importance, almost to the point of extinction. Fewer and fewer French people identify with the great national institutions of the past, or with the social movements inspired by May 1968. They identify far more with their localities, and are more willing to participate in local public affairs than ever before. Surveys show that there is no contradiction between local activism and participation or interest in national politics. On the contrary, whatever their social or professional category, those who are involved in local affairs tend to be more interested in national politics than those who are not. The renewed vitality of local life is a fundamental feature of the new French society.

Part III

The stages of life

8

The strength of kinship

Foreign observers agree with their French counterparts that the family performs a vital role in French society. Practically all French people claim to be extremely attached to their own family. Although everyone might agree that the family in general is in crisis, they also consider that their own family is a happy unit, which satisfies all of its members. This apparent contradiction can be easily explained: that the family in general is in crisis can be readily admitted, but that one's own marriage is in crisis is far less easy to acknowledge, since it is difficult to recognise that the fundamental choice made in choosing a particular marriage partner was the wrong one. The emergence of love as the sole criterion for the modern marriage makes this recognition even more problematical, since agreeing that love has faded undoubtedly provokes bitter personal disappointment. The search for personal happiness and the importance of love as the main reason for the modern marriage, rather than any social or economic factors, has increased the instability of the married couple, since little remains once love fades.

The bourgeois or peasant household of the nineteenth century remains an ideal for many French people. The patriarchal family, which perpetuated itself from generation to generation within the same household, used to be regarded as a source of unshakeable stability. In the traditional patriarchal family each individual knew his duties and his place, and all members respected the authority of the male head of the household, the most senior person within the family. It was he who dictated the rules determined by family tradition, and who was the source of knowledge for younger members of the family. Despite the formal domination of the patriarch, however, the *maîtresse de maison* used to perform the prominent role in the domestic affairs of the family.

It would be naive to imagine that this family community was a pleasant environment within which to live. In fact, historians have recently demonstrated that this model was little more than a myth, artificially constructed towards the end of the nineteenth century by conservative Catholic idealists. Even in peasant villages, these extended households were rare, and they could be found only amongst the nobles, the bourgeoisie, and the wealthier peasants who possessed substantial property. Most households were based on the nuclear family, for the simple reason that all they possessed was their own labour, which made it impossible to support a wider family unit. In addition, single people, unmarried couples, widows and widowers were all to be found in sizeable numbers. In order to analyse the real pattern of family life in modern France (with the help of evidence provided by demographers and historians), it is necessary to reject the historical myth of the universally present patriarchal family, which supposedly prevailed until well into the twentieth century.

The word family has a double meaning, in French as in most other Western languages, which has caused a great deal of confusion. In its limited sense, the word family means the parents and children who come together to form a home: this is what statisticians mean when they talk of the household. In its wider sense, the expression family in French signifies the whole of the kinship group, however distant or near, who share the same forebears. This would include ancestors, descendants, cousins, and indeed any known relative, however far removed. Marriage is the process whereby a man and a woman come together to form a new household and tie together two previously separate kinship groups. For more than a century, anthropologists have illustrated the extraordinary variety of kinship relations that exist throughout the world and the uses that can be made of these.

In many ways, France provides the perfect opportunity for comparative analysis into kinship to be carried out. For centuries, the principles of Roman law coexisted with those of Frankish and Norman law, and the many different legal systems of the pre-revolutionary (1789) period had to respect the particular structures of family relations which existed within each separate region of France. Despite the recent research carried out by anthropologists, historians and lawyers, the judicial confusion governing family relations in France's pre-revolutionary history has not been entirely sorted out. Rules guiding family organisation (authority, inheritance, obligations and so on) were simplified and made uniform in Napoleon's Civil Code of 1804, which decreed standards for civic behaviour in all areas of life, although these did not immediately transform existing regional customs.

FAMILY STRUCTURES

In order to explain why such strong and lasting contrasts persist between family structures in different regions, one prominent French sociologist, E. Todd, has proposed an original model based on three hypotheses: firstly, family structures are the most stable of all social structures: the family reproduces itself over and over again from century to century, whatever ulterior changes are occurring within society as a whole. Secondly, it is through the family that an individual learns a particular moral code, and it is the family unit which transmits fundamental social and political attitudes from one generation to another. Thirdly, three main types of family structure traditionally existed within French society: the patriarchal family; the stem family and the nuclear family.

In the patriarchal family, young married couples continued to live with the man's parents and remained firmly subordinated to the patriarchal rule of the male head of family. Sons and daughters, adult sisters-in-law and brothers-in-law all continued to live under the same roof, and were all subordinated to the authority of the male head of the family. The children of the various young couples were all brought up together, under the harsh rule of the grandmother. The basis of organisation of the patriarchal family was the need to preserve the *patrimoine*, and to pass it on to succeeding generations. No one person owned the *patrimoine*, which was collective property and which gave identity to every member of the family unit. In fact

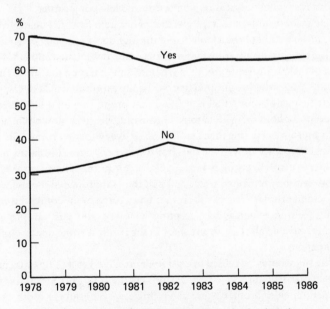

Figure 8 'Do you agree with the idea that "the family is the
only place where one can feel relaxed"?'
Source: CREDOC

the patriarch merely administered the *patrimoine* in the best interests of all family members. No individual could demand his share of the family wealth, in order to enable a young married couple to establish their own household. This severely limited the freedom of manoeuvre of younger members of the family, and reinforced the power of the patriarch. The only response to an act of rebellion by younger members of the family against the patriarch was that of exclusion from the family community. Such exclusion was likely to lead to financial destitution and social disgrace. For this reason, the patriarchal family used to be able to ensure that younger members respected the authority of older members, and placed the preservation of the family *patrimoine* above any other consideration such as personal happiness, or the desire for autonomy. This type of family structure bred a strong sense of equality amongst its members, since each individual was equally subordinate to the authority of the patriarch. The principal characteristic of such a family structure was an impatient submission of family members to the patriarch (who did not need to justify his authority), interspersed by periodic rebellion against the authoritarianism of the patriarch's rule. This rebellious undercurrent helps explain why those areas in which the patriarchal family prevailed (for example the north-east Massif Central) have traditionally inclined towards republicanism and left-wing parties.

The second family structure was that of the stem family. The survival of the *patrimoine* and of the family name throughout succeeding generations was the essential justification for the stem family. It was based upon the principle of male primogeniture: the first-born son inherited the entire family fortune. This structure ensured that the family's fortune would not bę subdivided equally amongst all heirs, and that property would be preserved intact throughout the generations. Girls would be given dowries, married off to appropriate young men and sent off to live with their parents-in-law. Younger brothers were given the choice either of leaving the family home in order to earn a living elsewhere, or else of remaining at home on the condition that they remained single and that they subordinated themselves to their eldest brother. The eldest brother was assured of inheriting the entire family fortune, whereas by accepting a dowry, the girls and younger brothers gave up all claim to any share in the family fortune on the death of their parents.

The stem family, as it used to exist in France, used to be a fundamentally inegalitarian structure, in so far as the old kept the young in a position of subordination, elder brothers were given priority over younger brothers and daughters, and men were more powerful than women. Within the stem family, each member was classed in a strictly hierarchical manner. The father incarnated authority over every member of the family: like the patriarch described above, he was in charge of administering the *patrimoine* and managing the family farm. The mother had authority over her daughters for as long as they stayed in the family home, and over her daughter-in-law when the eldest son married, as well as over her grandchildren. The younger brothers who had remained single and stayed in the family home were reduced to the status of little more than non-paid servants, and they were expected to work and obey. The daughter-in-law found herself in an even worse situation: she had no authority either over her husband (whose status in the family's eyes was that of the first-born son and future head of family), or even over her own children, who were controlled by their grandmother. This social structure embodied a form of lasting stability, since the eldest son, daughters and younger sons all knew from an early age what their destiny was, and acted accordingly. Problems arose mainly when younger sons refused to conform to this pre-established family structure (which clearly disadvantaged them) and frequently brought disgrace upon themselves as a result. The stability of the stem family was best assured when the number of children was limited to two: a son and a daughter (who would later be exchanged for a daughter-in-law). The birth of younger sons threatened to disrupt this pattern of stability.

The hierarchical principle inherent in the stem family was repeated in the organisation of traditional village society. The village was composed of various different families, which were classed hierarchically in relation to one another: 'large' families as against medium-sized and small families, powerful families as against mid-ranking and uninfluential families and so on. Noble and bourgeois families would similarly be ranked in order of hierarchy, and they respected the same rules of inheritance and succession as peasant families. In areas where the stem family prevailed, the Catholic Church was the only institution superior to that of the family. Indeed, the church conferred ideological justification upon the family as an institution, as well as upon the hierarchical relations which were maintained between different families.

The existence of such social and family structures enforced respect for hierarchy and authority amongst members of the community. Indeed, it induced them to respect the authority and power of the dominant institutions within society: the nobility, the priests, the church and the government. It is hardly surprising that those areas in which the stem family traditionally dominated have been Conservative in their political allegiance and have exhibited a higher degree of religious observance than elsewhere.

The model whereby Conservative political allegiance and a high degree of religious observance could be related to the prevalence of the stem family was concentrated mainly in parts of south-west France. However, in other areas of south-west France (where the stem family was less strong) the opposite model prevailed: political affiliations were left wing and degrees of religious practice were low. In radical areas of south-west France, neither the church nor the nobility was revered; the parish priest was judged solely by his personal qualities, and not because of the office he held, and the noble was detested as the class enemy.

The third model of the family in France was that of the nuclear family. The nuclear family traditionally prevailed in the northern half of the country. By contrast with the South, customary law was the norm within the northern regions of France. Customary law usually provided for equal rights to inheritance amongst all of an individual's offspring. The right to equal inheritance was written into Napoleon's Civil Code of 1804, and has been a fundamental principle of succession for the whole of France ever since. This principle is fundamentally different from that which prevails in Anglo-Saxon law, whereby an individual can decide for himself who will benefit from his inheritance. In certain regions, young married couples would be given property and money from both partners' parents, in order to start their own farms, as well as their own homes. The family cell was a nuclear one, based upon recognising the equality of the sexes and the independence of adult offspring from their parents. In western France, the prevalence of the nuclear family was synonymous with the isolation of individual families and the poverty of community life. This isolation was counter-balanced by the authority that local priests and landowners were able to exercise in bringing together the various family cells of a rural community. The nuclear family also prevailed in eastern France, but here the effects of family isolation were overcome by long-established community traditions such as common grazing rights and possession of animals.

Where the nuclear family prevailed, there was a rule of equality between families and respect for established authorities. Such equality between nuclear families reinforced the principle of equality of inheritance between sons and daughters, as well as that of equality between men and women. These egalitarian traditions, coupled with the lack of any tradition of rebellion against established authorities, helped explain why the northern half of France has always been orientated towards the right politically, except in the large industrial cities and mining regions.

MARITAL STABILITY AND INSTABILITY

That 'love is the child of Bohemia' may be true. However, for centuries it has been subordinated to the Christian laws of everlasting marriage, to the duty of producing descendants to perpetuate the family line and passing down wealth to succeeding generations. These imperatives, essential to preserve families with wealth and an honourable name to pass on to succeeding generations, were not so important for less fortunate families with neither wealth nor prestige. Consequently the marital instability of poor couples was far greater. In contemporary France, where the importance of inherited wealth and property to the successful marriage is much less commonly accepted, the main foundation of the marital stability of old has disappeared. Even the principle of the transmission of the family name has been called into question: many women insist on keeping their own surnames and, indeed, on transmitting them to their children. The old bourgeois custom of the woman adopting her husband's Christian and surnames, as in 'Madame Pierre Martin', seems distinctly odd in contemporary France.

In 1981, 58 per cent of French people considered that 'love is necessary to make a couple's relationship work'. During the last century, the most important factor in a marriage was that the partners had to be well matched socially, at least amongst the bourgeoisie and peasantry, since marriage was a means for a family to consolidate its position within the social hierarchy. These days, a marriage is a form of consecrating the affection and love which exist between two partners. The contradiction which underpins the modern marriage is plain for everyone to see: the only real rationale for the modern marriage, an institution which has traditionally been conceived of as a model of conjugal stability, is passion, which almost by definition is ephemeral.

Until 1970 France experienced stable demographic tendencies. The long-term trend was towards a reduction in the number of single people and the lowering of the average age of marriage: all young people got married, and they did so at an increasingly early age. In 1974, girls got married at an average of 22.5, whereas boys waited until they were 25. Moreover, the gap was narrowing between those who married younger than average and those who waited longer than average. Those people who remained single after the age of 30 were a rare breed indeed, and the unmarried couple living together were virtually non-existent, except in the urban slums. However, from 1972 onwards, the marriage rate began to decline rapidly. Whereas there were 387,000 marriages in 1975, there were only 285,000 in 1984, which constituted a decline of 36 per cent, despite the fact that the number of young people at a marriageable age had remained steady. The average age of marriage began to rise correspondingly: the average of 22 for girls in 1975 had risen to 24 by 1984, and that for boys from 24 to 26. In addition, the gap between those marrying younger than average and those waiting until later had begun to increase again. Of course, some people continue to get married at a young age, whereas others wait until way beyond the average

age. The number of divorces, which began to rise after 1965, multiplied rapidly from 1970 onwards: the divorce rate (calculated as the number of divorces per 100 marriages) doubled between 1970 and 1980, increasing from 12 to 24, whereas it had remained stable at around 10 before 1965. Until recent years, divorced people usually got remarried, and consequently divorce was a means for changing marriage partners. However, an increasing number of divorced people do not get remarried, but either remain single, or live with a new partner on an unmarried basis.

Until around 1970, France was evolving towards a single model of the family, characterised by an early marriage and two children. The model of the single child, which had been predominant before the war amongst the peasantry and petit bourgeoisie within certain regions of France, had virtually disappeared. Couples without children were a small minority and were essentially limited to atypical social groups, such as intellectuals or artists. Likewise, the large family with four or more children, which had been fairly common amongst working-class and peasant families within northern France, was limited by the early 1970s to a small number of militant Catholic traditionalists. In opinion polls, the vast majority of married people expressed their preference for two children. Indeed, the small four-seater car and the two-bedroomed council flat corresponded to the average aspirations of this ideal family unit.

The young people of May 1968 found this uniform model of the family stifling and constrictive and sought to discover new ways of community living which would be the exact opposite of the family as they had known it. Several couples would live together, sharing a common budget and raising all children within their community. Indeed, this sometimes extended to shared sexual partners, in order to overcome the sentiment of jealousy and to ensure that the children considered themselves as the children of the whole community. These initiatives failed. By 1975, it could be confidently asserted that, despite the radical changes taking place, the family had weathered the storm, and that the family unit would continue to ensure that there was continuity within French society, albeit with several minor modifications. These modifications were the increased incidence of young unmarried couples living together before getting married, and a higher divorce rate. Indeed, because young people eventually did get married after a period of living together, and because most divorced people remarried, the institution of marriage itself did not seem to be in peril. This is no longer the case. The May 1968 revolution in morality eventually made its impact felt upon the institution of marriage (albeit with ten years' delay), which is under greater attack today than ever before.

Before analysing contemporary marital instability in France, it must be stressed that the couple of yesteryear were nowhere near as stable as is often believed today. This was due to the fact that death separated couples then just as frequently as divorce does now. The average potential duration of a marriage was extremely variable. There was a high risk that the woman would die in childbirth, while attempting to have her first child, and leave a widower and child after one year of marriage. Those couples who celebrated their golden wedding anniversary were rare indeed. In between these extremes, the statistical average for how long a marriage would last was short in comparison to today. Fathers who lost their young wives would remarry, which meant that the 'evil stepmother' was a classic figure in children's lives throughout the nineteenth century.

Within contemporary French society, the lifecycle (from birth to death) has been fundamentally transformed by increased life-expectancy. If an individual lives until 80 and marries at 25, a marriage may last for fifty years or more. Should the couple have two children, both born shortly after the marriage, when each partner is under 30, then assuming that the children leave home at the age of 20, the married couple will find themselves at 50 without any children living at home. The couple will have to live alone for a period of twenty-five years, which is longer than the time they spent with their children. This lifecycle seemed to be becoming the norm during the 1960s but it has been challenged, and even radically altered, by the later average ages of marriage and parenthood in the 1970s and 1980s. The delay in marriage has been partially forced upon young people by the creation of an unstable period of 'entry into life' from the ages of 18 to 30 (see chapter 10). The effect of this period of instability which young people are more or less forced to go through during their twenties has been to postpone marriage and having children by between five and ten years. In turn, this has meant that the final period when a couple live alone without their grown-up children has been considerably shortened. Parallel to this, the increase in divorces has led many individuals to change their partners after seven to ten years of marriage, frequently remarrying, and often having children within their new partnership. In these instances, the period spent by the new couple on their own, after the departure of the last grown-up child, will invariably be far shorter than that of the classic couple described above. Finally, the death of one of the partners, generally the man, opens a new period of widowhood.

During the nineteenth century, the number of single people and unmarried couples was high, as was the number of children born outside of marriage, which varied according to region. A strong contrast could be drawn between the instability of working-class couples, compared with the stability of the bourgeois and peasant family unit. This divergence led the dominant classes to attempt to inculcate the wayward working classes with 'better' moral standards. It is interesting to recall that in 1850, 37 per cent of all births in Paris occurred outside of marriage. Of course, this was a distressing scandal for the bourgeoisie, which swore upon the eternal character of family lineages and the indissoluble nature of marriage. In recent years, the number of unstable couples has again begun to increase, especially amongst the new middle classes of the central constellation; the example provided by the middle classes has rapidly spread towards the top of the social scale, and rather more slowly towards the bottom. Those social categories which remain the most loyal to the traditional model of the stable married couple are farmers, shopkeepers and artisans; in each of these areas, the stable couple have an important functional value, since they are responsible for running a family business.

This new-found instability covers a wide variety of different situations, such as single people, unmarried couples, and divorced people who either remarry or stay single. The number of single people has rapidly increased since 1975. The number of households consisting of only one person rose from 2,800,000 in 1962 to 4,800,000 in 1982, and within central Paris one person in two lives alone (two-thirds of these are women). The number of unmarried couples living together has increased from 450,000 in 1975 to 810,000 in 1982, representing respectively 3.6 per cent and 6.1 per cent of all couples. The vast majority of couples are still married, but the number of unmarried couples has almost doubled since the last census. Moreover, on the margins of these clear-cut situations, the number of complex and difficult cases is rising. These include married people who are separated, single people living alone but having a stable relationship, divorced people who occasionally live together and so on. The variety of these situations will undoubtedly make the next census extremely difficult to administer, and census agents will have the greatest difficulty in accurately deciding within which category particular people should be placed. Indeed, it is no longer true that everyone lives within one house, or that the notion of household can be defined by a house and the people who live there.

Lawyers rapidly understood what the impact of the swing away from the uniform model of marital stability was likely to be. Indeed, governments even anticipated it in certain respects by reforming the laws governing matrimonial status, in order to give children born outside of marriage exactly the same rights as those born within it. This has meant that the status of the illegitimate child has in fact disappeared. Parallels can be drawn between this new situation, which allows a man or a woman to have several partners *de facto*, and the existence in certain non-Western societies of polygamy or polyandry. The main difference, in France and elsewhere, is that these new forms of multiple partnership are not institutionalised in the form of marriage. A woman can have children by several different men and remain a single mother, recognised as such by the social services. Recent reforms relating to the choice of children's surnames have completed this evolution: the father's name is no longer necessarily the family name which has to be carried by all of his offspring (see below).

The underlying trend is a move from a preoccupation with the father's interests to a primary concern for the mother's. Comparisons can be made between the evolution of the unit of the couple in France and the family structures described by anthropologists in various other societies, notably in the Caribbean. The woman, who is responsible for ensuring that society reproduces itself, has a string of successive male companions who provide her with children, whether legally recognised or not. This is so common that the child really belongs to its mother rather than its father. The traditional Western anxiety that it is the father who should be legally responsible for his children (and ultimately in charge of them) disappears in these societies, in which the mother constitutes the central reference for the child. For this reason notions of adultery and illegitimate children are also devoid of significance. It would seem that France, along with other Western nations, is edging closer to this 'Caribbean model', both because of changes in the law and because of changes in morality. It would follow logically from this that the normal rules of descent ought to be based on the female line: grandmother, mother and daughter, rather than grandfather, father and son. In truth, of course, the rules of kinship never obey such a simple logic.

Until recently, the period during which young unmarried people lived together was labelled 'pre-marital', because the couple would marry as soon as they had had a child. In other words, living together acted as a period of engagement, during which either partner could break off the relationship. The only difference with the traditional pattern was that pregnancy or childbirth preceded marriage. In reality, this was less novel than was commonly supposed: amongst the popular strata of society, and especially the peasantry in certain regions, this pattern had always existed. A girl would become pregnant before getting married, and the boy would have a moral duty to marry her. If he refused to do so, he would dishonour the girl, and thereby her parents, and would create a scandal which was certain to rebound on him and his family. This form of relationship (birth of children preceding marriage) was a means of ensuring that the couple would have children, which was a major concern in these peasant societies, in which the continuity of the family line was regarded as essential.

However, for several years it has no longer necessarily been the case that unmarried couples get married after the conception of a child, particularly as many women want to have children without a stable partner. Single parent families create a variety of situations for children. If the father does not legally recognise the child, the child takes the name of its mother. Even if the father recognises the child, and gives it his name (as the law encourages), he will not necessarily live with mother and child. There are around one million single parent families in France today, some 6 per cent of all households. This small minority incarnates a model of existence which is certainly different from the norm, but which is no longer regarded by the rest of society as scandalous. Consequently, the unmarried mother or the child born outside of marriage are no longer objects of disgrace. The proportion of births which occur outside of marriage has increased dramatically in recent years: from a steady 6 per cent between 1945 and 1966 to 8 per cent in 1974, 15 per cent in 1985 and 25 per cent in 1989. In Sweden, almost one child in two is 'illegitimate'. The extent to which this new situation is fully accepted by society is illustrated by the fact that only one child in five born outside marriage was recognised by its father in 1971, whereas by 1985 the figure was one in two.

THE VALUE OF KINSHIP

The rich variety of situations within which couples find themselves has led to a strengthening of kinship ties. Anthropologists have long asserted that a sort of balance is naturally established between the importance for an individual of his kinship relationships (that is, all known relatives), and the importance of his immediate family unit (that is, partner and children). The more an individual is involved with the latter, the less he will have to rely on the former. By contrast, an individual in an unstable conjugal situation will rely more heavily for help upon his kinship relatives than the individual in a stable nuclear family unit. Research has shown that single people, widowed people and divorced people who live alone see their parents far more frequently than do married people. This is particularly true for unmarried mothers. On the other hand, parents with more than two children see their relatives less often than those with fewer than two children or none at all. In general, investigation has shown that very few people (1 per cent) never see any of their relatives outside the immediate family unit, whereas 20 per cent visit relatives at least once a week, and 57 per cent do so at least once a month. These figures illustrate that kinship relations are healthy and active within modern French society. The recent renewed interest in genealogical research constitutes one of many sources of evidence for this.

In previous times, kinship performed functions which were far more important for the bourgeoisie and peasantry than they were for the petite bourgeoisie or the working classes. Surveys carried out amongst working-class communities in the 1950s underlined the importance of neighbour-hood relations as a source of social interaction and mutual aid, which con-trasted starkly with the weakness of kinship ties. By the 1980s, a tendency had arisen for there to be an homogenisation of the functions performed by kinship across the boundaries of social class. Of course, young couples are no longer constrained to live with one of the partner's parents, but they do still tend to set up house near to their parents. Although successive gener-ations of the same family (grandparents, children and grandchildren) no longer live together under the same roof, as the largely mythical family of the nineteenth century did, relations between the members of the same kin-ship group remain extremely close. The 'localised kinship group' is an extremely widespread and popular structure in France: grandparents, chil-dren and grandchildren all live in different houses, but live within the same locality and maintain frequent contact. According to studies by T. P. Caplow (1982) of Middletown in the USA, the same pattern exists in America.

Within the 'localised kinship group', material support and services descend in a vertical fashion from grandparents to their children and grand-children, whereas in return affection filters up towards grandparents from their children and, especially, grandchildren. Of course, this is entirely logical since retired people have more time to devote to their children and grandchildren, as well as greater financial resources to be able to help them (see chapter 10). Kinship thus appears to be a network through which wealth is redistributed from the older to the younger generations. This movement helps to offset the fact that the older generations, who have accumulated a lifetime's wealth, tend to be more wealthy than their off-spring. The weakening of the nuclear family unit and the working lives of young mothers have combined to make the support of parents more necess-ary than ever. The most extreme illustration of this is that a young working mother can only usually bring up her children if she can rely upon the support of her own mother. Kinship thus ensures that there is a sufficient familial continuity and stability necessary for the upbringing of children when the nuclear family unit, for whatever reason, is no longer able to cope by itself. The weakening of the nuclear family unit and the strengthening of kinship ties are thus closely associated in daily life.

KINSHIP AS A SUPPORTIVE NETWORK

Kinship can be seen as a network of relations which is self-supporting and self-manipulating, in France as elsewhere. Within this network, the older generations are well placed to be able to bid for the affections of the younger generations. The older generations know each member of the kinship network, and are aware of the personal histories of each member of the family, as well as of disputes between individual family members. This leaves them in a strong position to be able to smooth away ill-feeling between family members – or to fuel them. Moreover, possessing a *patrimoine* (accumulated during a lifetime) gives them an important source of power within the family, which they can use with discretion in order to maintain their influence within the extended kinship group. Even though the *patrimoine* is no longer the principal means of enabling a couple to survive, it can retain a decisive importance at certain stages of the relationship. Indeed, the transmission of wealth to succeeding generations is the main economic function of kinship (see figure 9).

Around half of the wealth of a typical French household is on average accounted for by property ownership, whether this takes the form of the family home or investment property which is rented out. However, financial assets have become increasingly important in the last few years. Unsurprisingly, there are great differences between the various social categories: the industrial worker has on average only one-twentieth of the wealth of the independent professional or big businessman. When industrial workers are compared with *cadres supérieurs*, this gap narrows to one-sixth. The private wealth of the average French person is modest, but has increased in recent years, and spread itself into a number of different areas. Around 50 per cent of French households now inherit wealth at some time in their existence, although the top 10 per cent of households leave around half of all inherited wealth. In the past twenty years, the number of settlements made by old people upon their relatives before they die has increased dramatically. Whereas such settlements used to account for one-quarter of all inherited wealth twenty years ago, they now represent one-half. The increase in life-expectancy and the extension of generous pensions and retirement schemes have prompted many parents not to wait until their death before they pass on at least part of their wealth to their children. This is especially true of farmers and shopkeepers. Home ownership accounts for the bulk of wealth possessed by most French people: one French household in two owns its own home. The role of kinship in enabling young people to buy property can be extremely important, since parents or grandparents are frequently able to advance enough money to enable their children or grandchildren to secure a mortgage loan. Moreover, grandparents often own properties (whether main or secondary residences) which can be used as holiday homes by their children and grandchildren. Indeed, approximately one-quarter of French households spend their holidays in property owned by one or other of the couple's parents or grandparents.

The lengthening of the lifecycle (and the corresponding increase in the number of elder relatives a young couple can rely on) has led many young families to rely upon grandparents to look after children, as used to be the custom in peasant societies and bourgeois families. Looking after small children is undoubtedly the most common service rendered by grandparents, as well as being the most important. Indeed, more than one third of children below school age are looked after by their grandparents during the day. When both parents work, they are extremely grateful to be able to send their children to their grandparents during school holidays. Improvements in

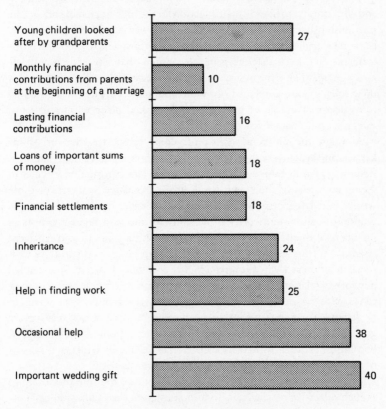

Figure 9 The economic functions of kinship: percentage of
young families who receive help from parents.
Source: INSEE, *Données sociales* (1984)

individual and collective forms of transport have greatly facilitated this, and on average half of French households send their children to their grandparents during school holidays.

In this way, children are exposed simultaneously to the values and behaviour both of their parents and their grandparents. These values are bound to be different, if only because the parents are working, whereas the grandparents are generally retired. It must not be deduced from this, however, that grandparents have been able to recover the authority within the family which used to be theirs during the nineteenth century. On the contrary, if they find themselves in a strong position to demand affection, they can no longer insist upon the subordination of younger members of the family to their authority. They must attempt to win the allegiance of their grandchildren, who are well aware of the strengths of their own position and who attempt to market their affection for the highest possible price. The relationship between grandparents and their grandchildren has certainly been transformed in the course of the past fifty years. The result of this transformation has been that the generous 'granny' has replaced an authoritarian grandfather as the best symbol of how the elder generations perceive their role, and are perceived of by the youngest generations. This transformation of the role of grandparents has taken place within all social categories (see chapter 10).

Amongst the different socio-professional categories, farmers, shopkeepers and artisans see their relatives the most often; indeed, it is almost as if running a family business makes these people attach greater importance to seeing members of their own family than do salaried workers, or those working in large organisations. In contrast, *cadres supérieurs* and people working in the intermediary professions are the least regular visitors of members of their family. Beyond the fact that they can provide material assistance for the younger generations, kinship ties perform an important social function as well. Within the higher echelons of society, an extended network of relatives, spread out across a wide variety of professional groups, can provide the individual with privileged and varied contacts, which might be decisive in career terms. Amongst the popular social classes, relatives are generally closer and provide a more permanent, diffused form of support. Kinship takes on the form of a localised extended family which acts as a sort of nest protecting its members from the misfortunes of life.

There has undoubtedly been a strengthening of the role of kinship in French society in recent years. Indeed, kinship ties are a fundamental network which affect the social relationships maintained by nearly all French people. People visit their parents, brothers and sisters far more regularly than they do friends, and this occurs in all social categories. It should be underlined, however, that familial sociability does not stop people from seeing their friends or neighbours; the evidence shows that the more an individual visits his parents, the more likely he is to see his friends and neighbours. Regular visiting of relatives is usually associated with traditional and conservative political and moral attitudes, as well as a pessimistic outlook on the future, almost as if kinship ties provided a means of refuge against future misfortunes. Moreover, strong links with relatives have traditionally acted as a brake upon geographical mobility, although the development of modern means of communication and transport has made this far less obvious.

If the family unit is considered as a part of a wider kinship network, and not merely as an isolated domestic group, then clearly it takes on another dimension. The fragility and instability of the nuclear family unit are no longer so worrying. It might be argued that the 'localised kinship' structure which exists in contemporary France is more satisfying than the real extended family of the nineteenth century, which was described in the introduction to this chapter. It is certainly more satisfying than the narrow family unit, comprised of mum, dad and two kids, which was becoming the only serious family structure in the 1960s. The 'localised kinship group' marks a radical departure from the older patriarchal family within which grandparents, parents and children all lived together under the same roof. However, the breaking up of the family into separate households has not meant the breakdown of relations between kinsfolk. On the contrary, it can be argued that it has created a new form of 'intimacy from a distance'. The relationship between grandparents, parents and children is all the more agreeable in that each party can avoid the conflicts which arise from living under the same roof.

The children of divorced parents, and unmarried mothers provide an interesting area of research for sociologists to analyse how important kinship ties are in situations which differ from the norm. Analysis of these situations illustrates that attitudes and behaviour are neither ritualised nor uniform. The single working mother's task can be a difficult one. She must be able to reconcile, or at least manage, the conflicting demands placed upon her by her occupation, her bringing up of her children and her living without a partner. Those single working mothers who are able to rely on the daily help of their own mothers are better able to cope than the others. For this reason, the single mother will often live close to her parents. The child of a single mother thus effectively lives in two different households – its mother's and its grandparents' – and is brought up as much by its grandparents as by its mother. Such a child will usually be surrounded by female company, and its kinship group will often be limited to its mother's side, depending upon the relations that are maintained between mother and father. In all probability, the kinship group of the child of the single working mother will be smaller than that of the child of a married couple (with relatives on both the father's and mother's side) or of a child with divorced and remarried parents.

At the other extreme from the child of an unmarried mother is the child whose parents have divorced and remarried. When its father or mother remarries, the child acquires a new series of relatives: a stepfather or step-mother, half-brothers and half-sisters and new grandparents (in addition to the existing ones). In other words, this child's kinship group is extended beyond its pure blood relations to include a new set of relatives resulting from the remarriage of one or other (or both) parents. We possess no studies of the relationship which developed between the child and its new relatives, and undoubtedly the relationship varies considerably according to case. Within these tangled networks of kinship relationships, children become skilful at playing different individuals, or rival branches of the family, off against each other. In fact, children, especially adolescents, often occupy a strong bargaining position within the family and the wider kinship group. They know how valuable they are to older relatives (parents, grandparents) and are quite capable of reserving their affection for the highest bidders amongst rival groups of adults. It is probable that children of divorced parents acquire a greater skill than others in manipulating their kinship group, and that this gives them distinct advantages in later social and pro-fessional life. For these reasons, the manipulation of family ties is no longer the exclusive privilege of family elders, as it was in the traditional extended family.

In the France of the late 1980s, the family was as varied in its composition as it had been a century previously. The major difference between these two periods was that by the end of the 1980s large households had almost entirely disappeared. Such diversity is likely to become a permanent feature of French society, and there is little likelihood that there will be a return to the model which prevailed in the 1960s of the homogeneous family unit com-posed of mother, father and two children. Likewise, the factors which led to a reinforcement of kinship relations, especially the increased incidence of female employment, are likely to remain.

9

Men and women

Varying patterns of relationships between the sexes have traditionally existed in different parts of France. This was illustrated by a comparative study carried out by an American anthropologist in 1970 into two French rural villages in Rouergue and in Lorraine. In Rouergue, where the stem family described in the previous chapter prevailed, female subordination was both apparent and real. On marriage, a woman would move into her spouse's household and would be expected to subordinate herself to her husband and her mother-in-law. The newly wed wife would bring a dowry of money or livestock with her, but not land, which was synonymous with power and was the monopoly of the husband. Because land was the really important commodity which allowed the family to survive, the wife was inevitably subordinated to those who possessed it, the husband and his mother. The prosperity of the 1960s did not diminish female subordination, as might have been expected, but rather reinforced it, with the result that many girls began to flee to the cities in order to escape being subordinated in marriage.

In Lorraine, on the other hand, relations between the sexes were based upon equality. Newly married couples did not live with the man's parents, but set themselves up in their own home. They would farm lands which they jointly owned, provided by both families. This was because the customary laws of succession in this part of France stipulated that men and women had to be treated equally in terms of the wealth they inherited. Within the family home, the woman was unquestionably in charge of domestic affairs, including control over the household, young children, the kitchen, the farmyard and the cowshed. Indeed, the man would almost be the wife's guest in the family home, and he would only really feel at home outside, in the fields, the café or the factory. Although the man, by working in the fields or the factory, would provide the finance when large sums of money had to be spent, it was the wife whose activity in the home ensured that daily life could continue. Moreover, the women had a strong influence over village life, since they would see each other and keep an eye on each other on a daily basis. They would know far more than the men about village life, and this control over information was itself a source of power. Whereas the men had no access at all to the female sphere of influence (the home), women would share influence with the men in the public domain (the village).

Within a bourgeois family at the end of the nineteenth century, the household's resources usually came in equal measure from the wife's dowry and the husband's various sources of income (from his *patrimoine*, and his professional activity). The equal contribution to the family's resources made by the man and the woman was a precondition for the equality that reigned between the two partners. A woman who brought no dowry with her was subordinated to her husband, while the woman who came with a large dowry was able to ensure that her authority was respected, even though her husband had responsibility for administering it. Within the average bourgeois family at the end of the nineteenth century, the distinction between female supremacy within the home and male concentration on matters outside of the home was as marked as in the peasant family of Lorraine. The man was in charge of administering the *patrimoine*, but it was the woman who controlled daily expenditure. Bourgeois society life had its own legitimacy, and the *maîtresse de maison* performed the pre-eminent role within the living room and at family dinners (see chapter 1). She was in charge of the grandest of family affairs, the marriage of children. Only women had sufficient information on their children's potential marriage partners to decide if such and such a marriage would be better than another one for the family's prestige. Family prestige mattered far more than the happiness of their sons or daughters in deciding whether a marriage should go ahead. The right marriage was of the greatest importance if the family was to increase its prestige; a bad marriage had to be avoided at all costs to save the family's honour.

This rapid survey illustrates that where there was a separation of male and female spheres, and where the duties performed by the two sexes were different and complementary (women prevailing inside the home, men outside of it), women had at least equal power to men. The women's situation depended upon how the social structure was organised and not merely on relations between individual marriage partners, or even upon the image that society projected of male and female roles. Until relatively recently, the whole of French society believed that a woman's role was to stay at home to manage the household and look after the children. This model was perfected amongst the bourgeoisie, but served as a reference-point which other social groups attempted to imitate as best they could. The model of the 'housewife' was considered by everybody as an ideal to which everyone ought to have the right to aspire. The fact that during the nineteenth century the wives of working-class men, peasants or shopkeepers were forced to work in order to feed their families was deplored by everybody as a social evil against which philanthropists struggled.

This model has been widely called into question during the past twenty years. It has been replaced by one according to which the woman leads a professional and a family life side by side, just as her husband does. Because the *patrimoine* has declined in importance as a source of family wealth, the woman who works increases her independence vis-à-vis her husband, as well as in relation to society in general. The daughters of the bourgeoisie were the first women to continue their studies past school-leaving age during the inter-war period. Some of these young women obtained degrees, which opened numerous career prospects for them, especially in the civil service and in the teaching profession. The example of these first career women soon became diffused throughout the rest of society. From 1965 onwards, the level of female employment increased so rapidly that by the mid 1980s virtually every woman under forty either had a job or else was looking for one. Only a fraction of workers remained loyal to the older model of the woman's place being in the home (even if their mothers had never enjoyed the luxury of not working).

This fundamental revolution can be explained partly by the ideological evolution which French society (along with other Western societies) has undergone during the post-war period. Work has become the most important aspect of life for most people, and in fact underpins virtually all other functions performed by individuals within society. In previous centuries, the bourgeoisie lived and enjoyed a life of leisure with a clear conscience. It

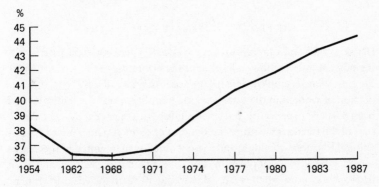

Figure 10 Growth in employment of women.
Source: INSEE

Table 9. *Percentage of working women
aged 25–54*

1954	43.1
1962	42.7
1968	44.6
1975	53.1
1982	63.7
1985	66.5
1989	69.4

Source: INSEE, *Ecoflash*

regarded such a lifestyle as a duty imposed upon it by its superior birth, and its possession of independent, inherited wealth. At the other extreme, industrial workers accepted the fact that they had to work long hours as a curse from God, to which they hoped that their wives would not be subjected. It was undoubtedly the Soviet Union which first mistrusted the ideal of leisure, and which elevated work as the supreme good. For the Soviet leaders, this ideal had to be shared by women, and no time was lost in conferring the hardest manual tasks on women. After the Second World War, the demand for economic growth meant that this idealisation of the work ethic was extended to all Western countries. To work hard for a long time became a source of pride, whereas the apparent indifference of underdeveloped countries towards their own development became an object of scorn for the West. At the same time, men's and women's interests began to be less exclusively concentrated upon domestic life, and more attention was paid to work. This process has gone so far that in order to exist socially, it is necessary for today's individual – man or woman – to have an occupation.

THE GROWTH OF FEMALE EMPLOYMENT

Between 1962 and 1965, women represented 33 per cent of the total working population, their lowest level since the beginning of the century. Since the 1960s, female employment has increased dramatically. By 1975, the proportion of women in the total working population was the same as it had been in 1906 (36 per cent), and it had climbed to 45 per cent by 1985. At the start of the twentieth century the number of women who worked as agricultural labourers was high, and these women were counted in the census as part of the working population. The wives of industrial workers also often had to work, although they did so less frequently than the wives of farmers. Amongst virtually no other social group, however, was female labour the norm, and, except in the case of shopkeepers, few women from middle-class or bourgeois families worked. From around 1965 onwards, the vast majority of women in all social categories have wanted to work, and the main differences that can be discerned today are those between generations, rather than between social classes. Three-quarters of women under 40 either have a job, or else are registered as unemployed, a figure which falls rapidly amongst the over-40s. The massive entry of women on to the labour-market has been a response both to France's post-war industrial take-off and to the development of the service sector of the economy. Women are often taken on as unskilled workers by employers who regard them as easier to dismiss than men. The birth of new industries and the expansion of the tertiary sector have both led to an increase in the number of routine tasks that employers like to consider 'feminine'.

Until 1936, women who worked did so because they were obliged to for financial reasons, and they kept their positions throughout their working lives. These women were mainly agricultural labourers or factory workers. This pattern changed during the 1960s, when a higher proportion of young women began to enter the labour-market. These young women would pursue a career until the birth of their children. Although they would stop working while bringing up their children, they frequently took up their old occupations again once their children had grown up. This pattern has been greatly modified in France today, in so far as young women hold on to their jobs at the same time as bringing up their children. By comparison with the 1960s, the age structure of the female working population in the mid 1980s has radically altered as a result of these changes. Whereas in the 1960s women would tend to take a break from work from 25 to 40, the highest concentration of working women in the mid 1980s is to be found in this same 25–40 age bracket. Two-thirds of today's working women are in relatively low-status clerical or service jobs, especially in the public sector. The development towards an increase in female labour has been a general one in Western Europe, but the form it has taken has varied considerably according to individual countries. In Sweden, working women are as proportionately numerous as in France, but many more have part-time jobs. In Holland, fewer women work. In Great Britain, the pattern of women working until around 25, then taking a break to bring up their children between 25 and 40 before returning to work in later life, remains important.

Despite popular belief to the contrary, no study has ever proved that there is a direct causal correlation between the rise in female employment and the falling birth rate during the past twenty years. On the contrary, the statistics show that the great majority of women who work have two children, the same number as those who remain at home. There certainly is a difference for those women who have at least four children (who are less likely to work), but they are increasingly rare.

In the last ten years the rise in unemployment has affected young people and women most. In those families where the man still has a job, but the woman has lost hers, the household largely resorts to the old traditional division of sexual roles: the man works, while the woman looks after the home. There is, however, one important difference from earlier days, since despite being unemployed, the woman has learnt a trade or an occupation. If she has the prospect of a future return to work, this is likely to lessen her position of absolute dependence upon her husband. In addition, she might also be able to claim unemployment benefit, giving her an independent source of income. Both developments give the unemployed working woman greater independence from her husband than the housewife could possibly have imagined fifty years ago. The effects of unemployment on women tend to vary. For some women unemployment might come as a welcome relief from having to work, whereas for others it can spell financial disaster, and a loss of self-respect.

At the same time as female employment was expanding during the 1960s and 1970s, public opinion on the subject of working women was also evolving rapidly. In 1979, almost 40 per cent of French people thought that women ought never to work when they have young children; by 1982, only 29 per cent did so. In 1979, 31.7 per cent thought that every woman who wanted to work should be able to; by 1982, 41 per cent did so. These opinions vary greatly according to age and social status. Amongst men, farmers, workers and the old are less favourable to women going out to work than the young and the higher social categories. Amongst women, the main difference is between housewives (who tend to be older) and working women (or those women who have worked in the past). Housewives are far more likely than working women to consider that women should go out to work only if there is a desperate financial need to do so. Those women who have worked (even if they no longer do so) are more likely to consider that the decision to work or not should be left to the woman and to regard work as a means of stimulating a woman's identity and personality, and of acquiring social status. The contrast between these two opposed sets of opinions is striking, and it illustrates that there are two competing models of what female behaviour ought to be within contemporary French society.

The conflict between these two models reappears in virtually every area which concerns the behaviour of women. Housewives express opinions and values which are markedly more traditional than those women who work, or have worked. For example, housewives tend to be more religious and more inclined to support Conservative parties than working women.

By contrast, working women and women who have worked are markedly more left-wing than housewives. This fact, in conjunction with the steady rise in female employment, has progressively narrowed the gap between men and women in relation to support for left-wing parties (women traditionally having been more right-wing than men). Indeed, in the last two elections, working women have voted more to the left than men. In addition, working women and men share an outlook which is similar on questions of morality, whereas housewives are distinctly more faithful to traditional moral values. For example, one survey showed that 55 per cent of housewives considered that female infidelity is unpardonable, whereas only 43 per cent of working women and 41 per cent of men shared the same opinion. Thus it can be seen that the growth in female employment has considerably narrowed the differences in behaviour, social roles and opinions which used to separate men and women so sharply. If the day ever arrived when no women had never worked, all such differences between men and women would logically disappear.

The passing away of the old bourgeois-and-peasant France of the nineteenth century, in which power was measured by the extent of the family *patrimoine*, has changed the nature of marriage as an institution. In the old France, social status and wealth were the essential prerequisites in choosing a compatible marriage partner. A 'good marriage' would be that in which the marriage partner occupied a superior social position, which would allow an individual's family to rise in the social hierarchy. The choice of such a partner would not be left to the individual, but would be vested mainly upon his or her parents; the young couple would initially be dependent upon their parents, who had provided both man and wife with the resources to marry. This situation has changed dramatically with the transformation to a society in which merit and competence have replaced birth and inheritance as determining factors of social standing. Notions of wealth and standing have been replaced by those of love and cultural compatibility as prerequisites in choosing a marriage partner.

A person's culture belongs to the individual alone, and cannot be controlled by anybody else. He is free to exploit this culture as he sees fit or is able, notably in the choice of a marriage partner. The influence exercised by parents over the selection of marriage partners for their children has been greatly reduced, and the modern married couple control their life in a way which would have been unimaginable during the nineteenth century. The social and familial conditions have at last been created in which love has become the only real rationale for marriage. As cultural capital has replaced inherited wealth as a source of power, the criteria for what constitutes a good marriage have evolved. The good marriage used to be evaluated in terms of buildings, land or income; now it is calculated by years spent at school and educational qualifications. The dowry in kind that a woman used to bring to a marriage has been replaced today by her professional qualifications and educational level.

In contemporary French society, the logic of love tends to coincide with that of social divisions, which results in a strengthening of *homogamy*: people marry other people with similar backgrounds, and of roughly equivalent professional standing. People are likely to be attracted to and meet others of a similar cultural standing, often within their place of work. This pattern often explains why people get married at a later age than previously, since marriage is not possible until one or both partners has a stable job, which tends to be the case only from the mid to late twenties onwards. Professional homogamy is almost the norm in modern society, as illustrated, for example, by the growing number of married couples where both partners are teachers or doctors. The reasons for this are easy to understand. People tend to fall in love with other people they can meet. But the tendency towards professional homogamy can also lead to celibacy, since it is not always easy to meet the perfect partner at work, and frequently impossible to do so outside of work.

The available evidence suggests that marriage enables most well-educated men to perform better in their careers than remaining single. By contrast, the well-educated woman who wants to lead a successful career ought to remain single. In other words, at a certain high level of educational attainment marriage enables a man fully to exploit the opportunities given to him by his qualifications and improves his career prospects, whereas it prevents high-flying women from realising their full career potential.

Children have the same effect as marriage on the prospects for their parents' careers. According to an American study, each child correlates with a 7 per cent loss of income for its mother, and a 3 per cent rise in income for its father. Similar conclusions are valid in France. The married man is more successful than the single man, and the husband with children is more successful than the married man without any children. The existence of children acts as a stimulant for their father in the pursuit of his career, especially at the top of the social scale. Unlike economic wealth, cultural capital can be transmitted intact to several children without any economic cost to parents. The ability to transmit a high level of cultural awareness explains why *cadres supérieurs* and the professional classes usually have more children than do groups lower down the social scale. Everything would point to the existence of children as a factor inciting the married man to succeed in his career, although this success often forces him to devote more time to his career and less to his family. For this reason, the man's success is frequently accompanied by the woman sacrificing her own career to look after the children and help her husband.

Many well-educated women make good use of their cultural level to attract a highly eligible partner on the marriage market, someone above them in the social hierarchy. Once they have concluded such a 'good marriage' these women are unlikely to exploit their education to the full, or to realise their career potential. Marrying someone above them in the socio-cultural scale, they are overshadowed professionally and, in support of their husband, limit their career ambitions. In other words, the 'good' marriage makes many women waste or give up their careers. Conversely, women who have made a 'bad' marriage (beneath their cultural level) often seek compensation in their professional life. These women are often of superior intelligence and lead more demanding professional careers than their husbands. This explains why they are more likely to hold on to careers which even if financially unrewarding are socially rewarding.

An analysis of the distribution of household tasks and power within the family leads to the conclusion that a woman's influence over important family decisions depends upon her professional situation. If we contrast professional women with successful careers and housewives, these differences are clearly revealed. The career woman not only controls domestic decisions, but also participates in those extending beyond the strict limits of the home, such as the children's future, housing, friends and holidays. In contrast, the housewife reigns supreme in the domestic sphere, but has little input into important family decisions. Successful career women often possess superior educational qualifications to their husbands, whereas housewives are usually less well educated than their husbands. In those families where husband and wife possess equivalent qualifications, there is no set pattern: sometimes the woman will take important decisions, sometimes she will be subordinate. Those women who have made a 'good marriage' with a husband of a higher social standing are usually willing to subordinate themselves to their husband. They feel that their husband is better qualified than they are to take the important decisions concerning the family's future. The woman who has made a 'bad' marriage will attempt to model her family according to her own principles, and as far as possible to exclude her husband from taking the main family decisions.

In terms of marital satisfaction, the 'good marriage' is more often considered to be a good marriage by the man than by the woman. The *hypergamy* model (marrying someone from a higher class) suits the man better than the woman; the woman's social status can be vital in the man's pursuit of his career, whereas women marrying above their position usually sacrifice themselves to their husbands' careers. Amongst people who care about their position within the social hierarchy, upwardly mobile couples are more likely to be happier than those who are static or in decline. As a general rule, upwardly mobile couples' marriages work best when the wife occupies a clearly superior social position and helps the ambitious husband to rise up the social scale: the grateful husband will respond by praising the qualities of his spouse. Those who are indifferent about their position within the social hierarchy tend to be happier when they have married partners of equal or inferior standing (the *homogamy* and *hypogamy* models). In other words, ambitious individuals are grateful to the spouse who has enabled them to rise up the social ladder through marriage, whereas individuals with few ambitions prefer someone who is their equal. If a general conclusion can be drawn, it is that women prefer partners who have at least equal educational qualifications to themselves, whereas men do not attach the same amount of importance to educational achievements, and might even prefer women who have lower qualifications than they do.

Beauty is also an important asset for finding a marriage partner, but it is more highly valued in women than in men. Although a woman's beauty will increase her chances of achieving a 'good marriage', it is less important than her level of education. It is, therefore, advisable for a woman who aspires to marry someone above her social status to concentrate on educating herself, rather than just relying on her physical characteristics. This is especially true of women from popular backgrounds, who must not only be beautiful but educated as well.

No analysis of marriage is complete without considering the people who are not married: celibates, unmarried couples, divorced people, widows and widowers. In general, widows and female divorcees who remarry take as their second husband a man whose social characteristics are as close as possible to those of their first husband. One survey discovered that 61 per cent of widows who remarried an industrial worker had a worker as their first husband, whereas 40 per cent of female divorcees whose first husband was a *cadre supérieur* remarried a *cadre supérieur*. Those women who married above their social status in their first marriage usually remarry someone with the same status as their first husband. The frequency with which remarriage occurs has strongly declined in recent years: it is more common amongst women without work and amongst men and women lower down the social scale.

The choice between the two competing models of the housewife and the working woman has placed every single woman in a dilemma which is likely to create dissatisfaction whichever alternative she chooses. House-wives no longer consider themselves as 'normal' and feel guilty about con-fining themselves to the home. But working women are torn between their professional duties and their domestic tasks, to which they feel they are pay-ing insufficient attention. In fact, the wide dissemination of the model of the working woman has not yet brought in its wake a correlative transformation in the behaviour-patterns expected of men and women. The statistics are unambiguous on this point: women continue to carry out most domestic duties.

Being single was traditionally more common amongst men and the poor than amongst women and the rich. However, this is no longer the case. People with the highest educational qualifications are those who are least likely to marry. Despite this, poor farmers and workers are the two social categories in which there are the largest number of single men, whereas single women are proportionately more numerous amongst *cadres* and medium-status professions. The fewer educational qualifications a woman has, the more likely she is to be married. Amongst women aged 35, only 5 per cent of those with a minimum primary-school qualification (*Certificat d'études primaries* – CEP) are single, as opposed to 18 per cent of those with a university degree. Traditionally, those girls with an attractive dowry from bourgeois backgrounds were the earliest to marry, but today the most highly qualified and eligible girls marry later than others: in 1982, women with CEP married at an average age of 22.3 years, those with the *baccalauréat* at 23.6, and those having completed four years at university at 25.2. There is at least one simple explanation for this, although undoubtedly an inadequate one: women want to have finished studying before they marry, and extending their studies postpones the age at which they are likely to marry.

Relations within the family have been governed for most of the period since 1804 by Napoleon's Civil Code, which re-established the paternal power written into Roman law. However, the Civil Code did not deal with unmarried couples, where the available evidence suggests that the woman is usually the dominant partner. Studies carried out into slums and shanty-towns illustrate that couples are just as stable whether they are married or not, but that within unmarried couples the dominant role is usually performed by the woman, who tends to be older. It is the woman who exercises control over the children and who represents the family in relation to the neighbours and the authorities. The development of unmarried couples, in France and in other countries, corresponds to the move towards greater equality between the sexes which was observed above, and frequently enables the woman to assert her position of equality or superiority within the relationship. Whereas marriage used to be a guarantee of stability for the woman, today it is often the woman who refuses to get married.

A study of young unmarried couples in Paris in the late 1970s showed that the idea of equality between men and women was a constant anxiety for both partners, and was the main principle which underpinned the organisation of household tasks, and relationships with the outside world. These couples were reacting against the situation they had experienced within their own families, which had been run on the basis of an extreme specialisation of roles: the father worked, and the mother looked after the household. In order to avoid repeating this state of affairs, the young couples institutionalised the instability of their relationship and their unwillingness to define specific male and female roles by refusing to get married. They considered that any legal ratification of their relationship would define rigid roles for each partner, and would ensure that the man was superior. Once sexual roles are not defined in advance, the carrying out of each domestic task must be agreed upon between both partners, and a form of bargaining establishes itself as a result. In order that this bargaining can be a completely free and mutually recognised process, the break-up of the couple must be able to be the ultimate consequence of a disagreement. The prospect of an ultimate split encourages each partner to develop his or her own occupation and to secure his or her own financial independence. Indeed, in such couples young women often work while their male partners stay at home.

In modern French society, love has become the only real motive for marriage. This has had the curious effect of increasing marital instability, since neither economic necessity nor social acceptability binds the family together so strongly as a unit as they did previously. In addition, there is less of a distinction than previously between the well-defined roles of man and wife, since in the event of a marital break-up each partner will need to be self-sufficient: the woman must be able to work in order to live, and the man must be able to look after himself within the home. Indeed, it is probable that the potential conflict between an individual's career strategy and his or her plans for married life have led to a greater marital mobility (increased divorce rate, greater incidence of unmarried couples and single people) than when only the man worked, and thereby assured his superior position within the family unit.

This expansion of female labour within all social categories has had serious consequences at all levels of society, and not only upon family life. It has transformed the organisation of companies and bureaucracies, which have had to adapt their internal structures in order to cope with an increase in the employment of women. Trade unions have been similarly affected, and have experienced most difficulty in ensuring that more women assume leadership responsibilities within their organisations. Finally, the development of female employment has had considerable consequences for the provision of social services and for the education system.

The first women to enter the labour force *en masse* were the wives of *cadre moyens* and *employés*; these women continue to be at the forefront of female labour. However, within all social categories, there has been a vast increase in the number of women who work. The two social groups which lag behind somewhat in this evolution are working-class women, and women from the highest rungs of the social scale. It is impossible to say whether these groups of women will catch up with other social groups in the future, or whether they will remain different. It is clear that whereas the model of the housewife was previously a sign of the cultural domination of the bourgeoisie, the prevalence of the working woman is now a signal of the cultural domination of the central middle-class constellation.

The extension of female labour has considerably complicated the pattern of neat social hierarchy which existed when only men worked. It has also strengthened the medium levels of society within which female labour is concentrated. For when it was common practice for men alone to work, the occupation of the head of the family was a sufficient criterion by which each member of the family could be positioned on the social scale. This criterion of using the man's occupation to place an entire family on the social scale continues to be feasible if the wife exercises a similar occupation to that of her husband: for example farmers' wives or shopkeepers often share their husbands' occupations, whereas most working wives of industrial workers are themselves either workers, or low-status clerical staff. However, the woman's occupational position coincides less and less frequently with that of her husband; hence the jobs of both men and women must be taken into consideration if a realistic picture of a household's position within the social scale is to be portrayed. In fact, the occupational position of the man is not necessarily more important than that of the woman in defining which social class a family belongs to. Everything depends upon the balance of power between the two and upon the respective strengths of the professional positions they occupy. In most instances, the higher position on the social scale, whether occupied by the man or woman, will define the family's class status as a whole, especially that of the children.

It seems clear that the desire of women to work is not about to change, and that many women have no wish to 'return to the home' and recover their traditional role as housewives (which at least had the merit of sparing them from the conflicting roles and contradictory demands that their professional, maternal and domestic duties impose upon them). In the same way that a new lifestyle is coming into existence for retired people (see chapter 10), a new family lifestyle will inevitably emerge in the future, which will spare women from the conflict of roles that their present position imposes. The new-style couple of the 1970s, who were influenced by the ideas of May 1968, sought to establish equality between men and women by refusing the differentiation of male and female roles. They considered that all tasks had to be able to be performed by either partner. This principle led to the establishment of a permanent bargaining-process, which became difficult to tolerate in the long run because it created new, intolerable tensions within the daily life of the couple. Despite the shortcomings of the 'new couple', the concept had the merit of calling into question the archetypal divisions of sexual roles which had traditionally prevailed within the married couple.

The real transformations which are beginning to appear within the power structures of the modern family have their root in the economic independence increasingly bestowed by the woman's socio-professional position. The increase in female employment has thus tended to strengthen the role of women within the modern family and appears likely to continue doing so in the future, to such an extent that the organisation of the family unit will become more subtle, based upon a more equitable distribution of roles between men and women. Indeed, the incongruous position of the working woman in today's society, who simultaneously goes out to work and continues to perform most of the domestic duties, has become so obvious that it is unlikely to continue indefinitely. Young women's career expectations are higher today than they have ever been before, which makes it extremely unlikely that there will be any return to the past strict demarcation of male and female roles. By redefining their role within society, women have been responsible for one of the most important social transformations of the Second French Revolution.

10

Young and old

The rejuvenation of the population which followed the post-war baby-boom (see figure 11) brought in its wake an enhanced status for youth, which led most adults to want to remain young for as long as possible. Once adults started behaving like young people, it became more difficult for young people to distinguish themselves from adults. In fact, the crisis of youth and the conflict between generations, so much talked about at the beginning of the 1960s, owed far more to the behaviour of adults (who were determined to remain young themselves) than it did to that of young people, who were simply attempting to affirm their own specific youthful identity. It was in order to reassert their difference from their elders that young people rebelled in the 1960s, in France and elsewhere, and adopted radically different political, social and moral stances from the rest of society. Youthful protest in the 1960s took numerous forms. Girls wore trousers or mini-skirts in order to irritate their mothers; boys let their hair grow long and cultivated beards, because their fathers had short hair and were clean-shaven. Indeed, hairstyle became a sign of independence for young people and a central element of inter-generational conflict.

By the 1960s, the pattern whereby adults attempted to channel young people into approved directions had been well established. During the inter-war years, a number of institutions had emerged which were created by adults, but which had as their objective the supervision of youth and the integration of young people into the adult world. This process was initiated by Baden-Powell, who invented the Scout movement for young bourgeois adolescents. It was followed shortly afterwards by the Catholic Church, which created a number of its own youth organisations: Young Christian Farmers (JAC), Young Christian Workers (JOC), and Young Christian Students (JEC). The left-wing government of the Popular Front (1936/7) established the first Ministry of Sports and Leisure, which concerned itself primarily with matters of interest to young people. At about the same time, left-wing activists began setting up youth hostels. The wartime Vichy government (1940–4) continued to devote considerable attention to youth affairs, partly in order to marshal the support of young people for the new regime. Efforts to channel the energies of youth into approved directions continued after the war. The sixties revolt might plausibly be analysed in terms of a reaction by young people against the idea that their elders had a right to dictate the norms they should respect.

Before the Second World War, young people's derision of their elders' authority was epitomised in the *monôme du bac*, a student rag procession which took place after eighteen-year-olds had completed their final school examinations. This ritual involved students marching through the streets and publicly mocking their elders. These rituals disappeared after the war. During the period of austerity immediately after the war, young people were impressed by the serious nature of the new era, as was the whole of society. It was hardly surprising that the constraints accepted by young people during the austerity of the forties and fifties should give way during the prosperous sixties to a new youth consciousness, based upon the desire to claim a youth identity which was separate from that of adults, and which rejected the adult culture of profitability and efficiency. The new youth consciousness came to fruition in May 1968. During the sixties, much was made of this youth 'civilisation' (in France and elsewhere) which appeared to conflict with the dull, work-orientated values, morals and rituals which then prevailed throughout society. The end of the sixties represented a dramatic reaction against the twenty years after the war, when French society as a whole seemed to have adopted the parsimonious work ethic which had previously been restricted to the middle classes.

The emergence of the new youth culture was clearly visible during the late fifties and early sixties. The films of James Dean and Marlon Brando, which presented adolescent heroes in revolt against adults, were the first signs of this new culture. These films were followed by the explosion of rock music, best represented in France by the singer Johnny Hallyday. The development of a youth press occurred simultaneously with the emergence of rock, illustrating that the pattern followed by young people in France was broadly the same as that in the USA or UK. Within this youth culture, a new ritual of social relationships emerged, whereby all social distinctions disappeared, and all ceremony was refused. A symbol of the familiarity of this new youth culture was the insistence on calling young people by their Christian names and a total disregard for surnames (and the position in society that surnames indicated). That these new cultural norms cut across social class boundaries was indisputable. Another aspect of the new youth culture of the sixties was the increased propensity for young people to demonstrate their opinions on the streets. The American model of civil rights marches and anti-war demonstrations was probably decisive in this respect. On 22 March 1968, it was a demonstration of sociology students at Nanterre, the first new university built in Paris since the war, that provided the spark which ignited the May 1968 'revolution'. The spectacle of youth demonstrating against the values embodied by their elders appeared to be a novel departure in the post-war period, but in fact it picked up a tradition of the pre-capitalist peasant communities.

May 1968 was a decisive date in the movement of transformation of French society. It began as a traditional *monôme* in which the emotions of a joyful youth overflowed on to the streets of Paris. It became transformed into a genuinely popular movement when the workers took up the students' cause and began a general strike (see chapter 6). For a while, the events appeared to endanger the survival of the government, and it was

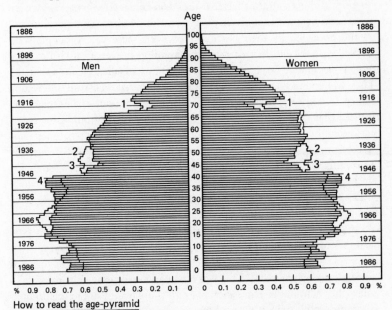

How to read the age-pyramid

The bold curve represents the European average; the horizontal lines indicate the percentage represented by each year's age-cohort as a proportion of the French population as a whole. We can see that the baby-boom started earlier in France than the European average; it began very markedly from 1945 and lasted until 1972. The baby-boom was more important in France than in other European countries.

1 Steep decline in the birth rate as a result of the First World War
2 Maturity of the 1914-18 age-cohorts
3 Steep decline in the birth rate as a result of the Second World War
4 Baby-boom

Figure 11 The French age-pyramid in a European perspective

widely believed that the May 'revolution' would overthrow both de Gaulle and the Constitution of the Fifth Republic, which clearly illustrated the new importance of youth as a social group in the functioning of French society. The political revolution did not materialise, and the events petered out as de Gaulle regained the initiative towards the end of May 1968 (consolidated by a crushing electoral victory in June). The failure of the political 'revolution' must not obscure the success of May 1968 as a cultural movement which profoundly modified the behaviour of French people.

In reality, the young university students of the sixties generation were particularly affected by the post-war transformation of society. They were the first generation of the baby-boom and in the main, products of the traditional middle classes (of modest means), whose children had never before managed to gain access to higher education. The young middle-class students of the 1960s thus felt that they had achieved a remarkable social promotion by entering university. They were reinforced in this sentiment by the pride felt by their parents. However, these young people soon realised that the number of students attending university itself devalued their achievement. In fact, many felt that they had fallen victim to a fraud. They had entered university in the expectation that well-paid, interesting careers would await them at the end of their degree courses, but they soon realised that they would be likely to find similar, medium-status occupations to their parents. That they reacted violently against what they considered an unjust deception on the part of successive governments (by expanding the university sector and promising a brighter future for graduates) was an understandable response.

Despite the May 1968 uprising, many students resigned themselves to accepting the inferior positions that they were being offered by society, although not without grumbling and postponing their entry into professional life. Faced with university graduates frequently delaying their entry into the labour-market, some critics diagnosed an allergy to work amongst young graduates. That was unfair and inaccurate. The increase in unemployment in the 1970s soon proved its unfairness, as did the findings of opinion polls, which showed that young people continued to place as much importance on their professional future as they had ever done. What was lacking was not willingness to work, but the availability of work, especially of interesting professional work.

'ENTRY INTO LIFE'

It was amongst the sixties generation that a 'young' lifestyle emerged for the first time in modern France. This was initially limited to a particular social category, but progressively extended to all groups within society. Many young people rejected family life, left their parents and went to live together in communities with other young men and women. Work was no longer seen as the individual's first imperative, and these young people often preferred part-time jobs, especially if they could rely on help from their parents. Their financial plight was made easier by the fact that they lived on next to nothing. Those members of the community who had 'serious' jobs would bring home money to the others, who would perform domestic duties. Children would be brought up by everybody. Such new communities came into being all over France, not just in rural areas or small towns, but in large cities as well. However, the purest exponents of the new lifestyle frequently took to the mountains, since living in a community in the mountains was regarded as the antithesis of traditional family life and the deadly routine of urban existence, as expressed in the formula *métro–boulot–dodo*. These communities were sometimes successful.

This refusal of the world could, in all probability, only have lasted for a limited period of time. After a brief period, the more traditional pattern of couples living together reasserted itself amongst the younger generation of the 1960s, even though the refusal of marriage persisted for many of them. These young rebels of the sixties eventually made their peace with the world. However, their example had a lasting influence in helping to define a new concept of youth, as an intermediary stage between childhood and full adulthood. The experience of the sixties generation, which has been repeated by successive generations, was that for around ten years after leaving school (18–28) young people respected different values and performed different rituals from those which prevailed in the adult world.

Those who remained the most faithful to their revolutionary ideals refused to enter any of the classic professions and took up one of the new 'society-conscious' careers which were beginning to proliferate during the sixties, such as social work, psychology or para-medical activities. This group was in every sense a new one. It was composed both of children of the traditional lower-middle classes, who were experiencing upward social mobility through their university degrees, and of downwardly mobile children of the old bourgeoisie. The latter had either been unable to obtain the type of qualification necessary for the careers which were usually pursued in their families, or had consciously refused to follow such traditional career paths. The sixties generation was in general characterised by a belief in the ideas of May 1968, which often set it apart from older members of society. Moreover, it lived within a context of extreme social mobility, which made people's economic futures far more uncertain and generally eroded social barriers. These two factors (ideology, and social mobility) combined to give a particular flavour to this new lifestyle, in which young people between the ages of 18 and 28 opted out of mainstream society before settling down to a more stable existence later on. The model created by the sixties generation has been repeated by subsequent generations; indeed, the rise in unemployment in the seventies and eighties has made it almost obligatory for young people to follow this route. As this lifestyle has become more widely diffused throughout society, it has become transformed into a standard model of behaviour. It is easy to forget in the eighties that such behaviour caused a scandal in the sixties.

During the 1950s, from the top to the bottom of the social scale, young people would either find a job, or go on to higher education immediately after leaving school. The precise pattern tended to vary according to social class. The sons of workers and farmers would start working straight away after leaving school at 16, whereas the sons of *employés* would enter their offices either at 16 or 18, depending upon their level of qualifications. The favourite institutions of young *employés* were the Post Office and the civil service. Those privileged young people who went on to university or a *grande école* would embark on their professional careers as soon as they had obtained their degrees. There was a tendency for people to get married at an increasingly early age, which effectively meant that the transition from adolescence to adulthood took place without the need to pass through the intermediary stage of youth. Military service continued to retain its symbolic character as the point of transition when boys were transformed into men. By the age of 22, almost everybody had left their parental home, had a job, was married and had settled down.

Since around 1970, this schedule has been completely disrupted. Although most sons of manual workers still leave school at 16, the scarcity of available employment has made it far from certain that they will find jobs. Those studying for the *baccalauréat* will obtain it on average at 18; should they go on to university, they may well be studying until the age of 25 (the latest age they are permitted to do their compulsory military service). In addition, since 1975 a majority of young people have not been able to find stable jobs when they leave school or university, or complete their military service. Only for the students of the prestigious and élitist *grandes écoles* is there usually no problem in finding secure, well-paid employment. Most young people in France today experience a more or less uncertain period during which they are unemployed, or else live off unstable, temporary jobs. Moreover, the average age of marriage has risen and modern French couples in all social classes tend to live together for a period before getting married. Some young people leave the parental home and form couples at a very young age, often under twenty, but the most recent trend is for young people to remain rather longer under their parents' roofs. This is especially true for the young unemployed, who are often obliged to stay at home through lack of money.

Leaving the parental home can involve a delicate decision, which has to take into account a number of conflicting constraints and desires. To leave home presupposes that an individual has both the financial and psychological means to do so. Curiously, young industrial workers, who generally start working at an earlier age than their contemporaries from middle-class families, tend to live with their parents for longer. Within the popular classes (industrial workers, *employés*), the 'installation model' is still dominant: an individual only leaves his parental home when he finds work and marries. These three events (leaving home, starting work and marriage) still tend to coincide for young people from the popular constellation, although couples will often live together for a period before getting married. Amongst children from the central constellation, these three events do not occur simultaneously, but are spread out over a period of ten years or so.

In all social groups, women usually get married earlier than men, and leave the parental home earlier. However, the greatest variations in the average age of marriage occur between different social classes. The higher one goes up the social scale, the later marriage occurs. A recent study showed that, amongst the children of *cadres supérieurs*, only 5 per cent of boys and 18 per cent of girls aged between 18 and 24 were married. The respective figures for children of working-class parents were 15 per cent and 33 per cent. Moreover, the children of *cadres supérieurs* were more likely to live together as unmarried couples than were those from lower social backgrounds. In addition, around 30 per cent of children of *cadres supérieurs* aged between 18 and 24 lived alone.

The extension of the time spent at school and the increase in unemployment have meant that many young people delay their entry into working life. At the age of 18, 75 per cent of girls and 70 per cent of boys were still at school in 1985, whereas ten years earlier these figures had been 56 per cent and 52 per cent. At the same age, 28 per cent of boys and 19 per cent of girls were working, whereas in 1975 these figures had been 45 per cent and 38 per cent respectively. The delay in entering the workforce is thus more strongly marked amongst women than men. This development has gone alongside an increase in the expectations held by young people and their parents in relation to school. Even amongst children from working-class or lower-middle-class families, expectations of what school can offer have increased dramatically. The extension of the period spent at school thus corresponds well to the increased demand from both children and their parents for more education. If their career ambitions are disappointed by the limited jobs that are available once they leave school, there is a strong like-lihood that today's young people will refuse to accept a permanent job which falls below their expectations. There is a tendency for them to opt instead for a further period of study, to remain unemployed, or to engage in temporary work for a period while waiting for a suitable job to arise. The suitable job will be one which corresponds to the knowledge a young per-son has acquired and the educational qualifications he has achieved. It is only towards the age of 28 that these ambitious young people find stable employ-ment, get married and have children (although in recent years marriage has often followed having a child, rather than preceded it).

It is undeniable that young people aged between 18 and 30 have come to form a separate, intermediary age category between adolescence and adult-hood, with its own identity and values. However, it is unclear whether this youth 'civilisation' is merely a generational phenomenon, linked to the current generation of young people, which is likely to fade as time wears on, or whether it represents a new, lasting social structure. It is true that until today, young people have been especially numerous as a result of the post-war baby-boom of the forties and fifties and that the new high levels of unemployment have had the effect of postponing their entry into active working life. To this extent, youth 'civilisation' might be considered as a purely generational effect. However, it might also be argued that the delay faced by young people in finding stable work and 'settling down' represents a new and lasting structure in French society, a society which no longer has enough work for everybody and which thus forces its youth to pass through an intermediary unstable period between adolescence and adulthood. Dur-ing this intermediary period of 'entry into life', young people are freed from the constraints of having a regular job or starting a family, and are invited to 'live differently', whether they like it or not. The latter argument is at least as convincing as the former one. There is no reason, *a priori*, why unemploy-ment should decline, unless society defines new rules about how to dis-tribute what work is available to it amongst its members.

We saw above (chapter 9) how female employment has increased steadily during the last twenty years, although the unemployment rate has grown even more rapidly. It seems almost as if French society has decided to keep its young people unemployed and to employ its women, despite the fact that the rise in unemployment might well have induced women to stay at home, or, indeed, created pressures to force them to stay at home. Another partial solution to the problem of unemployment (and youth unemployment in particular) might be to reduce the retirement age, now sixty, even further, and for employers to take on younger people for every older person who retired. This solution has not yet been considered seriously by any French party or government, partly because of the cost it would involve (in terms of expenditure on pensions), and partly because of the social problem which would arise from forcing people to retire in their mid fifties.

The emergence of a separate youth culture in France coincided with the development of the so-called 'consumer society' in the sixties. The wealth created by France's post-war economic boom (1945–74) was the essential precondition which enabled a variety of different lifestyles to emerge. From the early 1960s onwards, businesspeople began to realise that young people represented an important market which was increasing in numbers and which possessed a steadily growing amount of wealth. Of course, young people in their teens or twenties had less money than did those in their forties. Moreover, since the 1960s large numbers of young people had been unemployed. Notwithstanding this, young people's disposable incomes were often substantial, especially considering that they were interested neither in saving nor in insuring themselves against life's misfortunes, since they believed that if the worst came to the worst they could always rely on their parents. At the age of 20–1, one young person in three is still being provided for by his parents, although around half of this number have their own income. By the age of 24, almost all young people are financially independent, but can still rely on their parents for financial help when necessary. As a social category, young people are therefore frequently good clients.

Young people's lifestyles in contemporary France are strongly centred around socialising, leisure activities, sport and culture. Those aged between 15 and 25 use record players far more often than any other age-group and are more likely to play a musical instrument. The young's passion for music has revolutionised the music industry, in France as elsewhere. The production of records in France increased five-fold between 1960 and 1980, whereas that of cassettes multiplied sixteen-fold between 1970 and 1980, to respond to growing demand from the young. This concentration on leisure activities contrasts with a lack of participation by young people in politics or related activities: many young people are not even on the electoral register, and the abstention rate is high for those who are.

Thus, most young people aged between 18 and 28 in France experience a period of 'entry into life', during which they have not yet made a permanent career choice and when they rely on social security and help from their families to survive. This new lifestyle is neither adolescent nor adult, but a transition between the two. This situation is shared by most young people, except for the small élite of students of the *grandes écoles* who are destined eventually to occupy the top positions in the ruling class. However, this period of entry into life is experienced differently by young people from different social backgrounds. For example, young working-class people in the suburbs continue to live with their parents and spend their time as best they can, but are often reduced to boredom, and occasionally to delinquency. In certain inner city areas, delinquency has become a ritual amongst unemployed youngsters, which occasionally leads to prison. Parents are forced to accept such minor transgressions as the unwelcome consequence of long-term unemployment. In contrast, young middle-class people often continue their education through to university, live in their own flat or studio, are contented with a succession of part-time jobs and frequently live as unmarried couples. They are more likely than their working-class counterparts to travel widely, and make clear their intention to enjoy life when they are still young, before submitting themselves to the constraints of adulthood.

The contrast between a young student at one of the *grandes écoles* and a young middle-class student at a French university is striking. The former receives a salary at the age of 20, is taught by the best brains in France and is assured of a brilliant future career. The career prospects of the university graduate are far less bright. In order to maximise his career prospects by obtaining a master's degree, the university student will probably have to prolong his studies until the age of 25, and survive on part-time jobs. Even then, he is not certain of finding a job which matches his qualifications. The student who passes through a *grande école* costs the state 250,000 francs, whereas the university student costs 7,000 francs.

The major differences in young people's lifestyles correspond to French society's division into three main social categories: the ruling élite, the middle classes (the central constellation) and the popular classes (the popular constellation). The itineraries of different groups of young people within French society are extremely varied, although somewhat less so than prior to the sixties. The particular lifestyles which most young people develop have certain features in common, such as financial and occupational instability, and a concentration of attention on leisure activities. What distinguishes the current situation of young people from that which prevailed until the 1960s is that each individual has considerable freedom to decide whether he wants to prolong or reduce the period of youth. This relative freedom to choose within which age category the individual situates himself is greatest within the middle classes, where opportunities and lifestyles are most varied. It is less in evidence amongst the working classes, who have a narrowed range of opportunities open to them. It is scarcely in evidence at all within the narrow ruling class, where career imperatives dictate what course the individual must follow.

RETIREMENT FOR ALL

The rejuvenation of the population after 1945 came after the virtual demographic stagnation of the inter-war period, and this fact made the population explosion all the more unexpected. Whereas the French population had stagnated at around 40,000,000 throughout the inter-war period, by 1989 it had risen to almost 56,000,000. The dramatic increase in the birth rate was accompanied by an enhancing of the role of youth and young people. The young dynamic manager and the young modernising farmer became key figures in France's renewal, who cheerfully ignored the cautious management approach in industry and agriculture which had characterised their fathers' generation. Everything which was old was considered archaic and outdated; everything which was young was regarded as new, modern and geared towards the future. This rapid and complete turnaround in people's values did not appear to surprise anyone, not even those who had learnt to think that the impatience of youth must be moderated by the reflection of older, more experienced people.

However, since 1965 and especially since 1970, the birth rate has been falling, and – thanks to medical and social advances – average life-expectancy has been increasing. France is beginning to grow old once again. This fact has given birth to the traditional anxiety that an old country is one afflicted by sclerosis and turned towards the past, whereas a young country is dynamic and orientated towards the future. No convincing causal relationship has ever been established between the two. It is eminently plausible that young people might be forces of dynamism and vitality, but it does not automatically follow that older people cause inertia and stagnation. The response to this question is essential for predicting the future of French society, since for the first time in France's history old people represent one-fifth of the population. This has led to old people being considered as a specific social group again and has raised the prospect of virtually everybody being able to look forward to a new age of retirement.

The prevailing political morality in France continues to attach overwhelming importance to work and production. For that reason, old people, who are usually no longer working, have too often been regarded merely as recipients of welfare and as a social problem for the rest of the nation. Indeed, until the 1960s the old were frequently regarded as paupers, or even destitute people who had to be supported by their families or by the authorities. The transformation since the mid 1960s has been remarkable: old people have become the subject of government policy, especially in relation to their lifestyle and their integration into society. Moreover, their numbers have been swollen not merely by the increases in life-expectancy, but also by unemployment. Early retirement has been one of the main weapons at successive governments' disposal in an attempt to bring down the unemployment total. Consequently, the 'old' themselves now constitute a far broader range of people than ever before.

The idea that every citizen has the right to retire from work with a pension when he reaches a certain age is an invention of the last twenty years in France. Before this period, only civil servants benefited from an assured pension, which could explain the attraction of the civil service for the sons of the bourgeoisie and peasantry. The elderly bourgeois would be able to live off his private wealth, whereas the peasant would continue to reap the harvest of his lands, aided in this task by his children. The lower-middle-class shopowner would continue to work in his shop until he died. Farm labourers and industrial workers very rarely reached today's age of retirement. The ruin of the independent bourgeoisie after the war and the rural exodus gradually led to the invention of the idea of occupational pensions, first of all for wage-earners, and later for farmers, small businessmen and professional people. (These pensions are either contributory state-funded pensions, occupational pensions, or a mixture of the two.)

The income of the over-60s in France today is actually marginally higher than that of younger people. In 1982, the over-60s constituted 19 per cent of the total population but possessed 22 per cent of national wealth. If we compare the households of the over-60s with those of the rest of French society, we can see that retired people generally fare well. Although it is true that over-60s households have a marginally lower income than their younger counterparts, they also have fewer members, so that the average income for the over-60-year-old is in fact above that of the rest of the population. This advantage is likely to increase further in the future, since the number of households where both husband and wife work and where both will receive a pension has risen dramatically during the last fifteen years. Despite this, figures given for average wealth can be deceptive, since extreme differences in lifestyle persist amongst old people. The creation of a recognised age category of old people aged from 60 to 80 is one of the most fundamental developments in post-war France.

In order to understand the phenomenon of old age, it is important not to treat it in negative terms as a social problem. The creation of this new social category should be treated positively. What can old people contribute to society? What types of financial resources do they have? What are their activities? What social and economic functions do they perform? What services do they provide, and to whom? In other words, old people must be treated in the same way as members of the working population. The crucial question is no longer one of what society must do for its old people, but of assessing what they themselves do for others. Today's old people bear little resemblance to the often pauperised, destitute older generations of the 1950s and 1960s. They have become consumers in their own right and perform an important role within the economy and society. Since 1983, the retirement age has been fixed at 60. Statistics show that the consumption of medicines increases rapidly from an average age of 78 onwards, and that soon this figure will have risen to 80. We are not primarily concerned in this chapter with the period between the age of 80 and death, which tends to be one when health becomes the primary, if not exclusive, preoccupation of most people. The problems to be dealt with amongst this age category are obviously of a different nature. When we speak of old people, we are concerned with the age category 60–80.

The 60–80 age category represents about 20 per cent of the total French population, a proportion which is likely to remain stable for the next twenty years. The age of retirement is a highly political issue, partly dictated by economic constraints, partly by social preference. The only uncertainty relating to the number of retired people is whether future governments will lower the retirement age still further (to ease unemployment), or raise it (to reduce the burden of welfare payments). The alternative to a fixed retirement age would be to introduce a graduated scheme which would end the brutal transition from full-time employment to total retirement and replace it with a transitional stage of 'gradual retirement' between the ages of 55 and 70, during which period employment would be on a part-time basis. Other solutions have been envisaged to soften the transition from work to retirement, as well as to help people cope with the problem of unemployment. These include postponing the actual age of retirement until 70, but spreading out periods of 'inactivity' throughout a person's career, either by reducing the length of the working week to 25 or 30 hours, or by organising sabbatical years which would enable workers to undergo retraining at regular intervals. However, any further conjecture is hazardous, since future policies depend upon political decisions.

Old people are more heavily concentrated in the countryside and small towns than in the large cities: almost one-quarter of France's rural population is over 60, as opposed to 17 per cent in urban areas. This contrast has often created a false impression about the nature of the countryside, since it has helped encourage the belief that the rural exodus was accelerating so rapidly that entire regions composed of diminishing and ageing populations would eventually be deserted. However, the population in rural areas actually increased more rapidly than that of the urban zones during the last intercensal period (1975–82). For although old people eventually die, they are replaced by younger retired people, often attracted from the towns, with the consequence that the elderly population perpetuates itself without any difficulty. Moreover, that old people are more heavily concentrated in villages and small towns than in larger urban areas does not necessarily have a negative effect on the economic fortunes of these communities. It can even be an advantage, since old people, who themselves receive a pension and have accumulated considerable wealth throughout their lifetimes, often attract younger relatives with high incomes.

The elderly population of France is, of course, distributed throughout the nation, but there is an uneven population spread. High concentrations of old people are especially likely to be found within the traditionally economically backward rural regions (for example in central France), but also in regions where economic activity is intense, especially along the Mediterranean coast. In fact, old people prefer if possible to live in the southern half of France. The last census (1982) illustrated that the population of the southern half of the country had risen more rapidly since the previous census (1975) than that of the northern half, and that the proportion of retired people living in the South had increased still more markedly. Indeed, although French people in general were less geographically mobile between 1975 and 1982 than they had been in previous intercensal periods, the rate of mobility of the over-60s hardly declined at all.

The generation of old people who lived out their retirement during the 1950s and 1960s was possibly the most disadvantaged of all generations during modern times. The old independent bourgeoisie had lost its wealth, and often sank into penury during old age. However, an increasing number of industrial workers were surviving until retirement age, but had virtually nothing to retire on. Likewise, small peasants, shopkeepers and artisans, whose children had moved away and become wage-earners, ended their lives in misery tilling the land, or trying to run their shops. These various social groups all depended more or less upon their children to survive, as had been envisaged in Napoleon's Civil Code, or accepted whatever public charity they were offered. It was true that for this generation to be old was synonymous with misery, solitude and dependence. It was much less true for previous generations (who could rely upon the economic infrastructure provided by the extended family, or upon independent sources of wealth) and is no longer true at all today (since everybody is integrated into a public or private pension scheme). In the 1950s and 1960s, as a result of the post-war 'baby-boom', a large generation of children was brought up which spent considerably longer at school than its predecessors and whose entry into the workplace was thus postponed. That so many children could be brought up related in part to the fact that the number of old people was limited, hence people's resources could be used to bring up more children. For once, the support of young people cost society far more than that of the old. That situation is now reversed, since the number of old people has risen considerably and the proportion of the young in the population has diminished. The problems of financing France's expensive social security system are likely to become even more acute if the nation's age structure is not radically rejuvenated within the next twenty years.

Despite popular belief to the contrary, most people's wealth generally grows with age, despite a loss of income derived from professional activity. As someone gets older the income generated from his *patrimoine* tends to increase. Returns from property and from state bonds are on average almost twice as high amongst retired people in France as they are amongst those still

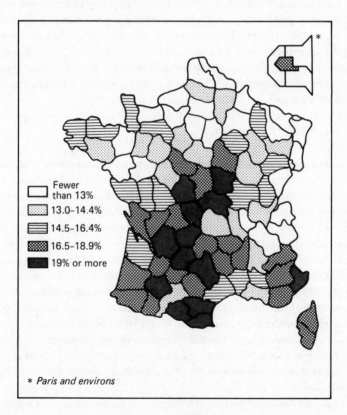

Figure 12 Proportion of people aged sixty-five or over in
1982. Source: INSEE, *La Population de la France en 1982*
(February 1984)

working. Moreover, those households composed entirely of the over-60s tend to be less indebted than others, since mortgages and other loans have been paid off. There are various other ways of measuring this relative affluence. The total private wealth of the average retired household is substantially higher than that of a working household whose head is an industrial worker, an *employé* or a *cadre moyen*; but lower than that of a working household which is headed by a company director, professional farmer, artisan or shopkeeper. Although they no longer derive an income from professional activity, and many are desperately poor, retired households possess one-third of the total private wealth owned by all French households. According to statistics given by the Bank of France, people over 55 own 57 per cent of the total number of shares and bonds, which account for 75.5 per cent of their total yield. The average portfolio of shares and bonds of someone over 65 (a value of 165,000 francs) is more than double that of people below that age (76,000 francs). In addition to this, to gauge the real wealth of France's over-60s, we would have to take into account other sources, such as gold, cash assets, personal property, household equipment and non-monetary incomes. In short, retired people constitute an active, often affluent market.

A LEISURE CLASS?

It is no exaggeration to say that most retired people do not know what to do with their money, or at least those with above average incomes do not. For that reason, they represent a clientele which is extremely active in certain markets, especially in property, tourism and food and drink. It is, of course, difficult to predict how future generations of retired people will react to their new-found freedom. None the less, one might expect that further transformations will occur as younger generations used to mass consumption gradually retire in future years. For example the septuagenarians of the 1980s had already formed their habits of consumption before the great consumer expansion and the profound revolution in lifestyles of the 1960s occurred. Tomorrow sexagenarians, on the other hand, will have experienced only 'modern' living, based on patterns of high consumption. Moreover, they will be vastly better educated. It is probable that the old people of the year 2000 will be scarcely recognisable in comparison to today's pensioners.

In theory, the combination of free time and disposable income ought to mean that retired people are able to concentrate upon 'leisure' pursuits. However, according to the available statistics, this is not yet really the case. In almost every cultural activity, the over-60s show less interest than the average for all age-groups: reading, sports, watching sporting events, cinema, theatre, concerts. The only exceptions are television, and reading a daily newspaper, a magazine or a journal. Once again, it is difficult to evaluate whether this can be explained by age or generation. It is plausible to argue that today's generation of retired people, raised in the austerity years of the 1930s and 1940s, has not been socialised into enjoying leisure activities, whereas the retired people of the year 2000, the products of the consumer society of the 1950s and 1960s, are far more likely to devote their energies in retirement to the pursuit of leisure. The habits of the over-60s are thus likely to be progressively modified in future years. A substantial market is opening up for the suppliers of goods and services for the leisure industry. The growth in foreign travel amongst retired people perfectly illustrates this: the senior citizens' clubs are important organisers of foreign travel for retired people, many of whom have never left France before. Indeed, as a category, retired people are excellent clients for the travel agencies, since their bookings account for some 37 per cent of all leisure flights.

The traditional French image of the old people in Mediterranean villages sitting on stools outside their front doors and chatting with the neighbours would suggest that socialising is the main activity of the old. Unfortunately, we possess insufficient data to give an accurate picture. The studies that do exist illustrate – unsurprisingly – that a person's daily routine varies immensely according to whether he is working or retired. One study compared people over 55 who were still working with those who had retired. Those who had stopped working spent far more time sleeping, engaged in leisure pursuits (including watching television) and in the bathroom than did those still working. The greatest contrast between the two was that the retired man began to participate in the housework, but the working man did virtually none. Gardening and DIY are extremely important amongst retired men, especially amongst the young retired of 55–64, who spend on average more than two hours daily on these activities. However, the time spent on gardening begins to diminish after 65 (one and a half hours daily) and even more so after 70 (one hour). Whether this can be attributed to age or to the effect of generation is again uncertain. Both men and women spend approximately one and a half hours daily on socialising. In contrast, retired men spend more time walking (three-quarters of an hour daily) than do retired women (one-quarter of an hour).

Young retired people are inventing their own novel position within French society, strongly bound up with the renewed vitality of local community life. The available evidence suggests that today's generation of retired people limits the scope of its social relationships to those of kinship, immediate neighbours and the local community. Retired people are often especially enthusiastic about engaging in activities and assuming responsibilities in local and family activities, since they now have time, financial security, and the experience acquired during their professional lives. Young retired people are active in all areas of civic and cultural life, and have placed themselves at the centre of a new network of poorly organised activities which are developing outside of the great established institutions. In this manner, they are contributing to a certain 'de-institutionalisation' of society.

One area to which old people devote considerable time is looking after their grandchildren. Active grandparents spare no effort in devoting themselves to their family. They constantly seek out the affection of their grandchildren. The role of grandparents, and of grandmothers in particular, is being reinvented by today's new generation of retired people. Young grandparents are able to hand down certain values and rules to their children and grandchildren, but no longer incarnate authority, because no member of the family is directly dependent upon them for their survival. It used to be the case in certain extended bourgeois or peasant families during the nineteenth century that the grandfather's position at the head of the family, and his control over the family's wealth, gave him considerable power in his relations with younger members of the family (see chapter 8). The breakdown of the patriarchal family has effectively ended this power. Because they no longer occupy a position of power within the family, grandparents must now compete for the affection of younger members of the family (especially their grandchildren) rather than demand obedience. They do this not by symbolising familial authority and hierarchy, as they used to, but by offering material and emotional rewards for their grandchildren's affection. The patriarchal grandfather, who commanded fear and respect, has largely disappeared in contemporary France. He has been replaced by the kindly and generous grandma, who best epitomises children's images of their grandparents. Because of their changed position within the family, grandparents must be tolerant of the ideas and morality of other members of the family, especially their grandchildren. Indeed, enquiries show that politics, religion and morality are often taboo subjects, discussion of which is avoided within the family, in order to maintain a harmonious relationship between the different generations. As far as many grandchildren are concerned, grandparents provide a vital link with the past in their search for their roots. For they incarnate the customs of their regions and social class, in a way that parents are too young, and too close, to do. This is especially the case when parents live in conurbations, but grandparents live in the countryside or in small towns.

Old people are in the process of creating a new lifestyle, based on organising various kinds of leisure activities. This development is certain to have an impact on the behaviour-patterns of other age categories, as they reach retirement age in the future. The new lifestyle of retired people invites comparison with that of the financially independent bourgeoisie of the nineteenth century. The main difference between the two is that, whereas the bourgeoisie was a social class, which elevated leisure activities into a *raison d'être*, today's generation of old people constitutes an age category, within which not everybody is capable of enjoying leisure activities, whether for financial, cultural or medical reasons. In addition, there is no pre-established pattern of leisure to which people have to conform, as was the case with the old bourgeoisie.

Each retired person has to invent his lifestyle in order to suit his financial and cultural resources, the nature of his kinship ties, his neighbourhood, and so on. Even if most aspire to a life of active leisure in retirement, some manage to achieve it more satisfactorily than others. The future models are only now being evolved by the current generation of retired people, and they will undoubtedly change as those generations who lived through the sixties reach retirement age. With retirement at the age of 60 in France, the person who retired in 1990 would have been born in 1930, and spent his childhood in the depressed and ossified France of the 1930s and spent his youth during the war and post-war austerity. In contrast, the person who retires in 2010 will have been born in 1950, will have only known a wealthy, open society and will probably have led an enriching social and cultural life which will have prepared him well for leading a life of leisure in retirement. Moreover, the latter person will have been able to benefit from his parents' experience of retirement, which may serve as a model to perfect, or reject.

Ancient wisdom used to declare that leisure had a noble quality about it. This rediscovery is being made by today's old people. During the nineteenth century, a section of the bourgeoisie ostentatiously led a life of leisure, because this was a means of illustrating that it possessed wealth and was respected for it. Today's senior citizens are looked upon unfavourably by many because they no longer work. For over a century, work and production have been the supreme values in our industrial societies. That being 'unproductive' is considered as being decadent is no longer justifiable in modern societies such as France. Indeed, in France and in other industrialised nations, the production of goods is no longer the only thing which matters in the modern economy, which also needs consumers of goods and services if it is to be efficient. It is probable that the leisurely and comfortable way people live out their retirement will be increasingly envied by the rest of society, and, consequently, that older people will recover the prestigious position they once occupied during the nineteenth century. If that is the case, they will once again serve as a model, especially for their grand-children, whom they will have helped to bring up. In this way, old people will gain greater respect from society as a whole, and a broader pattern of social values, no longer pinned exclusively on the work ethic, will gradually become accepted throughout society.

Part IV

A new civilisation

11

Changing lifestyles

The growth in the wealth of the average French citizen has led to an increased standard of living for all social groups, although the overall position of these groups within the scale of incomes has not altered. The general increase in wealth has opened new possibilities that were previously denied to the lower social groups, the peasantry and the working class in particular. In 1979, industrialists, large traders and the liberal professions consumed three times as much as unskilled workers or farm labourers as opposed to 3.6 times in 1956. In between these two social extremes came firstly the *cadres supérieurs* (whose level of consumption was 15 per cent below that of the first group), and then *cadres moyens* and small shopkeepers (who consumed some 33 per cent less than the first group). Slightly further down the social hierarchy came *employés*, artisans and foremen, who consumed close to the overall average. Finally, skilled and unskilled workers experienced a level of consumption some 20 per cent or more below average, as did farmers. It must be pointed out, however, that variations within a particular social group are frequently far greater today than used to be the case. Within each social category, individuals can organise their lifestyle as they wish, within the constraints imposed by their incomes: there are no longer codes of consumption behaviour to which particular social classes are expected to conform. None the less, certain salient tendencies can be distinguished which illustrate that social class models continue to influence patterns of consumption.

THE WORKERS AND THE OTHERS

In contemporary France, it is no longer possible to distinguish per se between a working-class lifestyle, a lower-middle-class lifestyle and a bourgeois lifestyle, as it undoubtedly was at the beginning of this century. The pattern of a family's expenditure no longer depends on social category as much as it does on the overall income of a particular family. With the overall rise in the standard of living, the particular features of a working-class lifestyle have become blurred, and working-class expenditure patterns are now broadly similar to those of other social categories. For example, the proportion of a working-class family's income spent on food decreased from 56 per cent to 32 per cent between 1956 and 1979, and that of a *cadre supérieur* from 30 per cent to 23 per cent, thereby reducing the overall difference from 23 per cent in 1956 to 9 per cent in 1979. Working-class expenditure on cultural activities increased over the period, whereas that of *cadres supérieurs* declined.

In spite of this evolution, it remains true that even when a working-class household has the same level of income as that of a *cadre moyen*, the two do not have the same lifestyles and patterns of consumption. Differences in consumption patterns between the workers and the others are clearer when they have the same income: the *cadre moyen* spends comparatively more on new products, culture, leisure and holidays, whereas the worker spends more on food. It is obvious that the proportion of a family's income spent on food will be greater the lower the income is. However, for those on low incomes, the consumption of non-alimentary goods (especially in relation to quality of life and leisure products) depends more on social expectations than it does on income *stricto sensu*. Although *employés* may earn no more than industrial workers, they are likely to aspire to climb the social hierarchy and to imitate middle-class lifestyles. It is not usually the case that when women go out to work this changes the structure of the family's lifestyle: the income contributed to the family budget by working women usually serves to raise the family's lifestyle without fundamentally altering its structure. However, evidence does exist to suggest that the woman's salary is frequently used to pay off mortgages.

There is one important respect in which a manual worker's lifestyle is different from that of all other social groups: his working conditions remain radically different from those of all non-manual workers. One example is the number of hours worked daily: one urban industrial worker in four has left the house before 6.30 a.m., compared with 13 per cent of clerical workers. Likewise, night-time shiftwork continues to be the fate of many industrial workers, including women: this type of work has increased in recent years. Of course, working conditions vary considerably from one firm to the next, because of the state of technological developments and the skill of management. Taken as a whole, however, the working conditions which industrial workers are forced to accept (noise, monotonous rhythms, physical effort, and so on) are radically different from those which apply to clerical workers.

The incarnation of the working-class model is provided by the foreman.

The foreman shares the principal characteristics of other members of the working class, but represents them in an exaggerated form. His working conditions are similar to those of other workers, although he is given more responsibility, is better paid and has a degree of authority over fellow workers. The foreman not only supervises the workers, but acts as their spokesman and understands their grievances. The lifestyles and leisure patterns of foremen are much like those of other workers. Finally, foremen remain firmly attached to working-class culture and ideology. At home, working-class households spend more time on housework than their middle-class counterparts: an average of seven hours per day, as opposed to six. This can undoubtedly be explained by the fact that women from working-class households are less likely to go out to work than those from other groups in French society: in families with children, one working-class woman in two stays at home, compared with the average of one in three for other social groups. Moreover, working-class men are less willing to help with the housework, or to engage in DIY activities than their middle-class counterparts. Finally, working-class households are less likely to be equipped with luxury consumer durables such as washing-up machines, an omission which makes domestic duties more onerous for the housewife. The average male manual worker is shorter than the average male, but weighs no less; the obvious inference to draw from this is that the industrial worker is stouter than average. The clothes worn by adult members of the working class tend to be less varied and of less high quality than average, although parents make sure that their children are well dressed. In the long run, the proportion of the workers' budget spent on clothes has decreased faster than in the other social categories.

Because of the physical nature of their work, leisure for the worker tends to mean relaxation rather than physical activity; this sets him apart from most other members of society, for whom leisure is associated with activity (e.g. sport or DIY). Workers are more likely to bet on horses, to play Loto (the state-sponsored lottery), to watch sporting events or to spend their time in cafés. However, these pursuits are usually limited to male workers, and for this reason men and women lead very separate social lives. The café is the male bastion; the home, the female bastion. The whole family comes together for the annual summer holiday, usually a camping excursion to the sea or the mountains, rarely abroad. The workers are the social category within which ownership of caravans is the most extensive; the caravan represents the only expensive consumer durable which is more prevalent amongst the working class than higher up the social scale.

Kinship relations perform an essential role for all categories of French people (see chapter 8), but differences between social classes are important.

Visits to brothers and sisters are far more frequent amongst industrial workers and *employés* than in the rest of the population. *Cadres moyens* and *cadres supérieurs* place great emphasis on receiving friends at home, participating in meetings and joining local associations of all sorts. Popular patterns of life are far less formal than amongst the middle classes: manual workers or *employés*, for example, are unlikely to join an association (fewer than 30 per cent compared with 60 per cent for *cadres supérieurs*), or to attend meetings. For members of the working class, family relations (brothers, cousins and so on) tend to be closely interwoven with neighbourhood relations, since various branches of a working-class family are likely to live in proximity to each other. This is more rarely the case in middle-class families, in which relatives are more likely to live in another town; visits to relatives thus involve leaving one's area. None the less, for both the working class and for the middle-class groups of the central constellation, contact with relatives outside of their locality provides the most frequent link with the 'outside world'. Even those who leave their home town frequently usually do this in order to socialise with relatives living elsewhere.

Working-class sociability is characterised by the warmth of human relationships between individuals who feel themselves part of a community. Various forms of practical cooperation and help between friends and neighbours result naturally from this feeling of community. Working-class sociability is thus largely spontaneous and takes place outside of the home. Within the central constellation, however, social relationships are more formally organised, concentrated around the dining table: people invite friends for dinner-parties at fixed times and dates. From this angle, the programmed form of middle-class social life appears more 'superficial' than the more spontaneous working-class conviviality. It is probably fair to remark, however, that for its participants the middle-class variety of social life is far from superficial. The context and surroundings within which social relationships are formed and maintained vary considerably according to social class. Within the working class, social relationships tend to be limited to a narrow geographical area: home, neighbourhood and workplace. Relationships are forged through the force of daily repetition. Travel outside of the immediate vicinity is relatively rare. This restrictive pattern is not repeated with the central constellation, whose members more frequently have access to friends and relatives outside of the immediate surroundings of work and neighbourhood.

Patterns of home-ownership and types of residence are a further form of differentiation between the working class and the central constellation. The middle classes have a preference for home-ownership (if financially possible) and favour the model of the individual detached one-storey house, introduced into France by builders influenced by American building techniques. The working class are less likely to be able to aspire to home-ownership, and (whether renting or buying) tend to prefer houses with more than one storey. Differences in preference can be explained by the financially more unfavourable position of working-class families: the homes they are most familiar with are usually flats within multi-storey buildings. There are considerable variations within the working class itself. Foremen are far more likely to own their own homes, and to equip them with luxury consumer durables such as washing-up machines.

The analysis so far has been on distinctions that can be drawn between social classes, but increasingly important divergences separate members of the same social class. Indeed, French society is caught between the tendency towards homogenisation brought about by the breakdown in traditional class barriers, and the tendency towards diversification, because members of the same social class (or social constellation) are less likely to conform to any particular class models. The effect of centrifugal forces on the cohesion of a particular social group can be illustrated by looking at: public versus private sectors, generational differences, female employment and size of locality.

The division between the public and private sectors in France is probably of more relevance than in any other industrialised nation. The expression the public sector covers a variety of different realities in France. Public-sector workers include civil servants working for government departments, who are guaranteed security of tenure; workers in para-public agencies (such as nationalised industries, local councils, state hospitals, other govern-ment quangos and agencies), who generally enjoy favourable working con-ditions by comparison with their counterparts in the private sector, and teachers, who are guaranteed security of employment, unlike in Britain or the USA. Public-sector workers tend to vote more heavily for the left (especially the Socialist Party) than do comparative workers in the private sector, and look to the state to safeguard living-standards. Apart from the social groups of the independent constellation (shopkeepers, traders, small businessmen, professionals), who come entirely within the private sector, and teachers, almost entirely within the public sector, each main social group within French society can be differentiated internally by the division between the public and private sectors. This is one force which clearly leads to the internal diversification even of more homogeneous social groups such as industrial workers. The growth in unemployment in the last ten years has increased the antagonism between public-sector workers (gener-ally guaranteed security of tenure) and those in the private sector (occupy-ing a more tenuous position). Within the private sector, a further division can be made between the large firms, which offer workers relative security, and smaller firms, which are the first to lay off workers in a period of crisis. The fear and reality of unemployment is another factor of division within all social groups: no social group has been spared the threat of unemployment, which leads inexorably to downward social mobility for those afflicted, as well as to increased tensions within and between the main social groups.

Age is a further feature which might create differences within a social group. Those at both extremes of the scale enjoy far more leisure time than the mature working adults. It is important to distinguish between how these periods are lived by members of the different social classes. Amongst the youngest group (18–30), there is clearly a considerable difference between the charm of a university student's existence, and the petty criminality that the young unemployed are forced into in the deprived suburbs of large cities (see chapter 10). Likewise, amongst retired people, there is a world of difference between the comfortable existence of the well-off middle classes, surrounded by neighbours and relatives, and able to pursue cultural interests and so on, and the desperately poor, who often go short of essential food. Divergences between the lifestyles of different generations across the boundaries of social class can be very apparent, but so can tensions between different generations within the same social class.

A further source of differentiation within social classes might be that of female employment, between those households where the woman works and those where she does not. The impact of female employment is probably to blur the boundaries between social classes. This is especially the case in relation to the working class, since the effect of a woman working might be to allow a working-class family to rise up into the central constellation (a family's class being determined by the socio-economic position of the better placed of its two partners).

A final source of differentiation which cuts across class boundaries relates to the size of the locality in which people live. Patterns of social relationships vary according to whether people live in villages, small towns or large cities. In villages and small towns, people maintain often very close relationships with one another, and have many occasions on which to meet. In addition, all sorts of associations and groups propose objectives for the town, which gives people another opportunity to come into contact. The strength of identification with the village or small town is greater than with the large city. In these small towns, the hierarchy between different social classes is strong, and the higher up the social scale an individual is, the more likely it is that he will perform an active role in the life of the local community. Notwithstanding this, all individuals, whatever their social class, are more likely to play a part in the local community in these small towns and villages than in the impersonal large cities. The specific influence of social class upon behaviour is correspondingly likely to be less in small towns, especially when a working-class community lives in the midst of a predominantly middle-class environment and is influenced by middle-class lifestyles.

WITHIN THE HOME

The sharing of domestic duties by men has progressed less rapidly than is commonly supposed, especially if we believe the claims of Frenchmen and women themselves. Male participation in the household chores has increased most amongst the middle-class families of the central constellation. In contrast, both upper-middle-class and working-class families remain stubborn in their resistance to greater sharing of domestic work between men and women. In most French households, the DIY mentality has firmly taken hold, as the family attempts to achieve a degree of self-sufficiency in relation to maintaining the home, rather than continually calling in outside professionals to do essential maintenance work. Both men and women are often adept at do it yourself and gardening, and turn to outside professionals only as a last resort.

The growth in DIY can be illustrated by the increased sales of electric drills, garden tools, concrete mixers and so on. The take-off in the home improvement market in France in recent years has been impressive, as it has in other countries such as Britain. Home extensions have proliferated, usually resulting from DIY work carried out by members of the family themselves. Indeed, thanks to the emergence of many new products, home extensions and improvements can readily be carried out by the DIY amateur and there is no longer any need to pay someone to do the work. Even carpentry or plumbing is within the reach of anyone who knows how to use his hands. The money a household can save by DIY is considerable. Indeed, it is thanks to the growth of DIY that home improvements have flourished in the 1980s, a decade in which the official statistics point to a stagnation of living standards. Any evaluation of the extent and value of this domestic production is a hazardous exercise, but it is clearly of great importance in increasing the average household's living standards. Domestic production has a direct impact on the official economy, since any money saved through do it yourself can be spent on finished consumer goods.

The garden is another example of how attitudes have changed in the past thirty years. Until thirty years ago, the bourgeois garden was conceived of as an elaborate extension of the family home itself, an integral part of the domestic scenery, as well as being a pleasant place for after-dinner strolls (see chapter 1). Since the beginning of the nineteenth century, the bourgeois garden had served primarily an ornamental function and had been kept totally separate from the vegetable patch (hidden behind a wall or a hedge). The French bourgeoisie copied the meticulously organised gardens of the eighteenth-century English country gentleman. This nineteenth-century practice marked a breach with a still older custom, whereby the garden was a mixture of flowers, fruits and vegetables. During the nineteenth century, only the workers and peasants remained faithful to the older model of cultivating a vegetable garden, which served a valuable function in providing food for the family table.

In France today, more than half the population have a garden, either in their principal or secondary residence. All gardens tend to be organised in roughly the same manner: the front garden consists of a flower garden, a lawn, perhaps some trees; the back garden will contain a vegetable patch. The different ways in which a garden might be organised have lost all social significance, except in very subtle ways. The contrast between the front garden (ornamental) and the back garden (vegetable) prevails within all social classes, illustrating that the popular classes have become sensitive to notions of social standing and appearance. Whereas the vegetable garden used to be limited to peasant and working-class families, it has now become extended to the whole of society. The vegetable garden performs different functions according to social class. For those with a low income, fresh produce from the garden can contribute to the family's overall budget. For the *cadre supérieur*, however, the objective of the vegetable patch is not to save money, but to feel the satisfaction of consuming 'natural food' which one has produced.

At the core of 'domestic production' lies the calling into question of the distinction between consumption and production. To a greater or lesser extent, the household produces what it consumes, rather than buying it in the market-place. Such domestic production is in fact based on the main precept of the old peasant economy: there is no distinction between production and consumption, since both activities take place within the same household. The household is the sole economic actor involved. Activities such as gardening and DIY are perfectly suited to the middle-class groups of the central constellation. These activities promote all sorts of new social relationships and forms of mutual favour and exchange of services with other likeminded middle-class households. Whereas industrial workers have inadequate time or money for home improvements (although they tend their gardens conscientiously), and the very rich can usually afford to pay black-market workers to perform these tasks, the middle classes have become overwhelmingly converted to 'domestic production'. It is mainly within the central constellation that the social networks and leisure time combine to allow 'domestic production' (which requires both) to occur. The contrast is striking with unemployed manual workers. Once they leave the factory, such workers lose their entire social network – which makes it virtually impossible for them to find work on the black market. The importance of 'domestic production' within French society as a whole is a further illustration of the pre-eminence of the central middle-class constellation in France today.

INVENTING NEW LIFESTYLES

As a result of all the various trends identified above, the professional position occupied by the head of household is less and less of an indicator of the lifestyle a particular household chooses to adopt. In the last fifteen years, French society has become so fluid in certain respects that there has been a sudden, unexpected diversification in the different lifestyles that can be adopted. The reasons for this diversification are many, including the transformation of the nature of many professions and occupations; the high degree of social mobility resulting from this; and the various models portrayed by television. Social class is far less strong an indicator of lifestyle than ever before.

Before the transformations of the past thirty years, each family attempted to organise its lifestyle according to the norms of the social class to which it belonged, or more precisely, to which it aspired to belong. To incarnate the values of the social class to which a household belonged was the best way of ensuring recognition from other members of that same class and of reinforcing a household's social identity by defining itself as apart from other social classes. In today's France, individuals have far greater strategic liberty to decide which lifestyle to adopt, and are far less passively moulded by the norms of social class. In fact, lifestyle has become a matter of individual strategies, which can change over time. At each stage of his existence, an individual makes major strategic decisions which influence his future lifestyle. Examples of these choices are: whether to get married or remain single, whether to have children or not, whether to give priority to career or family, whether to save or spend, where to live, and which school to choose for the children.

The totality of these choices forms a sort of framework of the main different lifestyles, with infinite individual variations and modifications. In this new society, lifestyle can be analysed as 'the permanent arbitration between constraints and resources (time and money) by reference to an individual's value-system' (Curie et al. 1987). The distinction between constraints and resources is not always clear. For example, having relatives living nearby might initially be regarded as a constraint on an individual's time (the obligation of family visits), but might be transformed into a valuable resource if a grandparent can look after a couple's children. Whereas differences in income are being gradually reduced, non-monetary resources are more diversified than ever: the ability to manage a network of relatives, friends and neighbours, for example, can enable an individual to raise his material standard of living considerably.

The diversification in patterns of consumption and lifestyle between individuals is difficult to analyse because national statistics deal only with statistical averages, which bury differences in individual behaviour under a mass of generalisations. Assessing national statistics is thus of limited value in analysing behaviour-patterns. It is clear, for example, that lifestyle no longer depends only on the money a household has to spend, but also on the use it makes of all its resources, including non-monetary ones. In the mass consumer society, the range of goods and choices that an individual can procure with the same amount of money is immense. For example, an individual might buy a pair of light shoes, or a pair of hunting boots (probably indicative of two differing types of lifestyle). Or he might decide to spend his summer holiday travelling through France on a bicycle, or to stay on a camp-site. Moreover, the inequality of wealth within French society does not usually prevent the poorer sections of society benefiting from overall increased affluence. Virtually everybody can probably afford to take some sort of holiday on the French Riviera, although there is an enormous difference between a luxury villa with a garden going down to the beach, and the basic municipal camp-site next door. In reality, any individual has to make choices about his expenditure and activities. These choices and activities come together to form a lifestyle, underpinned by a coherent system of values and an individual strategy. Lifestyle is a concept of immense interest for the sociologist. However, the range of individual lifestyles can never really be gauged entirely accurately, since it is impossible to conduct detailed surveys of every individual.

The growth of the supermarkets is the best possible example of how individual choices have multiplied in the area of food. A rural housewife of the pre-1960 period was constrained to use an extremely narrow range of foodstuffs: produce from the garden and coffee, oil and noodles from the local grocers. Even within bourgeois households, where gastronomic standards were excellent, there was a narrow range of foodstuffs which could be consumed, limited to those available in the locality. This situation has been totally transformed by the growth of supermarkets, which offer a large variety of different foodstuffs and types of cuisine. The growth of ready-made frozen meals (which can be prepared rapidly in the microwave) has greatly expanded culinary choice: regional French dishes compete with exotic Mexican or Middle Eastern dinners. Alongside these ready-prepared dishes, the more active consumer can buy natural foodstuffs in bulk such as unshelled rice or bags of potatoes, or, indeed, can fill the freezer with a side of lamb (previously unimaginable in a less technological age). The supermarket promotes variety in all aspects of food consumption. It is through the supermarket, for example, that the French public has become aware of the existence of excellent cheeses from other countries, as well as of the great variety of French cheeses. The growth of supermarkets might be taken as one example of how individual choices help to shape lifestyles in a previously unprecedented manner. It is clear that the consumer society has been a factor promoting diversity in this respect.

During the 1960s, the French sociologist O. Guilbot carried out a series of surveys into how employees of traditional firms organised their households, compared with those who worked in modern companies. She discovered a correlation between the structure of a particular firm and the organisation of its employees' domestic life. The employees of the traditional firms adopted traditional modes of behaviour, especially in relation to finance: they were anxious to economise and save money to safeguard against future misfortune. The employees of more modern firms imitated practices of the company in their domestic lives. They were far more willing to go into debt in order to invest in equipment for the house, and were determined to enjoy the burgeoning consumer society because they had precise ideas and plans for the future. This second pattern of behaviour is that which prevails in today's France, especially amongst the younger generations and the *cadres*. This type of behaviour illustrates how individuals are less bound by tradition and more inclined to invent their own lifestyles.

For as long as the behaviour of consumers was strictly dependent on their income and their position within the social hierarchy, the task of salesmen and advertisers was easy. New products could be launched which appealed to the statistically proven preferences of particular segments of the population, and advertising techniques would be tailored to suit these preferences. Market surveys enabled a firm to identify which social groups favoured a particular product, and to ensure that advertising was targeted to appeal to the preferences of these segments of the population. But behaviour can no longer be crudely assigned to particular social classes: households from all social groups are inventing their own lifestyles in an unprecedented manner. This has made the task of advertisers far more difficult, since statistics can give a less accurate indication of the preferences of particular social groups than was previously the case. Advertisers must continually be on the lookout for new behaviour-patterns and changing ambitions. It must be stressed that in the new France, people are leading the advertisers, rather than the reverse. Certain advertisers have begun to identify different lifestyles as advertising categories replacing older notions of social class: for example, 'foxes', 'trendies', 'sixty-eighters' and so on. The same can be observed in Britain or the USA, with the explosion of 'yuppies', 'dinkies' and 'sinkies'. These are not real social classes with objective statistical boundaries; but they do correspond to groups with recognisable ideologies and discourses upon society. Recognition of such groups helps the advertisers anticipate movements in the market when social class has become an inadequate pointer. They cannot explain the functioning of society itself.

What is *fashionable* is of great importance in explaining how lifestyles are shaped in an extremely fluid and mobile society. The idea of fashion enables us to reconcile the image of homogenisation portrayed by advocates of mass society with that of diversification offered by sociologists. In traditional French society, fashion was virtually non-existent, limited to a few relatively unimportant areas such as dress. Fashion did not directly influence the main structures of society. In France today, however, fashion has penetrated all aspects of society, including patterns of demographic behaviour. For example, birth rates and the age of marriage are both subject to changing fashions in a manner which would have been incomprehensible to traditional French society. Fashion allows the individual a large degree of personal choice, but this personal choice usually lies within the conventions and underlying consensus accepted by most French people. Fashion is thus both an element of diversification (personal choice) and homogenisation (the range of choices usually falls within an accepted consensus). Of course, certain extravagant fashions, of dress for example, go well beyond what is considered normal by most people, but in so doing reinforce the feeling of consensus amongst the great majority. Fashion in France is no longer merely the preserve of the social élite, but can originate in any particular social group, especially within the middle-class groups of the central constellation.

We have seen in this chapter how lifestyles in contemporary France are composed of subtle blends of diversity and homogeneity, as well as how social location is far less important in determining lifestyle than it used to be. France is a nation undergoing a high degree of social mobility, in which most traditional ideas have become outmoded or have adapted. But a fluid social structure does not signify an unstable one: the process of calling into question established ideas and traditions is taking place within the framework of an overall consensus on the organisation and objectives of

French society. France is thus a nation characterised by growing social differentiation, but also by an underlying fundamental consensus which explains why the 'Second French Revolution' has been an entirely peaceful affair.

12

The cultural explosion

Prior to 1939, traditional French society was divided between a dominant bourgeois culture and a dominated popular culture. Popular culture (see below) attained its apogee during the interwar period, but this robust, jovial culture no longer exists. The victory of the left in 1936, the strikes and working-class celebrations which followed on its heels and the short-lived Popular Front government (1936/7) were the swansong of an urban popular culture which had been produced during the nineteenth century. After the Second World War, some well-intentioned left-wing intellectuals attempted to breathe new life into popular culture, in order that the 'people' might preserve its identity. However, this rearguard struggle was destined to failure: popular culture finally succumbed to the combined effects of the post-war increase in schooling, the gradual intrusion of television and the decline of the industrial working class.

By a similar process, rural peasant cultures had been fading away slowly since the end of the nineteenth century, and this process was accelerated in the immediate post-war years. It is difficult to imagine how peasant cultures could have survived for so long, considering that agriculture had occupied an increasingly less prominent position in the national economy after 1918. Since the nineteenth century imposed the obligation of universal education, the schools had been teaching French to generations of peasant children. One effect of this was to challenge the rationale for the continuing existence of a peasant culture distinct from that of all other groups within society. Traditional peasant cultures had been based upon the incredible regional diversity of the peasantry, partly expressed by the survival of regional dialects and languages (distinct from French) used in daily life. Once peasant communities began to lose their languages, they were on the way to losing their separate cultures. In many ways, the great paradox was that peasants themselves were determined that their children should learn French in order to give them access to national culture and improve their prospects of upward social mobility. The number and variety of regional dialects or languages which gradually succumbed to the universalist attraction of French was impressive: *oc, corse, provençal, breton, alsacien, flamand, basque, savoyard, normand* and so on. The Catholic Church contributed to the triumph of French by abandoning its traditional practice of conducting mass in Latin. The last generation of peasants, born before the First World War, who spoke a regional dialect before French, and who used to sing mass in Latin, is in the process of dying out in the 1980s. For the rural populations born during the inter-war period, French was universally the mother language, and even patois became diluted to include much of the French language. The efforts of the post-1968 regionalists have succeeded in preserving the existence of the most important regional languages, although these have disappeared from daily life. Indeed, these languages have been preserved as an extinct species might be preserved, and they are effectively dead. The best proof of this is that they are taught within universities, which refused until fairly recently to consider them as worthy objects of study. Regional languages are now taught like any other foreign or ancient language.

POPULAR CULTURE AND BOURGEOIS CULTURE

The 'dialectic' of the old confrontation between a dominant bourgeois culture and a subordinate popular culture is no longer relevant in today's France, moulded by the combined effects of universal education and the influence of the mass media.

The old bourgeois culture has lost its coherence, as well as its status as the example to be aspired to by lower social classes. The study of the classics (Latin and Greek), introduced first by the Jesuits in pre-revolutionary France and given great importance in Napoleon's *lycée*, has gradually faded away into oblivion. The classics no longer transmit a coherent vision of the world and a specific value system setting the bourgeoisie apart from the rest of society. It used to be accepted by the governing élite that the classics inspired a humanism based upon ancient Greek and Latin culture, which reinforced the eternal values of Christian morality. The knowledge of the classics possessed by a student who had obtained his *baccalauréat* in 1900 was far superior to that of today's high-flying candidate for entry into one of the *grandes écoles*. The successful *bachelier* of 1900 had a profound knowledge of Latin verse, had translated Homer and Sophocles into French and had learnt the works of Virgil and Horace by heart. Indeed, Greek and Latin mythology was familiar terrain; and the heroes of the ancient world became models to which the young bourgeois would refer to justify his superior position within society. That it was necessary to have studied ancient Greek in order to be able to pass the entry examination for Polytechnique illustrated the importance of the classics in preserving a sense of élite bourgeois culture. Only the best students, usually from bourgeois backgrounds, would study Greek at the *lycée*. Those who were to go on to one of the *grandes écoles* would be selected from this narrow social group. The importance of ancient Greek and Latin in contemporary France has decreased dramatically, not least because a sound competence in mathematics has become the essential ingredient in passing the entry examination for one of the *grandes écoles*.

One-half of French schoolchildren now receive no religious education whatsoever. This has meant that the Christian worldview shared by everybody in previous generations is totally foreign to many of today's young people. Whereas the committed anticlerical of old knew exactly what he hated about the church, his children are indifferent because they have no religious knowledge. It seems inevitable that the current generation will lose all trace of classical art and literature, no longer on the school curriculum because they are considered to be antiquated subjects. What used to be the central tenets of culture for all cultivated people have become rarefied subjects limited to a diminishing band of scholars.

The decline of bourgeois culture has meant that popular urban and peasant cultures have lost their autonomy and coherence. Both the old working-class and peasant cultures were dominated (either positively or negatively) by the learned, religious culture of the bourgeoisie. It is false to assume that the peasantry invented its own culture and folk-history independently of any reference to the dominant bourgeois class. Such assumptions are frequently made, since they respond to romantic sentimentality, according to which the old peasant cultures were in some sense pure, untainted with the corruption of urban society. This romantic vision of the peasantry is largely inaccurate, since peasant culture itself imitated traits of the dominant bourgeois culture at every turn. In reality, historians and anthropologists have demonstrated unambiguously that all forms of innovation within the peasant village (including technical innovation) came about because of pressures from outside, or in imitation of the dominant bourgeois culture. The influence of the dominant bourgeois culture on the culture of the working-class urban districts was even more obvious.

For at least a century, admirers of peasant culture have collected objects of peasant furniture or working utensils and kept them as collectors' items. In fact, such objects of peasant furniture, far from originating in rural France, were directly copied from models produced in the towns, influenced by the eighteenth-century Louis XV style. A similar process occurred in relation to peasant folklore and dress. 'Traditional' peasant clothes can in fact nearly all be dated from the nineteenth century, and were themselves copies of older urban fashions. Of course, imitation was not synonymous with slavish reproduction. On the contrary, peasant communities shaped the models they copied from the towns according to their own customs and regional traditions. This could be seen in relation to spheres as diversified as folk-history and 'traditional' songs, as well as in the types of furniture, dress-styles and tastes adopted by the peasants.

The influence exercised by bourgeois culture on the industrial working class was also considerable. Unlike the peasantry, the working class did not seek to imitate the bourgeoisie, or to aspire to its social status. However, by defining itself as being against the bourgeoisie, the French working class inherently recognised the importance of the class adversary's culture. More-over, the great French 'proletarian' thinkers, such as Proudhon, Jaurès, Guesde or Allemane, were all themselves products of the bourgeoisie. Although indirectly influenced by bourgeois culture, the French working class consciously rejected it, and formed itself into a defensive social group, determined to reject and rebel against the dominant bourgeoisie. Popular culture thus praised the struggle of the little man against the powerful. Underpinning the workers' culture was an unshakeable moral certainty that the 'people' were honest, but that those in positions of power were inherently corrupt. The vestiges of working-class culture which remain today are best embodied by the French Communist Party (see chapter 4).

The model outlined above of the dominant bourgeois culture and a sub-ordinate, dominated popular culture is no longer relevant. The emergence of the middle class as the central force in French society, in between the working class and the old bourgeoisie, has broken the dichotomy between dominant bourgeois and dominated popular cultures. In its place, a multi-faceted 'middle-class' culture has emerged. The new culture is one based not upon domination – as was the old bourgeois culture – but upon the dif-fusion of varied cultural influences to other groups within society. Culture no longer obeys the same rules. The 'ruling class' has lost its power to dictate cultural norms for the rest of society to follow. The most pervasive influ-ences on society as a whole are usually those which emerge from dynamic groups forming part of the central constellation, cultural influences and innovations which are subsequently extended upwards to the ruling élite and downwards to the popular constellation. In this new, far less regimented society, each social group has a large freedom of manoeuvre to decide what cultural influences it will obey, and how these will affect its behaviour. What is fashionable no longer depends upon what the bourgeoisie declares to be fashionable; instead, any group within society can invent modes of behaviour which are subsequently widely diffused throughout all other social groups.

CULTURAL POLICIES

Since around 1960, cultural activities of all sorts have blossomed in France. It was in 1960 that the well-known writer and art historian André Malraux became France's first minister at the head of a new culture ministry. Since then, the annual budget of the Ministry of Culture has grown three times more rapidly than that of any other ministry. In addition, the cultural budgets of other government departments represent approximately the same figure again. Finally, the amount that local authorities spend on cultural activities is considerable, having grown by an average of 10 per cent per annum since 1970. By the latter half of the 1980s, local authorities were spending twice as much on cultural activities as the central state. Cultural policy represents one of the proudest achievements of governments and enterprising local authorities in the past twenty years. A number of new para-public authorities have been created in recent years: the National Fund for Contemporary Art (FNAC) and the various Regional Funds for the Acquisition of Museums (FRAM) are two of the more important such organisations. Moreover, the amount given to museums and art galleries in private donations has increased dramatically.

The most rapid growth area has been that brought about by the local and regional authorities: regions, departmental councils and municipal councils have all promoted a broad range of cultural activities, including music, the plastic arts, libraries, museums, historical monuments, theatre and dance. Those towns and cities in the centre of a large conurbation spend more than other towns on the periphery of a conurbation, or than isolated towns. The structure of expenditure on cultural activities varies according to the type of town: those in the centre of large conurbations spend on average one-third of their cultural budgets on promoting musical activities, whereas towns in the suburbs spend 42 per cent on specialised cultural institutions and activities. The towns which spend proportionately the most are the medium-sized ones of around 100,000 inhabitants: the southern town of Avignon, famous for its annual festival, spends comparatively more than any other, devoting 22 per cent of its overall budget to culture in 1981.

These figures only partially reveal the extent of cultural activity in France, because they take no account of benevolent activities. The sphere of culture is one in which performers and artists are often willing to offer their services for free. The extent of such amateur activity is impossible to gauge, but it has probably increased even more rapidly than professional culture. Frequently sponsored by local authorities or other bodies, amateur groups attract large numbers of people to theatres, concerts, art displays and the like. Various sorts of paid organisers of cultural activities have developed in recent years such as museum curators, lecturers in art history at university, librarians, ethnographers, and music teachers in the numerous conservatories. The influence of these professionals can be of great importance in promoting the development of local and regional artistic circles, in which professionals and amateurs come together to appreciate art, music, literature or theatre. Such circles have proliferated in recent years, especially in medium-sized towns and regional capitals. Provincial artistic circles often maintain direct contact with the great Parisian art galleries. One consequence of this development in the field of art has been that the market for works of art is no longer limited to the specialists.

Under pressure from the development of these decentralised artistic circles, central governments have taken a great interest in the sphere of culture. In fact, governments and parties have realised that culture is of considerable political importance, and that the result of a toughly fought election can depend on it. The provincial circles of artists, musicians, or amateur dramatists constitute a new sort of clientele that can be courted by governments (and oppositions) in an attempt to win their support at election time. The political stakes are also real at local and regional levels. During the 1960s, far-sighted town councils constructed swimming pools to satisfy their electors' demand for sporting facilities; in the 1980s, they have been building museums and organising artistic festivals. In the course of the 1970s, many of the new Socialist Party activists devoted considerable attention to participating within cultural and artistic associations; it was within these decentralised organisations that PS activists became experienced *notables*, as well as immersing themselves in new cultural demands (many of which sprang from May 1968). But the right has also laid great stress on the importance of cultural activity, and certain Conservative-dominated local councils can point to their own achievements in this area.

The new prominence of culture within French society is reflected in the increasing amounts of money spent by the average family on cultural activities (3.3 per cent of the family budget in 1985). The real growth area is that of television and domestic audiovisual equipment, which has expanded greatly since the early 1970s: home videos, television, radio, tape-recorders, compact discs and so on. The audiovisual market represents 70 per cent of the total money spent by consumers on cultural products. The importance of various other sorts of cultural activity in France can be illustrated by some basic statistics. In 1980, 62 per cent of French people visited a *vieux quartier*, the frequently charming older districts well preserved in most French cities; 54 per cent visited a church, 48 per cent an antique shop, 46 per cent a local festival, 39 per cent a museum, and 18 per cent a château. Visits to the cinema remain extremely popular: in 1980, 52 per cent declared that they had been to the cinema at least once. However, certain forms of cultural activity retain a rather élitist character. Displays of modern art attracted only 20 per cent, the theatre 19 per cent, and concerts or opera 15 per cent. The dramatic increase in visits to museums, châteaux and exhibitions illustrates that the cultural public is growing and is consuming more cultural products than ever before. The latest cultural product is industrial archaeology, involving visits to old factories to observe early industrial techniques, working patterns and lifestyles.

Cultural activity has never been as healthy as it is in contemporary France. The attraction of culture can be gauged by the numbers of visitors the great monuments receive annually: even if we exclude Paris, the figures are frequently impressive. The picturesque old city of Carcassonne (in the southwest), for example, receives 200,000 visits from tourists per annum, and the religious monument of the Mont-Saint-Michel (Normandy), some 600,000. Of course, Paris continues to be one of Europe's great cultural centres, its attraction being reflected in the number of visitors received by its museums and historic monuments. The Louvre museum and the splendid Palace of Versailles (symbolising the grandeur of the old French monarchy) both doubled their number of visitors between 1960 and 1985 from 1,000,000 to 2,000,000. The intense public demand for culture recently forced the French Ministry of Finance to move its headquarters from the Louvre in order to increase the capacity for visitors. In 1984, the national museums received a total of 10,000,000 visitors. In addition, mention should be made of the Pompidou Centre, the modern library and art gallery which has been transformed into a major tourist attraction since its opening in 1978 (1,750,000 visitors in 1984). The most recent addition to the impressive array of French museums is the Musée d'Orsay, an old railway station superbly reconstructed as an art gallery. Finally, the bicentenary of the French Revolution in 1989 provided the occasion for the opening of the Opera of the Bastille, the latest monument in a long tradition of French culture.

The development of local festivals and markets has been substantial during recent years. In whatever region of France local festivals take place, they are capable of mobilising enormous energies from local populations. In 1987, for example, 35,000 people participated in the annual festival at the Château d'Hautefort in Périgord, far exceeding the population of the outlying villages. Markets provide another example of the vitality of local cultural life. Even the fleamarket organised by local traders and shopkeepers is often able to attract considerable interest from the local community. There has also been a revived interest in antiques, and more specifically in anything which revives the traditions of a bygone age: this can explain the rapid development of antique and second-hand shops. After a period during which everything new and modern was in fashion, French society adopted a preference in the 1980s for old objects, reminding citizens of a more traditional France which no longer exists.

The extent to which what is old and traditional has come back into fashion can be illustrated by the renewed importance of local folklore, especially in rural areas. Inhabitants of rural villages are only too willing to put on commercially profitable displays for town dwellers of how peasant communities used to live in the past. Similarly, old artisans put their old tools on display and give talks about the working methods they used in the past. In many senses this is largely artificial, geared towards commercial exploitation of urban sentimentality, but it is undeniable that such practices give the local communities a means of reviving their collective memory and strengthening their identity. They also correspond to a strong demand amongst the public as a whole for greater knowledge of and continuing reference to the past. It is as if social transformation has been so rapid that most people feel the need to find their bearings in a highly fluid and mobile society. Folk history is one central element of the increased cultural awareness of many French people. We saw above how during the past thirty years, the old pattern of culture being transmitted intact from generation to generation has broken down. The current interest in local cultures, especially amongst young people, can be interpreted as a means whereby the new generations are looking back to older cultures in order to decide which aspects of these can be integrated into the new cultural models and identities they are constructing for the future

DIVERSITY OF TASTES

Differences in cultural tastes and activities vary greatly according to social class, age, and level of education received. There are few differences between men and women, however. The current generation of young people engages in more numerous, intense and frequent cultural activities than its elders. But here the effect of age can probably be combined with that of generation: today's old people grew up at a time when cultural activities were reserved for a narrow élite. When the current generation of young people retires, the situation is hardly likely to be comparable, since they will have received an intensive cultural 'training' from youth onwards. Cultural activities are far more widespread in the large cities than they are in smaller towns and rural communes, with the exception of local festivals. In addition, the higher up the social hierarchy, the more active involvement in culture there is, especially amongst educated people.

In 1981, the French Ministry of Culture carried out a survey in which it classified people into four different categories with regard to their cultural behaviour. Firstly, there were the 'interested eclectics' (33 per cent of the survey). These were people who were interested in all sorts of culture, contemporary as well as more classical. Secondly, there were the 'less interested eclectics' (28 per cent of the survey), whose preferences were diversified, but whose commitment to culture was far less strongly marked. Thirdly, the 'ancients' (26 per cent) were primarily interested in the cultural legacy of the past. Finally, the 'modernists' (15 per cent) were interested in contemporary culture. The last category was composed mainly of young people cutting across class boundaries, whereas the 'ancients' were more likely to be older, concentrated in the private-sector middle classes (small businessmen, shopkeepers, artisans). The first group, the 'interested eclectics', was composed largely of *cadres* and the liberal professions. Within each of these categories, there were very few differences in cultural preferences amongst the various social groups forming the central constellation. The central constellation is inventing a new 'focal culture': i.e. cultural fashions are mainly determined within this group, and then subsequently spread out to influence the rest of society.

The vast majority (80 per cent) of French people own books, and a strong minority (41 per cent) declare that they own over 100 books. A comparison can be made between those who have the *baccalauréat*, and those with no educational diplomas. Unsurprisingly, the differences are strong: those with the *baccalauréat* all possess books, compared with only 61 per cent of those without any qualifications. Moreover, those with the *baccalauréat* are far more likely to possess books of a philosophical or political character (86.5 per cent) than are those without any qualifications (22.3 per cent). These differences are far less marked for history books, dictionaries, encyclopedias, practical books (gardening, cooking, DIY) and cartoons.

Sporting activities in France have known a similar explosion. This began in the 1960s: in 1957, there were 2,000 official sporting federations in France; by 1985 there were 12,000. Likewise, only 5 per cent of French people formed part of a sporting association in 1957, compared with 22 per cent in 1985. Sport is engaged in most by young people, especially by young men (although women are fast catching up). Once young people get married or live together, their enthusiasm for sport diminishes: whereas 32 per cent of single people declare that they participate in at least one sport regularly, this figure declines to between 20 and 25 per cent for people living in couples. The inclination to engage in sport rises with an individual's level of education. Students are the most enthusiastic category of the French population (as elsewhere), followed by *cadres*. Those higher up the social scale, such as industrialists, *cadres supérieurs* or the liberal professions, prefer individual sports to team sports, especially walking and jogging. Industrial workers, however (imbued with a higher sense of collective action and class solidarity), prefer group sports, especially football. Sport in France is engaged in more in the large cities than it is in small towns or rural villages. Proportionately more people engage in individual sports in Paris than anywhere else. The same is not true, however, for team sports such as football, which accounts for 70 per cent of people participating in team sports. Other forms of sport have grown rapidly in the past twenty years: martial arts (especially judo and karate); winter sports (especially skiing) and tennis (from 100,000 players in 1960 to 2,000,000 in 1985). In contrast, certain of the more traditional French sports, such as boule, have stagnated.

According to most studies of popular versus middle-class culture, there are easily recognisable differences between the two. Popular culture is centred around the neighbourhood and the household, whereas the focal culture of the central constellation is far more diversified in space and in time. To take just one example, workers tend to frequent the same local neighbourhood café, whereas the middle classes will move from café to café depending upon how fashionable any establishment is at a given time. There are qualitative differences between popular and middle-class cultures. Popular culture lays great importance on activities as ends in themselves: the neighbourhood café is a centre of social life breeding its own satisfactions, where workers can express their comradeship. Middle-class leisure patterns, by contrast, are more likely to be means to ends: whereas the worker will play boule for pure amusement, the *cadre* will go jogging in order to keep fit. Working-class leisure patterns lay great stress on ideas of solidarity and collective enjoyment. Workers frequent the café in order to be with other workers. They attend football matches in order to share a collective emotion. They récognise few constraints on letting their emotions be felt. In contrast, middle-class leisure patterns lay far greater emphasis on individual activities and satisfactions. Within popular culture, contact is spontaneous and informal, whereas within middle-class culture, contact with other people tends to be far more formal, and emotions are more strictly controlled. For this reason, the middle classes participate far more often in formal associations and groups; are more likely to invite friends formally to dinner (rather than meeting them in cafés), and go to pre-arranged functions such as concerts or theatre.

In contemporary France, certain cultural traits may be more prevalent in one class than in another, but few cultural practices are limited exclusively to one class. The internal coherence of both the popular and bourgeois cultures used to lend a totalitarian appearance to both which no longer exists.

The weakening of the older cultures has given each individual of whatever social class far greater liberty to determine how to behave than ever used to be the case previously. Each individual is free to pursue his tastes in accordance with what his financial means permit. Within the higher social categories, people will possess superior financial means and a more educated background, which will probably permit them to engage in more varied, demanding pursuits. However, there are only a few élitist cultural practices which are in reality the preserve of a small minority. Most cultural activities and leisure pursuits are prevalent in different proportions throughout all social classes. For example, a predominantly collective, working-class sport such as football attracts many middle-class players and supporters; similarly, an 'élite' sport such as tennis is not confined to the middle classes. The only group which can really be distinguished in leisure terms from other groups in the population is that of the 15–30-year-old age cohort, which leads a far more active and diversified cultural life than do older generations.

Music provides a good illustration of the cultural transformations that have taken place in post-war France, as well as of the different tastes prevalent within the main social groups. Although the French have never had a musical tradition as vigorous as that of the Italians, Germans or Russians, there is a wide variety of strong regional musical traditions in France. French musicologists are currently sparing no efforts to save traditional songs and dances from extinction; they have succeeded so well that many nearly forgotten folksongs have once again become popular in local folk festivals. Another form of preservation is that exercised by the church, which has carefully preserved religious chants and hymns, especially in regions where religion is widely practised. During the nineteenth century, village bands developed rapidly, partly under the impact of the popularity of patriotic songs. These local musical traditions declined during the inter-war period and appeared on the verge of disappearing until a musical revival started towards the end of the 1960s. Since the late 1960s, there has been an explosion in the number of local orchestras, choirs and musical groups of all types.

Traditionally, two different musical instruments symbolised the division between popular and bourgeois cultures in the sphere of music: the accordion and the piano. The accordion was the popular instrument par excellence, and would be danced to in the working-class cafés. It was no coincidence that the accordion symbolised popular culture during the Popular Front era. The piano was the main musical instrument in bourgeois circles. The grand piano was a prerequisite of any bourgeois living-room, whereas the petty bourgeoisie would display a more modest upright piano in the dining-room. The past omnipotence of the accordion as the main popular instrument no longer survives; it has been replaced by the guitar. One French person in two can claim to play the guitar at least to some extent, especially amongst the young (whereas the accordion used to be played by all age-groups). Piano-playing became extremely rare during the decades immediately following the war, although it has somewhat increased during recent years. Finally, wind instruments are becoming more popular, with 20 per cent of households possessing at least one in 1981, compared with 13 per cent in 1973. However, the guitar and the piano are the two most commonly played instruments.

Recorded music erupted into French households during the 1960s. In 1981, 70 per cent of French households possessed at least a record-player and a record collection. The types of people who listen most to music are those with a high degree of cultural awareness: university graduates, educated single people, the young (especially students), *cadres supérieurs* and Parisians. However, no social group is excluded from enjoying music. Although *cadres supérieurs* (81 per cent) are the most likely to listen regularly to music, over half of the unskilled worker category (57 per cent) regularly appreciate music, the least musically conscious group being farmers (29 per cent). The degree of education is also an indicator of the musical awareness of an individual, since 76 per cent of those with the *baccalauréat* regularly listen to music, compared with only 38 per cent of those with no educational qualifications. The type of music most frequently listened to is the song, with most households now possessing record-players and a record-collection. Rock, pop and folksongs (with 49 per cent of regular listeners) are clearly more popular than classical music (41 per cent), and are continuing to increase their popularity. More élitist forms of musical entertainment, such as dance (17 per cent) and opera (13 per cent), are restricted to a more select public, itself a diminishing proportion of the population as a whole. Rock, pop and folksongs are generally listened to by the youngest age-cohorts, whereas classical music and opera remain largely the preserve of the *cadres supérieurs*. One consequence of the penetration of recorded music is that French people are now less likely than in the past to perform in public themselves.

A nation's language is the main instrument of its culture, and the best means of differentiating between different groups within society. Speaking in a refined, precise and elegant manner is a sure sign that an individual possesses a high degree of culture. When foreign observers analyse France, they usually consider that it is a country which attaches great importance to the need to speak French correctly. This is especially the case for politicians, who must be able to express themselves well in a grammatically and linguistically correct manner. Such a ritualistic attitude is illustrated by the importance placed on spelling in primary and secondary schools. That the Académie française is the only institution in which antiquated rituals and ceremonies have survived testifies to the sacred status of their language for the French. The Académie française consists of a small group (forty) of highly learned and distinguished scholars, men of letters and artists, dedicated to the propagation of the French language and culture. In its ceremonial detail, the Académie française offers a spectacle whose only parallels are the British monarchy and the Vatican. The uniform has completely disappeared from French society, except for army officers. The Académie française is the only institution in which the wearing of uniforms retains a great symbolic importance. To don the cloak of the Académie and to carry the sword is the sign of admission into the small band of immortal scholars.

The 1960s probably marked the high point of correctly spoken French throughout the country as a whole. Classical, scholarly French was taught in the nation's schools, and even spoken by policemen in their dealings with ordinary citizens. The need to speak French correctly was widely accepted throughout society, even amongst those who were incapable of writing fluent, correct French. Since the 1960s, uniform standards of French have been increasingly neglected by certain groups within society, and patterns of speech have become more dependent on social background. Purists of the French language have profoundly regretted what they consider as a lowering of standards, and have blamed poor methods of teaching French in schools. In fact, it seems that a whole series of popular variants of the official French language are being recreated. These variants are bound both by social class and regional linguistic differences. The new forms of popular French have their own syntactical norms and particular uses of vocabulary. The popular varieties of French that have been emerging since the 1960s are considered legitimised by the language used in certain popular songs and in films on the television.

The role of the mass media, and of television in particular, is a complex one. Television has reached every French household, complemented by the growth of other media (radio, the press). The expansion of television has helped promote a unified national cultural market (based on a number of consensual cultural beliefs shared by all French people), as well as encouraging the development of more specific cultural markets, appealing to particular segments of the population. Each viewer is able to select what interests and satisfies him, and this selectivity has brought about a diversification and specialisation of programmes. Growing specialisation can be illustrated in all areas of culture: for example, the music industry has expanded rapidly by catering for a broad range of tastes, from opera to reggae. In fact, although tastes vary somewhat according to social background, it is no longer true to argue that there exist two mutually exclusive bourgeois and popular patterns of leisure. Evidence to support this assertion can be provided by the classic bourgeois sports, such as tennis, horse-riding and golf, which are all becoming open to everybody.

We have illustrated above that France used to be a society which was highly polarised between mutually antagonistic bourgeois and popular cultures (each portraying total, and hence incompatible, visions of society). Alongside these two conflicting cultures, there existed a number of relatively autonomous peasant cultures. In today's France, there is one national culture (albeit a pluralistic one), the elements of which are accepted by all French people. This culture is essentially based upon aspects of the older bourgeois culture which have been extended to cover all groups within society. Despite the existence of one national culture, a large number of particular, even particularised, cultures have developed. In this way, the same individual can share with everybody else an acceptance of the main traits of the national culture, as well as investing time and effort in particularised cultures. Within the confines of the national culture, individuals are free to invent their own particular cultures, which need not conform with any pre-established models. This is in stark contrast with the traditional pattern whereby the duty of the 'honest' citizen was to aspire towards the ideal of a good grounding in the classical humanities, and being a good Christian. Each individual can now invent his own culture. For that reason French society is radically different from what it has been at any stage in the past.

13

A moral revolution?

The 'revolutionaries' of May 1968 rediscovered the old revolutionary themes of 1789, of 1848, and of the libertarians of the nineteenth century. May 1968 came after a period of intense moral austerity during the 1950s, when France stiffened its moral fibre in an effort to stimulate the nation's rebirth, and adopted a new work ethic. It took the form of an explosion of youthful joy. In comparison with the drab attire worn by the workers, *employés* and *cadres* in the 1950s, the young demonstrators of May 1968 dressed themselves in colourful, provocative clothes to illustrate their desire for personal freedom. In May 1968, the generation of young people born in the post-war 'baby-boom' noisily rejected the puritanical atmosphere within which it had been brought up.

The ideological commotion given expression by the events of May 1968 divided France into two. Conservatives refused to see in the demonstrations anything other than a riot aimed against the immutable moral order, which had to be defended against the activities of an irresponsible youth. In the other camp, the students' act of defiance heartened the souls of all those alienated by the technocratic society created under Gaullism. For its supporters, May 1968 signified the momentary triumph of the joy of living over false rationality and boredom.

What remains of May 1968 twenty years later? Most obviously, there is a continuing cleavage between those who regard May 1968 as a fortunate series of events, and those who condemn it as a menace to an ordered society. This cleavage cannot be reduced to one separating left and right, or even young and old. It is true, of course, that left-wing sympathisers and young people are generally favourable to the memory of May 1968, but so are many older people and right-wing sympathisers. Many of the young idealists of May 1968 have made a reluctant peace with existing society, and taken up functions in new, marginal institutions, where they have maintained the belief (or illusion) that they are helping to change society, without challenging the principal tenets of it. But the purest idealists have never adapted to the failure of May 1968 to achieve its more exotic ambitions. These puritans of May 1968 have become marginalised from society, and withdrawn into apathy. At the other extreme, within certain institutions (especially the universities), a number of *soixante-huitards* have not given up the struggle and continue to believe in the necessity for and possibility of a radical change of society. If we except these die-hards, most French people regard May 1968 as a symbolic cleavage between the Party of Order and the Party of Movement – just as the great French Revolution of 1789 was regarded during the nineteenth century.

The events of 1968 were not limited to France: in all Western industrial nations, protest movements by young people temporarily shook the existing political order, but without any lasting effect. Nowhere did these movements overthrow existing political institutions, which emerged strengthened in the 1970s, except briefly in Czechoslovakia. In the USA, passionate divisions over involvement in Vietnam gave rise to a protest movement which had lost confidence in American democracy, but which did not threaten its survival. In France, the events of May 1968 seriously damaged de Gaulle's authority and were followed by his retirement in 1969, but that year also witnessed the peaceful transition of power to President Pompidou which signified a strengthening of the Fifth Republic. In Germany and Italy, the legacy of the radical protest movements of the 1960s was the emergence of Communist-inspired terrorist groups in the 1970s, dedicated to using violence to overthrow the state.. These groups (Bader Meinhof in West Germany, Red Brigades in Italy) were marginal, overwhelmingly rejected even by Radical opinion, and did not succeed in their objective. In West Germany, the Greens took over the legacy of Radical protest from the Reds during the 1980s and have become a major political force. Only Great Britain escaped from the turmoil of youthful protest during the 1960s, despite the fact that British young people had been at the forefront of new fashions in music and dress since the beginning of the 1960s.

WHAT REMAINS OF MAY 1968?

In France, the decline of the great social movements of the 1970s, which expressed many of the aspirations of May 1968, has been quite remarkable and unexpected. Pacifist, ecologist, regionalist, feminist, extreme left and other 'alternative' groups assumed considerable importance during the 1970s but faded away during the 1980s. In 1981, the election of François Mitterrand symbolised the hopes of these various Radical, youth-dominated movements, but by 1986 he had lost credit in their eyes, and was 'cohabiting' as President with a Conservative government. The various original movements to which May 1968 gave birth have all been absorbed by the existing institutions of French society. Many considered that the Ecologists would form themselves into an effective anti-establishment Radical movement as the Greens did in Germany. Throughout the seventies, however, the influence of the Ecologists as an autonomous political movement remained slight, partly because the environment was recognised as a legitimate issue by existing political forces; and partly because of the divisions of the Ecologists themselves into left and right. The creation of a Ministry of the Environment testified to the importance of 'green' issues, but underlines that these could be dealt with by existing political machinery. The breakthrough of the Ecologists in the late 1980s could not be regarded as a direct legacy of May 1968, but rather as an indication that environmental issues had suddenly become a central preoccupation of society. The Ecologists in 1989 were far more 'respectable', far less eccentric than their predecessors of the 1970s. Their success itself reflected the absorption of green issues into the political mainstream. A similar pattern of absorption can be observed in relation to feminism: after many heroic struggles (and several historic victories), the force was taken away from the feminist movement by the creation of a Ministry of Women's Rights in 1981. Likewise, regionalism and regional cultures, which flourished during the 1970s, lost their zest in the 1980s. On a cultural level, the demand for regional awareness and self-expression became diluted into support for local festivals, folk music and regional dialects or languages. On a political level, the 1982 decentralisation legislation took the wind out of regionalist movements, since their leaders were coopted to serve on the new regional councils and were drawn into the system.

The various movements inspired by May 1968 have thus served mainly to place new issues on the political agenda, which existing political institutions have usually been able to absorb and articulate. In addition, the leaders of these movements have acquired positions of social and political responsibility and have themselves become *notables* in the institutions they previously fought against. The activists at the forefront of May 1968 have become journalists, advertising staff or university lecturers. Even the originally ultra-left newspaper *Libération*, which symbolised many of the more extreme demands formulated in 1968, has been transformed into a highly respectable daily, whose original style has influenced other sections of the press.

How can we explain the fact that such an imaginative and enterprising generation as that of May 1968 has not been imitated by succeeding generations of young people? When they reached adulthood, the children of the baby-boom were determined to shake up existing society in order to secure their own place within it, by ensuring that it took greater account of their aspirations than did the austere 1950s. By loudly demonstrating its demands, the 1968 generation was able to call into question certain established behaviour-patterns and attitudes. However, once society had recognised its existence, the May 1968 generation integrated itself within the social main-stream. The next generation failed to follow in the radical early foot-steps of its predecessor and showed little disposition to reject society. Arguably, it was too preoccupied by the onset of economic crisis in the 1970s and by the threat of unemployment to allow itself the luxury of protest. Some would argue that the influence of the May 1968 movement, which had been fuelled by the new aspirations stimulated by post-war economic growth, disintegrated with the onset of economic crisis; others, that May 1968 was a movement limited to a minority of young middle-class students and that the mass of the population supported the demonstrations and strikes but never really accepted the demands.

Many people believed that as a result of the libertarian values expressed in May 1968, permissive attitudes would extend into every sector of society. In the sphere of values, morality and behaviour, it was widely predicted that a profound revolution would occur, and even that Western societies would begin to consider themselves and the world from a fundamentally different viewpoint. When the record is set straight twenty years later, it is an ambiguous one: those areas in which nothing has really changed are prob-ably more important than those where there has been substantial change. Of course, the question whether society has been fundamentally transformed is partly a subjective one, depending upon the relative importance accorded to different criteria, and upon varying methods of analysis or nuances or appreciation. No comparative studies exist to allow us to make a detailed judgement on the extent of change after May 1968 in France.

One of the most forceful themes expressed in May 1968 was that of 'everything straight away'. This slogan was an extreme expression of the gradual advance of hedonistic values in French society. The fact that the pursuit of pleasure and enjoyment, previously considered as bad and dangerous, is today recognised as legitimate and desirable, is more of a change in moral norms than in actual behaviour-patterns. The bourgeoisie of the nineteenth century professed a respect for rigorous moral codes in public and in the workplace, but insisted upon pleasure and comfort in its private life. The bourgeois *maîtresse de maison* devoted considerable time and attention to ensuring that the house lacked no material comfort: lined sofas and armchairs, festooned curtains, and above all the finest dining table, where the best food and wines were served with the highest-quality silver, porcelain and crystal. The work ethic and the puritanism preached in schools and in church were reserved for the factories and the fields, but gave way to the pleasures of good living at home.

This curious mélange of opposing principles was rediscovered in many different spheres, in relation to sexual morality, attitudes towards money and work, and in the general outlook on society. It was the very essence of bourgeois morality (some would say hypocrisy) which was in stark contrast with the sense of honour of the English gentleman or French aristocrat, of the ascetic puritanism of the industrial entrepreneur, or – at the other extreme – of the carefree attitude of the worker. The inter-war economic crisis forced all social groups to economise and cut back; this was followed by the imposition of a work ethic in order to favour national economic reconstruction after the Second World War. Thus for a total of some fifty years, French society experienced grey austerity. Only after 1965 did 'the spirit of enjoyment triumph over that of sacrifice'.

The Catholic Church shared in this general evolution. Until the Second Vatican Council (1965), the church expressed a moral theology which presented earthly existence as a vale of tears, from which the only escape for the righteous was eternal life after death. This theology was replaced by another which preaches that happiness on earth is a premiss for eternal happiness after death. Work was no longer regarded as a divine curse to punish mankind for original sin, but as an opportunity for the individual to realise his full potential. This message had been preached by Protestants since the sixteenth century. A morality based on failure and suffering gave way to one which encouraged earthly success and licit pleasure. The chaplains of the Young Christian Farmers (JAC – see chapter 1) were undoubtedly the first to express this ideological turnaround, which appeared all the more radical in that they addressed themselves to the children of peasants who had been brought up according to the old theology. The leaders of the JAC instructed their followers in the need for economic and technical success, which should be justly rewarded by financial profit. They despised the small peasants in the process of proletarianisation, and gladly abandoned them to the Communist union MODEF. The biblical parable of the rich man having the greatest difficulty in entering the kingdom of God had suddenly been forgotten.

Material prosperity and the absence of serious world conflict have had the effect that since 1945, French people have felt themselves to be in greater material and physical security than ever before. The opening line of the Lord's Prayer, 'Our Father in Heaven, give us our daily bread', no longer seems relevant to the well-fed people of the West. Their material security is akin to that experienced by the bourgeoisie during the nineteenth century, a class which feared nothing except revolution, since it possessed its own *patrimoine*, and was secure in its position in society. The great majority of the French population today find themselves in a similar situation, except that their material prosperity and social status depend upon working (which was generally untrue for the bourgeois gentleman of the nineteenth century). Just like the bourgeois of the last century, the average French citizen, secure in his material prosperity, social security and status, is able to devote far greater time to aesthetic and intellectual needs and to resolving problems of personal identity than ever before.

OPINIONS, VALUES AND SENTIMENTS

Every opinion pollster knows that the opinions he measures are those of individuals at a given time in relation to a given subject in a particular context. These opinions are frequently volatile and unstable; indeed, fluctuations in public opinion are the professional norm which the pollster must register and interpret. Public opinion is especially volatile in relation to political issues and personalities. There is nothing more normal than a politician who is at the height of his popularity only months after being in the doldrums. But behind these temporary, variable opinions, psychologists identify a set of more stable attitudes, character predispositions and preferences. How, if at all, have these stable attitudes changed during the last twenty years? Which attitudes have changed, and which have remained stable? It is difficult to respond with any accuracy to these questions, since opinion surveys posing the same questions over a period of years are too recent an invention in France to be able to measure the variation of attitudes over extended periods with any degree of confidence. Surveys based upon international comparisons have taken place, but these are generally rather superficial.

Unfortunately, with the statistical evidence available it is impossible to judge France in a comparative context over an extended period of time. There is, however, one comparative European survey that can usefully be referred to (Stoetzel, 1983), in which it is revealed that three-quarters of Europeans declare that they are happy. The morality embodied in the Ten Commandments is still that which, *grosso modo*, governs European morality. It is true, of course, that there are fewer and fewer moral certainties, and that few now consider themselves competent or authorised to judge the morality of other people. The general air of permissiveness has bred a large degree of tolerance towards others, which makes it far easier than previously for each individual to construct his own lifestyle and set of moral codes. The values which Europeans espouse can be classified according to two different types: firstly, the 'traditional' values such a honesty, good manners, obedience, patience, careful housekeeping (*esprit d'économie*); secondly, the values of change (tolerance, sense of responsibility, perseverance, imagination). European citizens divide their preferences almost evenly between these two differing types of values. The most coveted value is that of honesty (73 per cent), immediately followed by tolerance (51 per cent), respect for others (51 per cent), good manners (49 per cent) and a sense of responsibility (46 per cent). The mix between 'tradition' and 'change' lends a strong element of balance and continuity to European values. It should be emphasised, however, that public opinion respects the rights of the individual more than the need to conform with the rules of society. For example, more people consider that respect for other people's rights is of greater importance than good manners. This shift towards respect for individual rights over deeply ingrained social conventions is of considerable importance in the new European value system: it testifies to the fact that we live in a new era of tolerant individualism.

The development of a more permissive society has not meant that the great institutions of social constraint have lost their prestige. A majority of European citizens are proud of their country, although only 5 per cent declare themselves willing to sacrifice their lives in defence of it. Most European citizens place their confidence in their police force and army; a rather weaker proportion in the law, the church and the education system; a mediocre proportion trusts Parliament or the civil service; and a weaker percentage still is satisfied with big business, trade unions or the press. Of all social institutions, the police are by far the most popular, coming far ahead of the next four (army, legal system, education system, church). This is in stark contrast with Parliament. A low level of confidence in Parliament throughout Europe correlates with little interest in politics: 58 per cent of the sample claimed to have little interest in politics compared with 36 per cent who were interested and only 5 per cent who participated actively.

The church provides an example of a European social institution whose prestige is in decline everywhere. This loss of prestige has occurred despite evidence pointing to the continuing strength of the basic tenets of religious belief: three-quarters of European citizens declare a belief in God, nine-tenths declare that they belong to a particular religion, and two-thirds proclaim that they are religious and believe in life after death (including reincarnation). However, barely more than half of European citizens express their total or partial confidence in their nominal church; Protestants have less confidence than Catholics. The institution of the church has thus lost prestige even though minimal religious beliefs appear to resist the trend towards secularism.

Opinion polls assess a large variety of values and beliefs; often disparate in nature, these beliefs can usually be articulated in terms of an opposition between left and right. Polls frequently situate beliefs on the basis of a left/right scale, going from extreme left to extreme right and passing through a varied number of intermediary stages. Despite the pitfalls in this approach it does enable pollsters to simplify a complex variety of beliefs into a given number of philosophical positions, and to impose a structure on otherwise disparate beliefs. The value of a left/right scale is that no one has any difficulty in identifying where they stand in relation to this most basic political division. A number of variables are likely to influence where an individual locates himself on the left/right scale, such as degree of religious practice, social class, importance of *patrimoine* and home ownership. Detailed analysis of these variables is outside the scope of this book; my concern is to assess the philosophical positions and character predispositions associated with left and right.

The more leftist an individual's views, the greater the likelihood that he will favour equality in relation to liberty, and vice versa. The spirit of obedience and attachment to country is far more strongly marked on the right of the political spectrum and declines the further left one moves. In contrast, freethinking and internationalism are characteristics associated with the left rather than the right. Interest in politics increases sharply the further left an individual is situated on the scale, as does active participation in voluntary groups and determination to persuade others of one's political point of view. Confidence in institutions is a characteristic associated more with the right than the left, except in the case of trade unions.

Positions on the left of the scale constitute a challenge to existing society, and are associated with a general anxiety about all aspects of life. Those who situate themselves on the left of the scale are more likely to consider that life has no sense, that the family is an imperfect source of satisfaction, that their work is unsatisfying and that their income is inadequate. It is, of course, true that those on the left are more likely to have lower incomes and less rewarding occupations, and are less likely to be property-owners. The further an individual is to the left, the more likely he is to be dissatisfied with everything. An example is health: the further to the left an individual is, the more likely he is to complain about his health. Values associated with the left which challenge the traditional order and belief-patterns appear to be more widely disseminated within society than they probably are, because they are frequently expressed in the mass media (a platform for spokesmen of minority interests). The frequent expression of such values (atheism, revolution, sexual liberty, permissiveness, excuses for terrorism) gives the impression that traditional values are dying out, but this is far from being the case.

Left-wing and right-wing extremists have a number of traits in common. Both stress the importance of political activism, both are relatively isolated (young and single people on the left, older and widowed people on the right), both are intolerant and worried about the future. Left-wing extremists consider that life has no sense, right-wing extremists fear war or revolution. In other words, neither left-wing nor right-wing extremists are happy: they are two and a half times more likely to declare themselves unhappy than are non-extremists. Right-wing extremists support order and condemn marginal behaviour-patterns. They place considerable import-ance on socio-economic status when judging other individuals. Finally, they are relatively satisfied with their social and economic position and their family life. Left-wing extremists, by contrast, are strongly individualistic, and tolerate marginal forms of behaviour (homosexuality, use of drugs). They have little confidence in existing institutions, participate regularly in demonstrations, and support all new forms of protest. They are generally dissatisfied with their socio-economic and occupational position, and favour notions such as equality, workers' control and citizen-participation in decision-making. Left-wing extremists usually declare that they had strict parents, whereas non-extremists on the left were brought up in a tolerant family environment.

In an extended survey of attitudes, one opinion poll organisation, Cofremca, has measured socio-cultural currents within French society over the past twenty years. Short-term developments often appear erratic and disparate, but long-term trends can be discerned which have been reinforced over a period of time. These long-term tendencies were first enregistered amongst a small number of dynamic social groups during the 1960s, but they have since become extended to all sections of society. Six main long-term socio-cultural tendencies illustrate how the ways of think-ing and moral codes of French people have changed. These are:

1. The French used to have a profound need for order in all aspects of life. For example meals had always to take place at the same time, the table to be laid in the same way and the courses follow in the same order. This ordered ritual has been replaced by disorder, with no set pattern prevailing. The example of the meal might be extended to illustrate a more general social phenomenon: disorder has replaced order, and the French have had to learn how to manage complexity and uncertainty.

2. The average French person used to believe that in order to protect him-self from danger, it was necessary to protect himself and his family from the intrusion of others. This pattern has changed, and greater sociability has modified a distrust of strangers. Social relationships have become far more

subtle, less governed by ritual and formality. This change in outlook was introduced by young people, but has spread to all age-groups in all different social categories.

3. This evolution has been accompanied by a search for one's roots. Young people have displayed an ability to become rooted in any new social and geographical milieu within which they find themselves. Such flexibility initially worried their parents, who had been brought up to believe that social and geographical mobility were both forms of uprooting, and hence destabilisation. The ability of young people to adapt and feel themselves at home in any situation has meant that roots have become mobile.

4. The need for self-expression and personal fulfilment has become a major motivation for most French people. Older values such as social standing, which limited personal self-expression to an individual's position within society, have become less important. The result of this development has been a breakdown of many old attitudes and behaviour-patterns.

5. Sight used to be the privileged sense in Western Europe, with beauty always in the eye of the beholder. During the past twenty years, the other senses have become more and more developed: music, gastronomy and fine perfumes correspond to the new importance of hearing, taste and smell.

6. The need for achievement has grown sensibly, although not in an entirely linear fashion. Towards the end of the 1970s, this urge seemed temporarily out of fashion with the new generation of young people, but this is no longer the case. Success is again considered an integral part of personal realisation.

The strengthening of socio-cultural undercurrents in French society during the past twenty years has stressed the primacy of individual objectives and the satisfaction of self over collective objectives and the construction of society. In the past, for example, *cadres* would work extremely hard in order to serve their company because they were proud to be associated with it. Today, they work equally hard in order to ensure that the company is competitive, but their motivation is no longer corporate pride so much as the knowledge that their own position depends upon the success of the company. Outside of the workplace, the French display endless initiative and savoir-faire. More and more people spend an increasing amount of time engaging in cultural, social and associative activities, from which they draw a direct personal benefit in terms of self-fulfilment. A parallel might be drawn between this evolution in the past twenty years in France, and the situation which exists in the USA, whose citizens have always believed that it is the role of the individual, not the state, to manage his own affairs. The development of individualism and the greater inclination to engage in voluntary group activity have thus brought France closer to the USA.

As behaviour-patterns and moral codes have become diversified, they have also become less of a constraint on the freedom of the individual; to a greater or lesser extent, everybody can now define his own model of behaviour without being rejected by others. The best example of this is in relation to personal sexual behaviour. Attitudes towards sexual behaviour have been radically modified since the austerity of the 1950s. The first signs of a relaxation of traditional attitudes towards sex and nudity appeared during the 1960s, when the first nudes appeared on the cinema, in magazines, on posters, and finally on the beaches. The taboo surrounding nudity has become so weak that parents do not hesitate now before showing themselves nude in front of their children. The extent and rapidity of this revolution is remarkable: nudity in public disappeared in any form over one thousand years ago, as Christianity gradually asserted its control over the Western world. The reversal of this trend was complete in a mere twenty-five years.

Likewise, taboos surrounding sex and attitudes towards virginity have completely changed. There can be little doubt, however, that it is professed opinions and values which have changed rather than actual behaviour-patterns (always 'laxer' than avowed in public). The Catholic, bourgeois norm of the absolute imperative of virginity at marriage was imposed only on women and not in practice on men, although in theory sex outside of marriage was strictly forbidden for both men and women. In many peasant communities, however, sexual relationships before marriage were widespread and accepted, since they were a means of ensuring that a couple would have children who would in time inherit the farm and preserve the family lineage. Marriage thus followed conception, rather than preceding it as in the bourgeois model. The peasant model was imitated in many working-class communities. In fact, the 'norm' of virginity at marriage, which was proclaimed by all moral and religious institutions and demanded by nearly all Frenchmen, was in practice rejected by a strong minority, possibly a majority, of Frenchwomen. This norm no longer applies in contemporary France, but it should not be deduced from this that no women are virgins at marriage: many young Frenchwomen will only ever experience one sexual partner.

The manner in which sex is talked about has changed even more radically than sexual morality. Within bourgeois circles, sex was not a fit topic of conversation, although the French stopped short of the English Victorians, who invented numerous periphrases to refer to different parts of the body, including the stomach. The subject of sex was never raised in the bourgeois family, but boys would talk secretly to each other about it, and overhear the servants' gossip in the kitchen. Within aristocratic or artistic circles, however, sex was a normal topic of conversation. This was even more true for the working classes, for whom sex formed the substance of jokes and malicious gossip. During the past twenty years, sex has become the most popular theme for women's magazines and is no longer a taboo subject, even in family conversations in front of young children. A recent French anti-AIDS television campaign was centred around the use of condoms in preventing the spread of the disease; such frankness would have been unimaginable even twenty years ago, when the magazine *Paris-Match* caused a scandal by asserting that masturbation was not harmful for boys.

As with sexual matters, the bourgeoisie is no longer distinguished from the rest of society by its attitude towards money. One of the classic traits of the aristocratic nobility was to know how to squander money without worrying about the future. An aristocrat would be willing to be ruined financially in order to maintain his rank (and the behaviour expected of his rank); the bourgeois, however, would accumulate wealth and carefully monitor his spending. The peasant, who survived in a self-sufficient economy, rarely came into contact with money, which had no day-to-day function. Money was used to pay taxes, to buy land and to bestow a dowry on a daughter who left the household. An extreme case was that of the farm hand, who would be paid once a year and would not know what to do with his money, often squandering it in bars or – like the aristocrat – buying extravagant gifts until it disappeared. Like the aristocrats, when poor people had money, they were always willing to spend it immediately. The bourgeois and the peasant, on the other hand, would economise every day, in order to accumulate and preserve a *patrimoine* that could be handed down to the next generation. They jealously guarded the *patrimoine*, because it ensured their status; to lose it would be followed by social decline.

For most French people today, money comes and goes. It is considered as a fluid resource which should be used as well as possible in the immediate sense, rather than as a solid reserve to be piled up and hoarded. Money is earned to be spent. Most people consider that there is little point in accumulating money, since its value is constantly diminished by inflation. It is valued for what it can buy, not for what it is. Money has become a means, and is no longer an end in itself. The transition from the old peasant and bourgeois view of money to the modern attitude took place rapidly during the 1960s. That virtually everyone has become a wage-earner or is assured of a regular money–income helps explain the speed of the turnaround in the population's attitude towards money. A more functional attitude towards money is a sign of the increased wealth of the population as a whole. Most people are financially secure and have adequate provision for retirement. This is not to suggest, of course, that inequalities of wealth have disappeared: the *employé* is continually having to economise to make ends meet on his meagre salary. Moreover, many young people choose or are forced to live a life of poverty before becoming fully integrated into society. Finally, the new paupers are genuinely reduced to living a life of misery.

INDIVIDUALISM AND AUTHORITY

The transformations mentioned above can all be analysed in terms of the ultimate progress of individualism. This has been the most important trend in Western society since the Reformation. It distinguishes the West from the rest of the world. In the Middle Ages the church declared that its objective was to Christianise the whole of society without exception, individuals being considered only as a part of a larger whole. This strategy was disturbed by the Protestant Reformation and then by the Catholic Counter-Reformation, which both placed the individual at the centre of their pastoral strategies: each sought to convert the individual to its way of thinking, and thus established a direct link between the individual and his Creator. Once a direct link between the individual and God was consented, the implications were momentous. If the existence of God was itself challenged, or denied, then the individual was all that was left. And if God no longer existed, anything was permitted.

Within contemporary France, most people are anxious to develop their individual interests, rather than to participate in strengthening society, or other forms of collectivity of which they form a part. This shift towards individual over collective concerns is a recent phenomenon. It is little short of revolutionary, and its consequences are still largely unimaginable. Individuals assert their greater independence as soon as they are able to: children leave their parents as early as possible, elderly parents live independently of their adult children for as long as their health permits, and even couples do not always live together.

Curiously, this concentration upon the individual has not led to a devaluation of the family. On the contrary, as we argued above, the French people, like the Americans, attach an increasing importance to their family, despite the saliency of individualistic values. In fact, this is more of an apparent contradiction than a real one, since the traditional relationship between the individual and his family is in the process of being reversed. The individual traditionally felt himself to be a member of his family rather than a separate personality, a link in the family chain, to which he subordinated himself as an individual. His whole personality was naturally conditioned by the character and needs of his family. Today, the family is at the service of the individual, who expects it to satisfy his emotional needs; the family is valued because it serves the needs of the individual. Should it fail to serve these needs (for instance through lack of emotional satisfaction), the individual will abandon the family (divorce) and start up another one. The family has thus lost its sacrosanct character. The new freedom accorded to the individual has not so much weakened support for the idea of family, but for particular family units which do not provide satisfaction for their members. In fact, the domestic group is far more varied than ever before (nuclear family, one-parent family, unmarried couples etc.) and is likely to become even more so in the future.

In traditional society, in response to the question 'Who are you?' the individual answered 'I am the son of my father.' This was sufficient to situate him in relation to his kinship group and to a particular place. When arriving in a village, a stranger would be asked his surname and which village he came from; attempts would then be made to relate him to a kinsman or woman. This conception of society (primacy of kinship over any other considerations) was shared by the French aristocrat, for whom qualifications bestowed by birth were superior to any professional qualification. In contrast, the French bourgeoisie situated individuals according to profession rather than family name. In response to the question 'Who are you?' the bourgeois would respond 'I am a doctor, dentist . . . ' Bourgeois parents were anxious that their children should associate only with other children from similar backgrounds. These two criteria for situating individuals in a wider context – kinship and profession – have declined in importance; they have been replaced by the universal preference for the use of Christian names in order to situate somebody. The use of Christian names corresponds to the triumph of individualism over other notions: 'I am myself, alone responsible for my acts and choices.'

The pre-eminence of individualism has been accompanied by a transformation of attitudes towards hierarchy and authority, which is undoubtedly the most profound change in the mentality and behaviour-patterns of the French people. May 1968 was a rebellion against authority and against the authorities. It was a rejection of the very notion of hierarchy. Today this rebellion has died down, partly because of changes in society which began during the fifties, which have established the less rigid, more transparent society, analysed throughout this book. American observers of France have painted superficially attractive portraits of French culture which have seduced many of their French colleagues, but these have become totally anachronistic. The most famous of them is that produced by Michel Crozier which had a certain explanatory value, but can no longer adequately explain the beliefs and values of French people. Crozier's assessment that the French are afraid of 'face to face contact' and that they are 'unable to cooperate' can be juxtaposed with the new importance of collective action and associative groups, and the creation of a culture of negotiation. These have been considered in detail in earlier chapters. A number of explanations help explain why the Crozier viewpoint is inappropriate in analysing today's France.

The first explanation for the emergence of a more open, communicative society can be found in developments in the education system, particularly the creation of the nursery school (see chapter 5), the most important but least commented upon change in the French education system. Every French child is educated from the age of three, well before children in any other country. Teaching methods in nursery school are based upon toler-ance, close emotional ties and face-to-face contact between teacher and pupils, rather than upon strict discipline. Even before the creation of the nursery school, relationships within the French family had been radically transformed; traditional discipline between parents and children had given way to emotional incentives and more direct contact. Finally, the hier-archical structure of the family has been transformed under the impact of the new indulgent relationship that has developed between grandparents and grandchildren (see chapter 10). This relationship has modified children's perceptions of patriarchal authority.

In 1957, the American sociologist L. Wylie published a far-reaching study of a village in Provence. Twenty years later, Wylie returned to the same village and found it radically transformed; this was especially the case in terms of patterns of authority and discipline between teachers and pupils and parents and their children. The traditional symbols of authority, the parents and the teachers, no longer exercised their power with much con-viction, which was only too apparent to the children. Wylie cites the example of a mother who, in 1950, insisted that her child be quiet because 'I told you to be quiet, because you are a little boy and I am your mother'. The fraught mother went on to explain to her child that both mother and child belonged to the same family, that each had a role which it was their duty to perform, and that each had to conform to the natural hierarchical order within the family. In his second survey, Wylie relates how the grand-son of the same woman was able to explode with anger in the middle of the street without his mother scolding him. In the traditional family structure prevalent in the first survey, parents possessed two weapons to ensure that their children conformed with their orders: parental authority, usually accepted by children as a reason in itself to obey; and the threat of shame, or making the child look ridiculous in front of adults and its friends. Today, attempts to humiliate children by making them feel ashamed are ineffectual (the child is usually more assertive): parents attempt to reason with children, rather than invoking their authority.

As we have seen above (chapter 10), the new relationship between grandparents and their grandchildren is one which attaches great importance to teaching young children to bargain and negotiate. A loss of authority has occurred within the school as well. The schoolteacher was formerly a distant, strict figure. Children had no choice but to behave well, or else to misbehave. Those children who persistently misbehaved came to form a 'delinquent community' within the classroom, with its own rules, conventions and principles. Its members displayed a sense of solidarity against the teacher, which ensured that once a delinquent, a child would not risk the ridicule of its peers by abandoning the group. Paradoxically, the existence of a 'delinquent community' within the classroom strengthened the authority of the teacher, since it justified the use of punishment to sanction transgressions. From the classroom situation developed a sense of 'Them' and 'Us' which accurately reflected French people's attitudes towards politics and government. According to this perception, it was essential to protect oneself against 'Them', the outside authorities perpetually interfering in 'our' affairs when they had no right to do so. Because negotiation did not form a part of this adversarial culture, the only reaction against unpopular decisions was revolt.

The opposition between Us and Them no longer accurately represents the structure of French society, or the norm to be adopted towards authority. It is clear that the unprecedented development of participation in voluntary groups of all sorts has helped to break down traditional patterns of distrust. Authority is no longer exercised in a strictly hierarchical manner, but involves greater face-to-face negotiation, bargaining and compromise. It is clear, for example, that when there are twenty voluntary associations in a small town with 1,000 inhabitants, the mayor must take these groups into account in formulating policy. Similar examples could be produced for all levels of authority and decision-making. The development of a genuine associative group structure has modified traditional patterns of authority, and made those in power seem less distant and less incomprehensible.

The modification of authority-patterns is visible within the workplace. In the traditional factory, unskilled workers developed a unanimity-culture (see chapter 4). They could only express themselves in collective ritualised forms of protest which excluded face-to-face negotiation. This was the popular version of a more general adversarial pattern of authority, which opposed a reactive crowd (with little notion of strategy) to the unpredictable behaviour of those in authority. Such confrontational social relations have gradually weakened, to be replaced by those prevalent in the world of the *cadres*, for whom negotiation forms an integral part of any conflict.

This transformation of personal relationships ought to lead to a change in the way that government departments and large companies are administered. Since the studies of M. Crozier, it has generally been accepted that bureaucracy in France is characterised by a strong sense of compartmentalisation (loyalty to department or section) and reluctance to take decisions or to strike bargains (individuals relying on their precise terms of employment to avoid taking responsibility). In the case of disputes between individuals or bureaucratic units, arbitration will always be demanded at a higher level, since each individual clings jealously on to his precise professional terms of employment. There is no tradition of bargaining at a decentralised level. It might have been supposed that the emergence of a greater bargaining culture would have led to a reduction in the importance of rigid terms, but this has not been the case. The existence of such ingrained, precise terms continues to act as a brake upon initiative within organisations.

Thus the secondary-school teacher possessing the *agrégation* (top teaching qualification) refuses to accept that the headmaster has a right to interfere in his teaching methods. He falls back upon his professional qualification to reject any interference in his teaching. Primary-school teachers react in exactly the same manner. The same applies to all other government departments. There has, however, been a transformation in the manner in which professional terms of employment are manipulated by their holders. Rather than being a purely defensive arm, the terms of employment have become an offensive weapon that the individual brandishes to ensure that his position is strengthened rather than weakened in any professional reorganisation. Innovation is no longer refused, but each individual attempts to ensure that it strengthens his position within the organisation. This change has fundamentally perverted the logic of the bureaucratic system: passive uncalculating resistance to change has been replaced by active calculation of how best a particular professional term of employment can be manipulated to ensure that innovation benefits its holders. New generations are likely to consider the professional term of employment as a strategic arm to be manipulated as gainfully as possible, rather than as a purely defensive protective shield.

The general enrichment of society has brought about a relaxation of the constraints which previously limited the individual's freedom of action. The fear of the future, for example, the feeling of subordination to and dependence upon authority, or economic privation previously prevented individuals from taking any risks, or from displaying initiative. The poverty of the inter-war period aggravated this situation. It is no longer the case today. Everybody is assured of enough to eat and adequate medical care, and most have experienced material prosperity. Social relations are no longer governed primarily by fear. The individual has acquired the potential freedom to say no, without fearing the direst of consequences. The novelty of this new situation is not so much the challenging of authority: the older tradition of rebellion represented a total rejection of authority, without proposing alternatives or compromise. Rather, it is that a challenge to authority can occur without the individual taking an extreme risk. Naked authority has lost its force. The exercise of authority now requires consent. Without the consent of those subject to it, authority is no longer recognised as legitimate; in order to obtain consent, compromises have to be made, and bargains struck. The new prevalence of a bargaining or negotiation culture has meant that power has become diffused throughout society, rather than being concentrated at the summit.

This relaxation of social relationships has not always led to a greater freedom for individuals. When traditional hierarchical patterns of authority prevailed, subordinates had to execute direct orders, but were able to enjoy an area of freedom in those spheres in which no direct orders had been given. However, a flexible society within which bargaining and negotiation are permanent is necessarily more open than a hierarchical, ritualised society. An open, transparent society prevents people from hiding and, consequently, ensures that all of their activities are clearly visible. In May 1968, both the technocrats and the young revolutionaries dreamt of creating a totally transparent society, albeit for diametrically opposed reasons (see the introduction above). Both forgot, however, that total transparence creates the conditions for the ideal prison, Bentham's panopticon, in which the individual is totally deprived of privacy and secrecy. Far from being an entirely open society, it is more accurate to describe France as an extremely complex and diversified society, in the sphere of values as elsewhere. This reality prevents us from portraying a simple vision of this society, such as used to be possible when a few great national institutions confronted each other.

STRATEGY AND IDENTITY

Stable societies, such as that of pre-1945 France, provide their members with a relatively simple means of building their identity from early childhood onwards. The individual is anxious only to conform to the role and identity that are expected of him as a member of a particular social group. The notion of identity is no longer so straightforward in today's complex societies. Now that the great symbolic institutions have either disappeared or else had their ideological attraction weakened, it has become far more difficult for an individual to identify with one particular group or symbol – and thus to distinguish himself from all other groups within society. The differences between the sexes and social classes are both becoming blurred.

In this new society, every individual is free to develop his own identity. With time, each person is able to assess his own strengths and weaknesses and act accordingly. The opportunity for trial and error is an essential element of this search for identity. Those who are better placed in society or in a particular organisation can permit themselves more errors and generally adapt better than those who are less well placed. Trial and error is also important in relation to social relationships, and to the management of family life. Social relationships are far more a matter of personal choice than used to be the case, when the family and neighbourhood acted as an all-embracing constraint.

This degree of personal strategic manoeuvre is not entirely new. In certain regions, for example Brittany, the peasants would learn from early childhood that social situations were unalterable, that everybody's position within society was fixed and that all had a particular social role to perform. The only means of succeeding in life was to accept one's position within society and the normal behaviour-patterns associated with it. In other regions such as the south-west, on the other hand, peasants were far less inclined to accept their position in society without manoeuvring to their own advantage. South-western peasants were tolerant of differences in others (unlike the more traditionally inclined regions), were ready to challenge authority, and had little esteem for the law, or respect for the authorities. Differences in character between peasant communities in northern and southern France might explain why today southerners perform better in modern organisations with their complex networks of relations. Northerners, by contrast, have always shown more respect for authority and the need for discipline; they have tended to adapt better to hierarchical organisations with a military-style chain of command. They were perfectly suited to the traditional large company organised on Taylorian principles, which is in the process of disappearing. The recent economic development of the South, at the expense of the North, cannot be explained merely by the more attractive climate, but must also take into account the fact that southerners have a greater cultural affinity with the more supple structures of the emerging society (based upon their traditional village practices) than do northerners.

Linguistic and regional cultures are both powerful forms of identification, since they are linked to family, and racial characteristics, some would say to the very nature of the individual. This can be seen clearly in the USA, where young third-generation Americans of 'immigrant' families often go to considerable efforts to rediscover their racial roots and original family identity. This will involve imploring their grandfather to teach them Slovak or Romanian, and a declaration of intention to return to the village of their ancestors. Similar movements emerged in France during the 1970s, when there was a strong resurgence of regional cultures and languages, especially *langue d'oc* and *breton*. These regionalist movements rapidly died away towards the late seventies and early eighties. Today, only Corsica presents an exception to this rule, and here regionalism has too often taken on the form of terrorism (which cannot, however, entirely be explained by demands for regional autonomy). Most French people still resort to reaffirming their regional origins in order to express their character, but not at the expense of renouncing their national French identity. Far from losing its attraction, the sense of belonging to the French nation is a more important source of identity than ever, although region, locality and Europe are also powerful symbols.

French society has changed dramatically during the course of the Second French Revolution. Rather than conform to pre-established roles transmitted from parents to children (or learnt during a process of upward social mobility), its members can choose between different alternative models, roles and lifestyles. In fact, the individual can even invent his own lifestyle and moral codes, which he is able to modify continually in the light of experience. The multiplication of social networks, groups and voluntary associations has meant that each individual is encouraged to belong to several different cross-cutting networks, which dilutes his identification with any one of them in particular. The possibility of a totalitarian identification with one sole network, the norm in traditional France, is lessened in this new multifaceted society. The individual is constrained to build his own personal identity, which is much stronger and autonomous than was ever the case previously. This identity is the synthesis of the various multiple sources of influence and inspiration to which the individual is subjected.

The search for an identity is a never-ending process in a complex mass society characterised by a wide diversity of different groups and divisions. It is subject to continual refinement and recomposition. The widely held belief that anomie threatens any society in which traditional structures and institutions have broken down does not seem relevant to the new France. Social regulations continue to provide a framework within which the individual has a large margin of manoeuvre to build his identity. Because different groups have become so numerous and specialised, they all need each other and are dependent upon each other. The new French society is one in which individuals and groups are freer than ever before to develop their own identities.

Bibliography

WORKS IN ENGLISH

Ambler, J. S. *The French Army in Politics 1945–1962*, Ohio, Ohio State University Press, 1966.

Ardagh, J. *France in the 1980s*, London, Secker & Warburg, 1982.

Cerny, P. and M. Schain. *French Politics and Public Policy*, London, Methuen, 1980.

Cohen, S. and P. Gourevitch. *France in the Troubled World Economy*, London, Butterworth, 1982.

Cole, A. and P. Campbell. *French Electoral Systems and Elections since 1789*, Aldershot, Gower, 1989.

Crozier, M. *The Bureaucratic Phenomenon*, London, Tavistock Press, 1964.

Dupeux, G. *French Society, 1789–1970*, London, Methuen, 1976.

Gaffney, J. (ed.). *France and Modernisation*, Aldershot, Gower, 1988.

Gallie, D. *In Search of the New Working Class*, Cambridge, Cambridge University Press, 1978.

Halls, W. D. *Education, Culture and Politics in Modern France*, Oxford, Pergamon, 1976.

Hanley, D., A. Kerr and N. Waites. *Contemporary France: Politics and Society since 1945*, London, Routledge & Kegan Paul, 1984.

Hayward, J. *Governing France*, London, Weidenfeld and Nicolson, 1983.

Hoffman, S. *Decline or Renewal? France since the 1930s*, New York, Viking, 1974.

Lagroye, J. and V. Wright (eds.). *Local Government in Britain and France*, London, Allen & Unwin, 1979.

Machin, H. *The Prefect in French Public Administration*, London, Croom Helm, 1977.

Machin, H. and V. Wright. *Economic Policy and Policy-making under the Mitterrand Presidency*, London, Frances Pinter, 1985.

Marceau, J. *Class and Status in France*, Oxford, Oxford University Press, 1977.

Mendras, H. *The Vanishing Peasant*, Cambridge, Mass., MIT Press, 1970.

Oxford Analytica. *America in Perspective: Major Trends in the United States through the 1990s*, Boston, Mass., Houghton Mifflin, 1986.

Rand-Smith, W. *Crisis in the French Labour Movement*, London, 1987.

Ross, G. *Workers and Communists in France*, California, California University Press, 1982.

Ross, G., S. Hoffman and S. Malzacher. *The Mitterrand Experiment*, Oxford, Polity Press, 1987.

Suleiman, E. *Elites in French Society*, Princeton, Princeton University Press, 1982.

Weber, E. *Peasants into Frenchmen: The Modernization of Rural France*, Stanford, Stanford University Press, 1976.

Wright, V. *The Government and Politics of France*, London, Unwin Hyman, 1989.

Wylie, L. *Village in the Vaucluse*, Cambridge, Mass., Harvard University Press, 1957.

WORKS IN FRENCH

Adam, G. *Le Pouvoir syndical*, Paris, Dunod, 1984.

Adam, G. and J. D. Reynaud, *Conflits du travail et changement social*, Paris, Presses Universitaires de France, 1978.

Angeville, A. *Essai sur la statistique de la population française, considérée sous quelques-uns de ses rapports physiques et moraux*, Bourg, Imprimerie F. Dufour, 1836.

Augustins, G. *Comment se perpétuer? Devenir des lignées et destins des patrimoines dans les paysanneries européennes*, Nanterre, Société d'ethnologie, 1989.

Babeau, A. *La Fin des retraites?*, Paris, Hachette, 1985.

Babeau, A. and D. Strauss-Khan. *La Richesse des Français*, Paris, Presses Universitaires de France, 1977.

Barthez, A. *Famille, travail et agriculture*, Paris, Economica, 1982.

Besnard, P. and G. Desplanques. *Un prénom pour toujours, cote des prénoms hier, aujourd'hui et demain*, Paris, Balland, 1986.

Boltanski, L. *Les Cadres*, Paris, Editions de Minuit, 1982.

Boudon, R. *L'Inégalité des chances*, Paris, Armand Colin, 1973.

Boulard, R. and J. Remy. *Pratique religieuse et régions culturelles*, Paris, Editions ouvrières – Economie et Humanisme, 1968.

Bourdieu, P. *La Distinction: critique sociale du jugement*, Paris, Editions de Minuit, 1979.

Bourricaud, F. *Le Bricolage idéologique*, Paris, Presses Universitaires de France, 1980.

Brulé, M. *L'Empire des sondages: transparence ou manipulation?*, Paris, Laffont, 1988.

Capdevielle, J. et al. *France de gauche vote à droite*, Paris, Presses de la Fondation nationale des sciences politiques, 1981.

Carré, J.-J., P. Dubois and E. Malinvaud. *La Croissance française: un essai d'analyse économique causale de l'après-guerre*, Paris, Le Seuil, 1972.

Chalvon-Demersay, S. *Concubins, concubines*, Paris, Le Seuil, 1983.

Chombart de Lauwe, J. *La vie quotidienne des familles ouvrières*, Paris, Presses Universitaires de France, 1977.

Commaille, J. *Familles sans justice? Le droit et la justice face aux transformations de la société*, Paris, Le Centurion, 1982.

Crozier, M. *Le Phénomène bureaucratique*, Paris, Le Seuil, 1963.

Curie, J., G. Caussade and V. Hajjar. 'Comment saisir le mode de vie des familles', in OCS, *L'Esprit des lieux*, Paris, Editions du CNRS, 1987.

Daumard, A. *Les Bourgeois et la bourgeoisie en France depuis 1815*, Paris, Aubier, 1987.

Donegani, J.-M. and G. Lescanne. *Catholicismes de France*, Paris, Desclée-Bayard-Presse, 1986.

Dubet, F. *La Galère: jeunes en survie*, Paris, Fayard, 1986.

Dubost, F. *Côté jardins*, Paris, Scarabée, 1984.

Dupuy, F. and J.-Cl. Thoenig. *Sociologie de l'administration française*, Paris, Armand Colin, 1983.

Dussourd, H. *Au même pot et au même feu*, Moulins, A. Pottier, 1962.

Fonteneau, A. and P. A. Muet. *La gauche face à la crise*, Paris, Presses de la FNSP, 1985.

Forsé, M. 'La Diversification de la société française vue à travers l'idéologie et le mariage', *Revue Tocqueville*, spring 1986.

Fourastié, J. *Les Trente Glorieuses*, Paris, Fayard, 1979.

Galland, O. *Les Jeunes*, Paris, La Découverte, 1985.

Galland, O. *Sociologie de la jeunesse*, Paris, A. Colin, 1990.

Gervais, M., M. Jollivet and Y. Tavernier. vol. IV in Duby and Wallon (eds.), *Histoire de la France rurale*, Paris, Le Seuil, 1975–6.

Girard, A. *Le Choix du conjoint*, Paris, PUF-INED, Travaux et documents, 1974.

Girardet, R. *La Société militaire dans la France contemporaine 1815–1939*, Paris, Plon, 1953.

Goblot, E. *La Barrière et le niveau: étude sociologique sur la bourgeoisie française moderne*, Paris, Alcan, 1925.

Godin, H. and Y. Daniel. *La France pays de mission?*, Paris, Editions de l'Abeille, 1943.

Grémion, P. *Le Pouvoir périphérique: bureaucrates et notables dans le système politique français*, Paris, Le Seuil, 1976.

Groux, G. *Les Cadres*, Paris, La Découverte-Maspero, 1983.

Grunberg, G. and E. Schweisguth. 'Profession et vote: la poussée de la gauche', in J. Capdevielle *et al.*, *France de gauche vote à droite*, Paris, Fondation nationale des sciences politiques, 1981.

Guillemard, A.-M. *Le Déclin du social*, Paris, Presses Universitaires de France, 1986.

Hamon, H. and P. Rotman. *Génération*, Paris, Le Seuil, 1988.

Herpin, N., O. Choquet and L. Kasparian. 'Les Conditions de vie des ouvriers', Paris, INSEE, collection M, no. 126, December 1987.

Hervieu-Léger, D. *Vers un nouveau christianisme?*, Paris, Cerf, 1986.

Isambert, Fr.-A. *Christianisme et classe ouvrière: jalons pour une étude de sociologie historique*, Paris–Tournai, Casterman, 1961.

Isambert, Fr.-A. and J.-P. Terrenoire. *Atlas de la pratique religieuse des catholiques en France*, Paris, FNSP-CNRS, 1980.

Jeanneney, J.-M. (ed.). *L'Economie française depuis 1967*, Paris, Le Seuil, 1989.

Jollivet, M. and H. Mendras. *Les Collectivités rurales françaises*, 2 vols., Paris, Armand Colin, 1971–4.

Kepel, G. *Les Banlieues de l'Islam*, Paris, Le Seuil, 1987.

Kriegel, A. *Les Communistes français dans leur premier demi-siècle 1920–1970*, Paris, Le Seuil, 1985.

Labbens, J. *La Condition sous-prolétarienne*, Paris, Bureau de recherches sociales, 1965.

Lamarche, H., S. Rogers and C. Karnoouh. *Paysans, femmes et citoyens*, Le Paradou, Actes-Sud, 1980.

Lambert, Y. *Dieu change en Bretagne: La Réligion à Limerzel de 1900 à nos jours*, Paris, Cerf, 1985.

Lavau, G. *A quoi sert le P.C.F.?*, Paris, Fayard, 1981.

Le Bras, G. *Etudes de sociologie religieuse*, 2 vols., Paris, Presses Universitaires de France, 1955–6.

Le Bras, H. *Les Trois France*, Paris, Le Seuil, 1986.

Léger, D. and B. Hervieu. *La Retour à la nature: au fond de la forêt, l'état*, Paris, Le Seuil, 1979.

Lemel, Y. *Stratification et mobilité sociale*, Paris, Armand Colin, 1990.

Lesourne, J. *Education et société: les défis de l'an 2000*, Paris, La Découverte, 1988.

Maurice, M., F. Sellier and J.-J. Silvestre. *Politique d'éducation et organisation industrielle en France et en Allemagne*, Paris, Presses Universitaires de France, 1982.

Mayer, N. *La Boutique contre la gauche*, Paris, Fondation nationale des sciences politiques, 1986.

Mendras, H. *La Fin des paysans, suivi d'une réflexion sur la fin des paysans vingt ans après*, Le Paradou, Actes-Sud, 1984.

Mendras, H. (ed.). *La Sagesse et le désordre: France 1980*, Paris, Gallimard, 1980.

Mendras, H. and M. Forsé. *Le Changement social*, Paris, Armand Colin, 1983.

Ministère de la Culture. *La Politique culturelle 1981–1985: bilan de la législation*, Paris, Ministère de la Culture, service Information et communication.

Morel, C. *La Grève froide*, Paris, Editions d'Organisation, 1981.

Mouriaux, R. *Les Syndicats dans la société française*, Paris, Fondation nationale des sciences politiques, 1983.

Noiriel, G. *Le Creuset français: histoire de l'immigration (XIX–XXᵉ siècles)*, Paris, Le Seuil, 1988.

Noiriel, G. *Les Ouvriers de la société française au XIXᵉ–XXᵉ siècles*, Paris, Le Seuil, 1986.

OCS. *L'Esprit des lieux*, Paris, Editions du CNRS, 1987.

Paty, D. *Douze collèges en France*, Paris, Documentation française, 1981.

Perrot, M. *Le Mode de vie des familles bourgeoises*, Paris, Armand Colin, 1961.

Pitrou, A. *Vivre sans famille? Les solidarités familiales dans le monde d'aujourd'hui*, Toulouse, Privat, 1978.

Pitts, J. 'Les Français et l'autorité', in J.-D. Reynaud and Y. Grafmeyer (eds.), *Français, qui êtes-vous?*, Paris, Documentation français, 1982.

Prost, A. *L'Enseignement s'est-il démocratisé?*, Paris, Presses Universitaires de France, 1986.

Ranger, J. 'Le Déclin du Parti Communiste Français', *Revue française de sciences politiques*, 1, February 1986.

Reynaud, J.-D. and Y. Grafmeyer (eds.). *Français, qui êtes-vous?*, Paris, Documentation française, 1982.

Roussel, L. *La Famille après le mariage des enfants*, PUF-INED, 'Travaux et Documents', 1976.

Roussel, L. *Famille incertaine*, Paris, Odile Jacob, 1989.

Sainsaulieu, R. *L'Identité au travail*, Paris, Fondation national des sciences politiques, 1977.

Sainsaulieu, R. *Sociologie de l'organisation et de l'entreprise*, Paris, FNSP-Dalloz, 1987.

Saint-Macary, P. 'Vivre l'arme au pied', in H. Mendras (ed.), *La Sagesse et le désordre: France 1980*, Paris, Gallimard, 1980.

Segalen, M. *Sociologie de la famille*, 2nd edn, revised and augmented, Paris, Armand Colin, 1988.

Singly, Fr. de. and C. Thélot. *Fortune et infortune de la femme mariée*, Paris, Presses Universitaires de France, 1987.

Singly, Fr. de. *Gens du privé, gens du public*, Paris, Dunod, 1989.

Sofres, *L'Etat de l'opinion, clés pour 1988*, Paris, Le Seuil, 1988.

Stoetzel, J. *Les Valeurs du temps présent: une enquête européenne*, Paris, Presses Universitaires de France, 1983.

Suaud, C. *La Vocation: conversion et reconversion des prêtres ruraux*, Paris, Editions de Minuit, 1978.

Tavernier, Y., M. Gervais and C. Servolin. *L'Univers politique des paysans dans la France contemporaine*, Paris, Armand Colin, 1972.

Thélot, C. *Tel père, tel fils?*, Paris, Dunod, 1982.

Todd, E. *La Nouvelle France*, Paris, Le Seuil, 1988.

Touraine, A., M. Wievorka and F. Dubet. *Le Mouvement ouvrier*, Paris, Rayard, 1984.

Verges, P. 'Approche localisée des classes sociales', in OCS, *L'Esprit des lieux*, Paris, Editions du CNRS, 1987.

Verret, M. *L'Espace ouvrier*, Paris, Armand Colin, 1979.

Vulpian, A. de. 'L'Evolution des mentalités: conformisme et modernité', in J. D. Reynaud and Y. Grafmeyer (eds.), *Français, qui êtes-vous?*, Paris, Documentation française, 1982.

Yver, J. *Egalité entre héritiers et exclusion des enfants dotés essai de géographie coutumière*, Paris, Sirey, 1966.

Index